D1613014

SOCIALIST CONSTRUCTION AND MARXIST THEORY

Also by Derek Sayer

MARX'S METHOD

SOCIALIST CONSTRUCTION AND MARXIST THEORY

Bolshevism and its Critique

Philip Corrigan, Harvie Ramsay
and Derek Sayer

First published 1978 by
THE MACMILLAN PRESS LTD
London and Basingstoke
Associated companies in Delhi
Dublin Hong Kong Johannesburg Lagos
Melbourne New York Singapore Tokyo

Typeset in Great Britain by
The Bowering Press Ltd Plymouth
and printed in Great Britain by
Redwood Burn Limited
Trowbridge and Esher

British Library Cataloguing in Publication Data

Corrigan, Philip
Socialist construction and Marxist theory
1. Communism – History
I. Title II. Ramsay, Harvie III. Sayer, Derek
355.4′09′034 HX36

ISBN 0–333–21245–2

Socialist society covers a very long historical period. Classes and class struggle continue to exist in this society, and the struggle still goes on between the road of socialism and the road of capitalism. The socialist revolution on the economic front (in the ownership of the means of production) is insufficient by itself and cannot be consolidated. There must also be a thorough socialist revolution on the political and ideological fronts. Here a very long period of time is needed to decide 'who will win' in the struggle between socialism and capitalism. Several decades won't do it; success requires anywhere from one to several centuries. On the question of duration, it is better to prepare for a longer rather than a shorter period of time. On the question of effort, it is better to regard the task as difficult rather than easy. It will be more advantageous and less harmful to think and act in this way. Anyone who fails to see this or to appreciate it fully will make tremendous mistakes. During the historical period of socialism it is necessary to maintain the dictatorship of the proletariat and carry the socialist revolution through to the end if the restoration of capitalism is to be prevented, socialist construction carried forward and the conditions created for the transition to communism.

Mao Tse-tung

Fifteen Theses on Socialist Construction

Contents

Preface

This book is a collective production. Not only does it result from the combined efforts of its three accredited authors; it also owes much to many others. Its roots lie in our participation in the Political Economy Group which Gavin Williams founded in Durham in 1973. It was in discussions there that we first became aware of the mutual relevance of our apparently quite disparate individual researches, and gained the impetus to write a first draft of this book during 1974. We circulated that draft, both within and outside this Group, and the comment and criticism we received helped us immensely in writing the revised text which follows. The result, we believe, is a better book.

At the same time, our revision has involved a good deal of distillation and some excision. Chapter 1, for instance, represents a summary of arguments which were originally developed over 150 pages. We attempt to make good such losses in other writings, some of them already published, others still in preparation. In particular, we are writing a volume which will be in many ways a sequel to this, extending our assessment of the theoretical contribution to marxism made by Mao Tse-tung (*For Mao: Essays in Historical Materialism*, Macmillan, forthcoming). In this connection, we would like to make clear that our discussion in the present volume deals only with the period preceding Mao's death, though we believe that the analysis we offer provides the resources for comprehending the struggles in China which have followed.

Finally, we wish to express our particular thanks to Val Gillespie, Sheila Ramsay, Teodor Shanin, Tse Kakui, and Gavin Williams, for their invaluable encouragement, assistance, and criticism throughout. Derek Sayer would like to acknowledge the help of the Social Science Research Council, whose award of a Postdoctoral Research Fellowship has enabled him to work on this project full-time during the last year.

PHILIP CORRIGAN
HARVIE RAMSAY
DEREK SAYER

January 1977

Introduction

At 10.00 a.m. on 7 November 1917, before attending the Second All-Russia Congress of Soviets at the Smolny Institute in what was then called Petrograd, Lenin, on behalf of the Petrograd Military Revolutionary Committee, issued an appeal 'To the Citizens of Russia' (Akhapkin, 1970: Document 1).[1] This, the first text of Soviet power, records that

> The cause for which the people have fought, namely, the immediate offer of a democratic peace, the abolition of landed proprietorship, workers' control over production, and the establishment of Soviet power – this cause has been secured. Long live the revolution of workers, soldiers and peasants!

The first session of that Congress of Soviets stretched from 10.40 p.m. on 7 November until after 5.00 a.m. of the next day. Shortly after 3.00 a.m. on the morning of the 8th news was received of the storming of the Winter Palace, and the Congress issued an appeal 'To Workers, Soldiers and Peasants' (ibid., Document 2). During its second session, which began at 9.00 a.m. on the same day, Decrees on Peace and Land were adopted, at 10.00 p.m. on the 8th and 2.00 a.m. on the 9th respectively (ibid., Documents 3 and 4). On 27 November the All-Russia Central Executive Committee elected by that same Congress promulgated 'Instructions on Workers' Control' (ibid., Document 10).

This book is concerned with the struggles which make such actions possible and meaningful. It is as well to recall, right at the start, of whose struggles we are talking. Much in these actions – including the textual content of the decrees – was a descriptive rather than a prescriptive commentary on political events. The workers, soldiers and peasants who were creating the Union of Soviet Socialist Republics had already established the material situation – regarding peace, land, and workers' control – that these political decrees and appeals registered, summarised, and attempted to carry forward to a new generalisation. This is no mere aside – a dramaturgical obeisance to the *fact* that the world (objective and subjective) was changed at the time that these decrees were issued and those congresses were taking place. It is a central constituent of the reasons why we have written this book and, in part, a description of how we were enabled to do so.

Hundreds of thousands of texts exist recording and commenting upon the world transformed by the Great October Socialist Revolution and extended through the longer struggles in China which culminated in the declaration of the People's Republic of China on 1 October 1949. But very few indeed appreciate just how Soviet power was made possible. This is, in large measure, because of two major distortions. The first is to remain at the level of appearances. This is true in two different ways. Visitors and commentators emphasise the phenomena that present themselves for inspection. It is noteworthy how many who claim to offer a marxist account concentrate upon 'queues', 'uniformity' or 'shortages' within the USSR or the PRC. One wonders what arena of capitalist experience they inhabit that is so queue-less, full of choices and marvellously diverse. It can only be that of the bourgeoisie with their direct telephone line to shop servants, luxurious freedom of choice and all the miracles of fashion and instant conjury. But, secondly, and relatedly, the level of appearances is sustained through adopting a perspective, vocabulary and appreciation essentially informed by the values and orientations of capitalism, however much this may be occluded by being considered the normal, everyday and obvious. Through this mesh the reality of socialist experience is constantly *translated* into equivalents of 'our' institutions, words, symbols and activities. The two go together very frequently in seeking a bourgeois explanation of why the bourgeoisie have had rather a miserable time of it in the socialist social formations.

Equally important, however, is the second distortion. Both 'theory' and 'historical experience' are misconstrued. This is very much a central part of what we try to argue through this book as a whole but a prefatory word here is in order. 'Theory' is frequently considered to relate to a body of *ideas* which guide (in the manner that 'orders' relate to, for example, an 'army') social practice, above all that of a revolutionary Party, and through that Party understood as a vanguard, that of the revolutionary class. This 'Theory', moreover, can clearly not be generated within the practice of the class, but has to be injected from outside; it is therefore generated, so the argument runs, by a particular kind of person (different, clearly from 'ordinary' members of the class) generally assumed to be an 'intellectual'. We think it impossible to understand what is central to how (and therefore what) theoretical revolutions were accomplished by Marx, Lenin, or Mao with this deformed notion of 'Theory'.

For us, as Stalin phrased it, 'theory is the experience of the working class movement in all countries taken in its general aspect' (Stalin,

1924a: 15). We therefore agree with Marx, when he wrote in a pamphlet, widely circulated within England, which tried to generalise the historical experience of the Paris Commune of 1871, that the working class

> know that in order to work out their own emancipation . . . they will have to pass through long struggles, through a series of historical processes, transforming circumstances and men. They have no ideals to realise, but to set free the elements of a new society . . . (Marx, 1871c: 73)

Armed with the knowledge he wrote about in his *Civil War in France*, moreover, Marx, along with Engels, urged a major 'correction' of the text of their 1848 *Manifesto of the Communist Party*. Theory is generated and sustained by social practice; revolutionary theory is generated and sustained by revolutionary social practice. Social practice considered cumulatively over time is historical experience, which, we emphasise, is not some thing(s) which we have or not, but it is some way(s) that we are. Historical experience is not a property of an object (the label attached to this or that thing). It is the social relations through and within which a human collectivity has its very being.

In this book we try to draw to theoretical attention the historical experiences and social practices of the people of the Union of Soviet Socialist Republics and the People's Republic of China, in order to make possible a fuller comprehension of the relevance of the sixty years since 1917 to present-day reality. We are arguing strongly here that marxism is not a dogma. Like Lenin

> We do not claim that Marx or the Marxists know the road to socialism in every concrete detail. That would be nonsense. We know the direction of the road, we know what class forces are following the road; but the concrete and practical details will be learned only from the experiences of the millions when they begin to take action. (Lenin, 1917e: 285)

After all, as Stalin remarked to the 18th Congress of the Communist Party of the Soviet Union (Bolshevik) in 1939 – on the eve of that Great Patriotic War which was to cause the death of over 20 million Soviet People and to be won through the siege of Leningrad and the battle of Stalingrad –

> It would be ridiculous to expect that the classical Marxist writers should have elaborated for our benefit ready-made solutions for each and every theoretical problem that might arise in any particular

> country fifty or one hundred years afterwards, so that we, the descendants of the classical Marxist writers, might calmly doze at the fireside and munch ready-made solutions. (Stalin, 1939: 659)

For, as Mao Tse-tung phrased the same point in the middle of the prolonged war during the Border Region years in the making of new China, if we merely read the works of Marx, Engels, Lenin and Stalin

> but do not proceed to study the reality of China's history and revolution in the light of their theory or do not make any effort to think through China's revolutionary practice carefully in terms of theory ['the general conclusion drawn from historical and revolutionary reality' is how Mao had just defined this theory], we should not be so presumptuous as to call ourselves Marxist theorists. (Mao, 1942a: 37)

That is to say,

> It is necessary to master Marxist theory and apply it, master it for the sole purpose of applying it. (Ibid., 38)

Some years ago, Paul Feyerabend suggested that one way of grasping what a *theory of knowledge* was involved an analogy with 'a new production of a well-known play' (Feyerabend, 1969: 228fn.). The Great October Socialist Revolution has become, in this analogy, such a 'well-known play' that many historians and commentators do not attend to its production at all, but debate the validity of competing reviews or the memoirs of major actors. In this procedure there is very little attention to the relevance or not of Marx's work for comprehending the production of socialist revolutions, their genesis and development. Indeed there is very little trouble taken to attend to the specificity of the theoretical resources, and *their* historical contexts, at the inauguration of the era of 1917.

What we have attempted in this book is to demonstrate the relevance of Marx's theoretical generalisations concerning production – above all the capitalist mode of production – to understanding the genesis and actualisation of, and the subsequent paths taken after, the Great October Socialist Revolution. This involves an interpretation of Marx in the light of historical experience (and armed with a whole range of texts not available to Lenin) which concentrates on how he illuminates *production forms*. We develop this interpretation, in general terms, in our first chapter.

But the bulk of our book concerns *socialist construction*: *Bolshevism and its critique*. Long before 1917, socialist construction – a sustained working-class achievement as Marx has made clear (1854, 1864, 1871a, b, c) – was engaged in the crucial 'muscle-building' that made 1917 and its world possible. 1917 relit the beacon which had flared briefly but clearly in Paris in 1871. 1917 created a space – productive, political, cultural, and epistemological – for the carrying forward of the socialist construction that made possible new collective, egalitarian, conscious transformations of circumstances and people. 1917 creates the possibility of a socialist world. There is, then, a progression to be studied. That progression was and is informed by a body of theories and practices – what we have called a 'social problematic' – *Bolshevism.* Bolshevism presents itself and is represented as *the* (or at least *a* dominant) theory of social formations in transition from capitalism to communism. Bolshevism was understood by Lenin and others to have been formed, through revolutionary historical experience, around 1903 and to have been extended and structured through the world-shaking upheavals of 1905 and February 1917 and beyond.

It is to make visible that Bolshevism that we devote the bulk of our book. To do so we have used, to repeat, those two inseparable resources – marxist theory and historical experience – in order to go beyond the obvious phenomena of the Union of Soviet Socialist Republics to try to discover the conditions that sustain them. What we have found is a struggle at the very heart of the social problematic of Bolshevism itself. We establish this in our second chapter and then discuss its detailed configurations in the work of the Bolsheviks Lenin, Trotsky and Stalin in our third. Since we believe that the only sustained, if largely implicit, *critique* of Bolshevism has been achieved through the theory and practice of the Communist Party of China and the transformations accomplished by the workers and peasants of China, we try to indicate the outline of this in our fourth chapter and return to the same points in subsequent discussions. Our work concludes with an emphasis upon how far the socialism that exists within the USSR and elsewhere is guaranteed and simultaneously restricted by Bolshevism. We show these twin continuities within the Soviet Union and China in our final two chapters.

Bolshevism guaranteed a massive and qualitative break from capitalism. It fractured totally the hegemony of the capitalist laws of world economy and created a surface on the earth where men and women were not units of labour-power and where surplus-value making was not the dominating motor of production. But that break – that space – was understood by all the Bolsheviks in a particular way. Bolshevik theory and practice centres around a contradiction which pervades the work of Lenin as much as any other Bolshevik. The marxism of the Bolsheviks broke decisively with the marxism of the Second International. Lenin would have no truck with those who saw the Russian people as 'too backward' to make a socialist revolution. Writing at a time when 'events are moving at a speed that at times makes your head spin' (Institute, 1958: 47) Lenin, against the 'strike-breaking' of Kamenev and Zinoviev, celebrated that the only way was to 'go forward *with the revolutionary workers*' (ibid., 119):

> This is the only way to make the workers' party healthy again, to purge ourselves of a dozen or so spineless intellectuals and, having united the ranks of the revolutionaries, go on . . . (Ibid.)

From the workers and peasants will come the defeat of Tsarism, on that Lenin was admirably clear. After all, as Lenin wrote in *Can the Bolsheviks retain State power?* (1917k: 120):

> 'What a painful thing is this "extremely complicated situation" created by the revolution,' that's how the bourgeois intellectual thinks and feels.
>
> 'We squeezed "them" a bit; "they" won't dare to lord it over us as they did before. We'll squeeze again – and chuck them out altogether,' that's how the worker thinks and feels.

But the break concerning political and cultural relations was accomplished without challenging a particular reading of Marx's general social theory which above all involved understanding base and superstructure relations in a particularly restricted form and simultaneously sustaining a very narrow conception of 'production'.

The contradictions at the heart of Bolshevism are in fact the basis for the long, protracted, fierce and sustained class struggles that persist throughout the whole era of transition from capitalism to communism. We agree here with Mao, who has argued consistently that it will take one or two centuries before socialism (let alone communism) will be secure. Central to Bolshevism is a struggle between two roads and two lines. Socialist construction was hampered in so far as certain clearly capitalist techniques and relations (i.e. forces) were considered necessary to create the material basis for socialism. Socialist construction was liberated and accelerated in so far as its resources were coherently and consistently recognised to be particular productive collectivities (i.e. relations), that is to say, when socialist construction was seen to turn on the simultaneous conscious, collective and thus egalitarian transformation of circumstances and people. Only that continuous and extremely complicated struggle will enable the *complete* victory over capitalist ideas, habits, assumptions, images, symbols and so on, and enable socialism *to be secured*. We stress this at some length because it is extremely difficult to sustain this constant representation of struggle, contradiction, movement, tension throughout our text. As soon as only one side is taken as representing the whole life of Bolshevism, we lose sight of what is distinctive and peculiar to all socialist construction. As soon as we elect one Bolshevik – usually Lenin – to stand as judge over the erring others (Trotsky, Stalin) we do the same violence to historical experience. We are not in an either/or world – we are in a world in which socialism and capitalism are struggling for mastery, and their struggle rages over its entirety.

It is as well to conclude this Introduction with some indication of possible misunderstandings of our project. We are aware that there are two areas of our presentation that require amplification. First we need to sustain our interpretation of Marx through a more extended presentation and a *critique* of alternatives. In part we have tried to make these materials available elsewhere and they will be added to shortly. Secondly, we need similarly to sustain our argument concerning the critique of Bolshevism that has been accomplished within the People's Republic of China. We are at work upon and will shortly produce a book devoted precisely to this theme: *For Mao: Essays in Historical Materialism* (Macmillan, 1978). But, we stress, the relevant materials have been available in English for some twenty or more years.

This book is a work of theory. It is not a historical study, although we stress its basis within historical experience. There is no substitute, however, in that direction, for a study of such works as those of E. H. Carr, whose value we wish to acknowledge. But as a work of theory, in the sense that Feyerabend intends in his remark we have quoted, our text may operate as prolegomena for subsequent historical work, above all a sensitive provision of context for many of those texts of Bolshevism which are still ripped from their situation and treated as dogma.

Finally, this is not a geopolitical exercise in which one country (China) is seen to be 'better' than another (USSR). Neither is it hagiography, placing Mao 'above' Lenin in the heavens. At a time when many 'Friends of China' adopt such a superficial and geopolitical analysis it is necessary to emphasise this with some vigour. Contemporary events in China demonstrate – as they have since the 1920s – that a similar struggle between two roads and two lines is as ever-present in China and the CPC as in the Soviet Union and the CPSU.

This book, then, is offered as an initial analysis to further socialist construction. It celebrates the giant strides taken by the people of the socialist formations and sees their collective achievements as demonstrating just how extensively can necessity be transformed into freedom, just how what are taken within capitalism to be natural constraints can become ingredients for construction of a better, fuller, more secure life for all. For, let us also be clear on this, socialism offers a better life *for all* – social formations that are transitional between capitalism and communism, that is that are socialist, are the site of extensive class struggles to ensure that *everyone* as of right has enough to eat, is well clothed and housed. That is to say that people can have more only by being more. If we are critical of Bolshevik achievements it is only because we are conscious that our world is full of potential and actual emancipation of labour because of the achievements of 1917. We are also very aware – as are the people of China – of how far subsequent socialist revolutions and construction have been possible *because of* Bolshevism. But if 'theory' is 'to be alive to what has taken place', then we must be able to learn from error as much as celebrating correctness. Indeed we must admit the need to make mistakes and learn from them.

For our part this book is provisional in the sense that we hope that it will be used by being superseded, by being transformed into what was clearly a preliminary formulation of a range of problems. For we have tried to produce a book that will encourage certain questions (to which, it is thought, 'we all know the answers') and discourage certain all too available obvious interpretations. These questions and those answers, finally, have as much to say about England now, as they have about those events in November 1917 in Petrograd.

I Marx[1]

There are certain fundamentals that no marxist would ever dispute. Amongst them is *The German Ideology*'s claim that 'the first premise of all human existence and, therefore, of all history' is 'the premise . . . that men must be in a position to live in order to be able to "make history" ',[2] with its implication that 'the production of material life itself' is 'a fundamental condition of all history', and one which 'in any interpretation of history one has first of all to observe . . . in all its significance and all its implications and to accord it its due importance' (Marx and Engels, 1846a: 39). But if marxists would agree to accord production 'its due importance', they would be less than unanimous in their views of what observing it 'in all its significance and all its implications' actually entails for their theory and method. For this reason, we think it essential to make our own understanding of the fundamentals of historical materialism explicit before proceeding further.

1 PRODUCTION

For Marx, it is reasonable to speak of 'production in general' and to construct concepts which refer to features universal to production. We can do this because 'all epochs of production have certain common traits, common characteristics' (Marx, 1857: 85) by virtue of there being such things as 'general preconditions of all production . . . conditions without which production is not possible' (ibid., 86). The concepts through which we grasp these general preconditions, it follows, are concepts without which 'no production will be thinkable' (ibid., 85). They are therefore transhistorical, applicable to all modes of social production. We will begin by defining the major such concepts in Marx's work.

Production always involves a relation between producers and nature, which Marx terms the *labour process*. Regarded 'independently of the particular form it assumes under given social conditions' (Marx, 1867a: 177), this process in every case combines '1, the personal activity of man, i.e. work itself, 2, the subject of that work, and 3, its instruments' (ibid., 178) – labour, raw materials, and technology of some sort or another. Marx refers to the subjects and instruments of labour as *means of production* (ibid., 181).

In addition to relations between people and nature, production also involves relations between people themselves, or *social relations of production*. That production is social as well as material, and irreducibly so, is a point on which Marx is emphatic:

> In production, men not only act on nature but also on one another. They produce only by co-operating in a certain way and mutually exchanging their activities. In order to produce, they enter into definite connections and relations with one another and only within these social connections and relations does their action on nature, does production, take place. (Marx, 1847b: 28)

The claim, we should note, is not that production causes but that it involves social relations. For Marx, there can be no material production without them; material and social dimensions of production are related internally.[3] Unlike many of Marx's followers, we take 'social' here in the broadest possible sense, to mean, as Marx and Engels put it in *The German Ideology*, 'the co-operation of several individuals, no matter under what conditions, in what manner, and to what end' (Marx and Engels, 1846a: 41). By social relations of production we therefore understand *all* 'the social relations within which individuals produce' (Marx, 1847b: 28), in the sense of all those relations necessary to any given mode of production. The nature of such relations cannot be specified *a priori* for production in general, but remains in each case an empirical question.

Production, then, is both a material and a social process, an activity whereby people transform both their circumstances and themselves. Each of its facets, in Marx's view, conditions and constrains the other: he writes both that 'social relations . . . vary according to the character of the means of production' (ibid.) and of 'social relations and the level of development of the means of labour corresponding to them' (Marx, 1866: 1056). Means and relations of production can be equally salient in their productive consequences, and equally constitute *productive forces*. By this latter notion we mean, very simply, *any* force through which people enhance the productiveness of their labour, and, as with relations of production, we make no attempt to specify the nature of such forces concretely in advance of empirical enquiry. Here we again part company with many marxists, though not, we shall argue, with Marx.

2 THE SOCIAL FORCES OF PRODUCTION

Conventionally, the concept of productive forces is understood technologically, as a virtual synonym for the means of production, and Marx does indeed on occasion use the notion thus.[4] His employment of it elsewhere, however, is sufficiently broad to include what *Capital* refers to as 'all new developments of the universal labour of the human spirit and their social application through combined labour' (Marx, 1865a: 104). He makes clear, in particular, that amongst such 'developments' must be numbered those in men's social relations. We find, for instance, that 'technology' is only *one* out of a long list of productive forces beginning 'co-operation, division of labour within the workshop . . .' (Marx, 1866: 1024), the rationale of which Marx makes quite explicit elsewhere:

> The production of life . . . appears as a double relationship: on the one hand as a natural, on the other as a social relationship . . . It follows from this that a certain mode of production, or industrial stage, is always combined with a certain mode of co-operation, or social stage, and this mode of co-operation is itself a 'productive force'. (Marx and Engels, 1846a: 41)[5]

This recognition of social relations as productive forces is equally evident throughout Marx's substantive work: as in, for example, the *Grundrisse*, where he remarks of the 'primitive commune' that 'the community itself appears as the first great force of production' (Marx, 1858a: 495); or as in *Capital*'s seminal account of the transition from feudalism to capitalism, where Marx insists not only that the combination of producers brought about by their 'formal' subordination to capital as wage-labourers constitutes a 'productive power' (Marx, 1867a: 326 *et seq.*) in its own right, but also that this formal subordination precedes and creates the conditions for their 'real' subordination in a form of labour process which technologically requires such combination (ibid., 510; Marx, 1866: 1025 and *passim*).[6]

This last example also instantiates a corollary of our reading of Marx's concept of productive forces which it is worth our bringing up at this stage. Marx, it is well known, explained transition from one mode of production to another by the conflict of incipient forces and moribund relations of production, and on one famous occasion went so far as to assert that 'no social order is ever destroyed before all the productive forces for which it is sufficient have been developed' (Marx, 1859a: 21). On the orthodox view of productive forces, we have no alternative but to interpret such claims as professions of technological determinism;[7] professions which manifestly cannot be reconciled with Marx's own prognoses for revolution in such 'backward' social formations as mid-nineteenth-century Germany or Tsarist Russia. On our interpretation the dilemma is a false one. There need be no inconsistency between the generalisations of the 1859 *Preface* and, say, Marx's opinion that given the co-operative aspects of the relations implicit in its peasant commune, Russia could advance to socialism without undergoing 'all the fatal vicissitudes of the capitalist regime' (Marx, 1877: 292). One has only to recognise the social relations of the *obshchina* as a productive force fettered by existing production relations, as our definition allows, and as does Marx himself when he writes that in the wake of a revolution 'the rural community . . . will soon become the regenerating element of Russian society, and the factor giving it superiority over the countries enslaved by the capitalist system' (Marx, 1881a: 226). The superiority Marx has in mind is a *productive* one.

With Marx, we perhaps need constantly to remember that we are dealing with a man for whom even *theory* 'becomes a material force as soon as it has gripped the masses' (Marx, 1844a: 182). To define the concept of a productive force in a way that can provide for such possibilities is not to descend into idealism, but merely to follow through the logic of Marx's conception of production in general. Having asserted that production is indissolubly both material and social, it would make no sense to define the forces through which it is effected in a manner that excluded phenomena of either kind. Marx makes this abundantly clear in a passage whose authorship many of his disciples might be hard put to recognise:

> Man himself is the basis of his material production, as of any other production that he carries on. All circumstances, therefore, which affect man, the *subject* of production, more or less modify all his functions and activities, and therefore too his functions and activities as the creator of material wealth . . . In this respect it can in fact be shown that *all* human relations and functions, however and in whatever form they may appear, influence material production and have a more or less decisive influence upon it. (Marx, 1863a: 288)

3 THE SOCIAL RELATIONS OF PRODUCTION

That '*all* human relations and functions' may 'have a more or less decisive influence' on material production is a conclusion equally germane to our formulation of Marx's concept of production relations. For here too marxism has suffered from unduly restrictive definitions.

Traditionally, marxists have divided people's social relations into two categories: those belonging to the 'economic base' of society, and those comprising its 'superstructure'. The base is usually held to consist of relations technically entailed in the labour process and relations of *de facto* property in the means of production; the superstructure, of all other social relations, including, specifically, ones of a legal, political or ideological character. Only the former are classed as production relations. The justification for this restriction of the category lies in the substantive claim that base 'determines' superstructure; 'superstructural' relations, by implication, are secondary, not essential, to production. This inference is not affected by Engels's[8] much-cited qualification of the determination as 'ultimate'. For such a causal claim to be meaningful at all, the ability of the base to subsist independently of its superstructure must logically be presupposed.

The base/superstructure metaphor is Marx's own, and passages can undoubtedly be found in his work which when taken in isolation appear to support the 'classical' interpretation of it we have outlined. The 1859 *Preface* is a paradigm case. But, as we have argued in detail elsewhere,[9] this conception cannot be reconciled either with the conclusions of many of Marx's empirical analyses or with their methodology. First, let us consider his conclusions.

Two examples will suffice to indicate the readiness with which Marx identifies as *conditions* of production social relations which should, according to the orthodox view, be unambiguously 'superstructural' and thus mere epiphenomena of a 'base' capable of existing without them. We shall see shortly, when discussing the concept of the State, that these are far from being the only illustrations we could have chosen. The first is taken from that section of the *Grundrisse* quoted above concerning the 'primitive commune'. This 'clan community', Marx asserts,

> is the first presupposition – the communality of blood, language, customs – for *the appropriation of the objective conditions* of their [the producers'] life, and of their life's reproducing and objectifying activity (activity as herdsmen, hunters, tillers, etc.) . . . The *real appropriation* through the labour process happens under these *presuppositions*. (Marx, 1858a: 472)

The second comes from Marx's discussion of feudal 'labour rent' in *Capital* III. This form of compelling surplus labour, he argues, one basic to feudal society, is dependent upon 'other than economic pressure' of a decidedly political kind;

> . . . conditions of personal dependence are requisite, a lack of personal freedom, no matter to what extent, and being tied to the

> soil as its accessory, bondage in the true sense of the word. (Marx, 1865a: 791)

In neither instance does the 'base' subsist independently of, far less 'determine', its 'superstructure', as these terms are conventionally understood. On the contrary: in the first case 'communality of blood, language, customs', in the second a 'direct relationship of lordship and servitude' (ibid., 790) – classically 'superstructural' relations – are diagnosed by Marx as *internal* to production. In so far as it remains appropriate to talk of 'economic' bases at all, these supposedly 'non-economic' relations must be numbered among their *constituents*. For they are, quite simply, 'social relations within which individuals produce' and without which they could *not* produce in these particular ways. As such, they are clearly in substance as much social relations of production as those which have traditionally merited the appellation. It would be perverse, not to say misleading, to refuse to broaden the category accordingly.

What specifically justifies the empirically open-ended definition proposed above, however, is the methodology behind both these analyses and the rest of Marx's substantive work. *The German Ideology* expresses the relevant point succinctly:

> . . . definite individuals who are productively active in a definite way enter into these definite social and political relations. Empirical observation must *in each separate instance* bring out *empirically*, and without any mystification and speculation, the connection of the social and political structure with production. (Marx and Engels, 1846a: 36)[10]

On this premise, marxism could sustain *no* general theory of the 'connection of the social and political structure with production' comparable to the classical base/superstructure conception. For any such theory must involve either *a priori* or inductive generalisation, and Marx rules out the first when he requires that we ascertain this connection 'empirically', and the second when he enjoins us to do so for 'each separate instance'. Only such a theory, however, could justify a decision to term certain of 'the social relations within which individuals produce' *bona fide* relations of production while excluding others from the category. Without it, the boundary becomes completely arbitrary. Any but the open-ended definition of the social relations of production that we have advanced, in short, must be based either upon the abandonment of a key tenet of Marx's methodology or in sheer caprice.

4 CLASS AND THE STATE

The German Ideology argues (of class societies) that

> The conditions under which definite productive forces can be applied, are the conditions of the rule of a definite class of society, whose social power, deriving from its property, has its *practical*-idealistic expression in each case in the form of the State. (Marx and Engels, 1846a: 86–7)

Classical base/superstructure reasoning would incline us to interpret such a proposition somewhat as follows. 'Forces of production' refers here to means of production, 'property' to their ownership. Property in the means of production is the 'economic basis' of a ruling class's social power because it confers the power to determine the conditions under which the direct producers will be allowed to employ these means to produce the wherewithal for their own subsistence. These conditions will ordinarily include the performance of surplus labour on behalf of the owners, and it is this that renders them conditions of class rule. The social power of the ruling class is thus essentially 'economic' in nature and origin. The *State*, the political 'expression' of this power, is part of society's 'superstructure'; that is to say, a distinctive (but not unrelated) and secondary (but not unimportant) formation. Superstructures in general have a 'relative autonomy' and corresponding capacity to 'react back' upon their economic bases, and the State is no exception. It may therefore exert considerable economic influence. But its relation to production remains *external*: the State 'intervenes' in, but is not in any sense part of, the economy. The same holds for politics in general.

Marx and Engels left us a confused, and sometimes a contradictory, legacy in their writings on the State.[11] We intend to present only what, in the light both of the evolution of Marx's own ideas, and of subsequent historical experience, we see as the most enduring and fruitful aspects of that legacy. Our argument, briefly, is that the State should not be viewed as a superstructure at all but as *a set of relations of production*. For (to return to our foregoing quotation) Marx understood by property not just a relation of people to things but a social relation between people: as the same work defines it, 'the power of disposing of the labour power of others' (ibid., 44). *This* is the power Marx refers to as the ruling class's 'social power'. *The Poverty of Philosophy* (a text of the next year) draws the obvious enough inference that to define any particular form of property hence entails elaborating all the social relations through which this power is constituted.[12] Marx frequently, and emphatically after the Paris Commune of 1871, makes it clear that the social relations whose totality comprise the State fall precisely among these latter. The State, in sum, is a *conditio sine qua non* of all forms of social production predicated upon the command of alien labour.

In what follows, we shall first develop a concept of the State consistent with this perspective. We shall then say a little on what this means for a marxist understanding of the State as an instrument of class oppression. Finally we will spell out what we see as the political implications of our thesis.

Engels, in a celebrated passage in *Anti-Duhring*, clarifies exactly what 'the State' is, and how it is (internally) related to production. He defines it thus:

> . . . an organisation of the exploiting class at each period for the maintenance of its external conditions of production; that is, therefore, for the forcible holding down of the exploited class in the conditions of oppression (slavery, villeinage or serfdom, wage labour) determined by the existing mode of production. (Engels, 1894a: 306)[13]

Note, first, that Engels defines the State not (as is normal amongst marxists) by a coercive but by a productive function; and, second, that he infers the former from the latter. It is, he says, because the State is an organisation for maintaining a class society's conditions of production that it is *therefore* an apparatus for enforcing 'conditions of oppression'. It clearly must be, for reasons which should by this stage of our argument be apparent.

Production always presupposes social relations. These relations vary with each mode. A *class* society is one whose production is premised on relations of *exploitation*; social relations, that is, within which surplus labour is compelled and its product appropriated by a non-productive minority. It follows that to maintain the conditions of production of a class society is *ipso facto* to enforce conditions of oppression; for the latter are a part of the former. Once this has been grasped, the internality of the State to production becomes clear. Whatever the social formation, for reproduction to take place the conditions of production (including its social relations) must be secured.[14] Some 'organisation' to ensure this is therefore universally necessary, and the relations which constitute it essential to production itself – relations of production, on our definition. In class societies, Engels tells us, that 'organisation' is the State. The social relations whose ensemble is 'the' State must in consequence be regarded as relations of production.

We propose to take the passage we have quoted from Engels as specifying a marxist *concept* of the State. 'The State' is thus, for us, the entire repertoire of activities by means of which a ruling class endeavours to secure its collective conditions of production. This concept (like those of the productive forces and relations of production developed above) is an empirically open-ended one. What defines the State is not any set of concrete institutions. These in fact vary historically, State-forms being constructed and reconstructed continuously in the course of class struggle. The State is defined by a (productive) *function*; it is this, and this alone, that enables us empirically to identify in any particular context a particular institutional arrangement as 'the State'.

From here, we can move directly to an important confusion in marxist thought concerning the sense in which we can speak of the State as 'nothing but a machine for the oppression of one class by another' (Engels, 1891c: 17).

The class character of the State, both as a product of class antagonisms and an instrument of class rule, are implicit in the concept we have proposed. We have already explained why, in a class society, any apparatus for maintaining conditions of production is inherently an apparatus of class rule. Conversely, were there no classes, there could be no State, in the sense in which Marx and Engels understood the term. If, as they contend, 'political power, properly so-called, is merely the organised power of one class for oppressing another' then clearly in a classless society 'the public power will lose its political character' (Marx and Engels, 1848a: 76). The 'legitimate functions' (Marx, 1871a: 69) of maintaining conditions of production would remain; but their performance would no longer be carried out by 'repressive organs' (ibid.), because the social relations of production would no longer be relations of exploitation. The 'public power', in short, would no longer be a *State*. As the *Anti-Duhring* passage from which we commenced this discussion concludes, 'the government of persons is replaced by the administration of things and the direction of the processes of production. The State is not "abolished", *it withers away*' (Engels, 1894a: 307).

Marxists are therefore quite correct to stress the class nature of the State. But to do so is not at all the same as to identify the State with the visible machinery of governmental oppression, and define its concept accordingly. This is, unfortunately, exactly what many marxists have tended to do. Even *The State and Revolution*, one of the finest texts on this topic we have, straightforwardly equates the State with 'special bodies of armed men, prisons, etc.' (Lenin, 1917b: 393); a practice, of course, thoroughly consonant with the superstructural conception, within which the 'political' must have its own institutional embodiment.

But, in terms of the preceding argument, first, the State is much more than its manifest apparatuses of coercion, and second, its repressiveness derives not from any intrinsic qualities of these apparatuses themselves (like the capacity of armies to kill) but from the very function that defines it as a State. The State is *all* the activities employed by a ruling class to secure its collective conditions of production. Some of these, like Lenin's standing armies, are overtly oppressive; others, like the provision of public libraries[15] or old age pensions, are seemingly innocuous. But what makes them all intrinsically repressive is precisely what makes them part of the machinery of State: *the end they serve*. From this point of view, planning agreements are just as repressive as baton charges. For, as we have seen, to maintain the conditions of production in a class society is *itself* to perpetuate the oppression of class rule. Thus, the State is indeed, for a marxist, 'nothing but a machine for the oppression of one class by another'. But it is a 'machine' (we shall see that this image can be misleading) far more extensive, subtle and pervasive than the one singled out by Lenin. Marx was once moved to comment thus on capitalist production:

> What a convenient arrangement it is that makes a factory girl sweat twelve hours in a factory, so that the factory proprietor, with a part of her unpaid labour, can take into his personal service her sister as maid, her brother as groom and her cousin as soldier or policeman! (Marx, 1863a: 201)

If we have suggested that we are talking about the State long before we reach the words 'soldier or policeman' we will have begun to suggest the right questions. The State *is* that 'convenient arrangement'.

Now to the political implications of our thesis.

Socialist strategies towards the State have historically been dominated by two radically opposed orientations, which we will term the 'capture' and 'smash' views. We referred above to contradictions in Marx's and Engels's writings on the State; both views (though this is truer of the latter than the former) can claim some basis in Marx. The capture thesis is most clearly expressed in the programme of 'revolutionary measures' which closes the second section of the *Communist Manifesto*, which hinges on 'centralisation . . . in the hands of the State' and the subsequent use of this State 'as a means of entirely revolutionising the mode of production' (Marx and Engels, 1848a: 75, 74). It is also (ambiguously)[16] present in various of Marx's remarks on the possibilities that might be open were universal suffrage to be achieved in Britain. The smash view is most explicitly articulated in response to the 1871 Commune, in *The Civil War in France* (and, notably, its drafts), the *Critique of the Gotha Programme*, and the Preface to the German 1872 edition of the *Manifesto*, in which the *Civil War*'s conclusion that 'the working class cannot simply lay hold of the ready-made State machinery, and wield it for its own purposes' is advanced as an overt criticism of the political programme of the *Manifesto* itself (Marx and Engels, 1872a: 8). This is not to say simply that the experience of 1871 made Marx change his mind. Rather, the actions of the Paris working class brought home to him, in practice, positions he had long before reached theoretically in the studies that led up to *The German Ideology*, especially the 1843 *Critique of Hegel's Philosophy of Right*, and enabled him to develop their strategic implications.[17] It is, incidentally, of no small importance that the bulk of these 'early works', within which the State is a central issue, were unavailable both to the marxists of the Second International and to Lenin and the early Bolsheviks.

The capture strategy rests on a conception of the State as a relatively autonomous superstructure (and thus supposes an appropriately economistic notion of production). The State is viewed purely as an apparatus of political coercion which relates only externally to production. Its class character is not, therefore (as for us), understood as inherent in its productive role, but viewed simply as a consequence of the fact that the ruling class (by dint of its 'economic' power) *controls* it. The State as such is thus politically neutral, not in the sense of being 'above' classes, but in the sense of changing its political complexion with the class controlling it. It is, precisely, a machine. Hence, to capture this machine becomes the focal point of a socialist strategy and the 'seizure of power' thus construed *the* moment of 'the Revolution'. By the same reasoning, the State can be *used*, after the Revolution, to transform the social relations of production. Was it not Marx, after all, who wrote of the methods of another (the bourgeois) revolution that

> they all employ the power of the State, the concentrated and organised force of society, to hasten, hothouse fashion, the process of transformation of the feudal mode of production into the capitalist mode, and to shorten the transition. Force is the midwife of every old society pregnant with a new one. It is itself an economic power. (Marx, 1867a: 751)

We believe this passage (and the superlative historical analysis from which it derives) indicate something altogether different: what *Capital* III describes as the *simultaneous* construction, in the course of one and the same class struggle, of a mode of production and 'the corresponding specific form of the state' (Marx, 1865a: 791). We take it, in other words, as supporting exactly the 'relational' concept of the State argued above. The smash strategy is the only one that is consistent with this perspective.

If, as we have contended, the State is a nexus of social relations *internal* to a mode of production, it cannot be seen as a 'machine' to be captured and used. On the contrary its very *form* will be one appropriate to the defence of the conditions of production the socialist revolution seeks to uproot. The capitalist State is, specifically, 'wrought after the plan of a systematic and hierarchic *division of labour*' (Marx, 1871a: 64), within which 'administration and political governing were mysteries, transcendent functions only to be trusted to the hands of a trained caste' (Marx, 1871b: 169) – a division of labour Marx indicted as the most fundamental relation of all commodity production[18] and thus the most basic and enduring of capital's fetters upon socialism,[19] a system of production in which the producers *themselves* collectively determine the use of their labour and its products. Hence, for the Marx of 1871, 'the political instrument of their [the workers'] enslavement cannot serve as the political instrument of their emancipation' (Marx, 1871c: 228). It cannot, because that 'instrument' is itself an integral part of precisely the production relations which block that emancipation. It must, accordingly, be destroyed with them.

From here, a number of other points follow. The 'seizure of power' must be envisaged very differently than it is within the capture thesis. There is no such thing as a unitary 'State power' to be captured (and used) because State power is not a *thing*, but one dimension of the *relations* whose ensemble adds up to the ruling class's 'property' and 'social power'. It is a question, rather, of constructing new *forms* of power, as appropriate to the emancipation of labour as is the State to its suppression. The Commune, the Soviet, the Councils of Action (whether in the Italy of 1920, the Britain of 1926 or the France of 1968) are such forms; organisations not of the ruling class but the producers themselves, through which they can begin to revolutionise their social relations of production from below. Not the seizure, but the destruction of State power is the condition for the flowering of organisations like these; there is no paradox in Marx's assertion that 'the first condition for the hold[ing] of political power, is to transform working machinery and destroy it – an instrument of class rule' (ibid., 227), because the communist revolution[20] is not a struggle for control of the same political edifice but a struggle to replace one form of power (exploitative and oppressive) by another (popular and emancipatory). The same internal relations, in short, obtain between popular political forms and socialist production as hold between State-forms and production grounded in appropriation of other people's labour. This has an important corollary. If the emancipation of labour demands the creation of popular forms of power, it is equally the case that making that power 'solid' requires acceleration of that emancipation. Both conclusions follow from the internality of the politics/production relation. We cannot, therefore, continue to conceive 'the Revolution' as an *event*. It is an *ongoing practice*: a continuing dialectic of self-emancipation (or in Marx's phrase, a 'permanent revolution')[21] which, we shall see, turns not on suppressing but on unleashing class struggle and extending its fronts. At the heart of that dialectic is the spiral of political and productive liberation which so impressed Marx in the Commune:

> . . . it was a thoroughly expansive political form, while all previous forms of government had been emphatically repressive. Its true secret was this. It was essentially a working-class government, the produce of the struggle of the producing against the appropriating class, the political form at last discovered under which to work out the economic emancipation of labour.
>
> Except on this last condition, the Communal Constitution would have been an impossibility and a delusion. The political rule of the producer cannot coexist with his social slavery. The Commune was therefore to serve as a lever for uprooting the economical foundations upon which rests the existence of classes, and therefore of class rule. With labour emancipated, every man becomes a working man, and productive labour ceases to be a class attribute. (Marx, 1871a: 72)

5 MARX'S CRITIQUE

We have several times insisted on the *empirical* nature of Marx's project. For this reason we have offered open-ended definitions of the basic general concepts of historical materialism, and polemicised against those interpretations that seek to draw from Marx trans-historical 'models' of the connection of production with the social and political structure. In Marx's view, what can validly be asserted of 'production in general' is extremely limited.[22] 'Production in general', he writes, is 'an abstraction' (Marx, 1857: 85), and all the concepts through which we grasp its 'general pre-conditions' (forces and relations of production, etc.) are in themselves merely 'abstract moments with which no real historical stage of production can be grasped' (ibid., 88). These concepts specify classes of phenomena present in all material production, but not the phenomena as such. Empirically, we never confront 'production in general' but always some determinate *mode of production*, or 'way in which men produce their means of subsistence' (Marx and Engels, 1846a: 31). To grasp a 'real historical stage' of production is to apprehend such a mode (or more frequently, a combination of modes). To construct an adequate concept of a mode of production, for Marx, involves describing the particular nexus of forces and relations of production (in his expression, the *essential relations*) necessary to it. Now, we clearly cannot derive these historical concepts, as we shall term them, by permutation of the concepts of the preconditions of production in general; to attempt to do so would entail the absurdity of trying to infer what differentiates members of a class from the concept of the class itself, i.e. from precisely what they share. Nor, as we have seen, will Marx allow us to elaborate historical concepts *a priori* or by induction. They must, on the contrary, emerge out of empirical analysis.

To say this, however, does not at all mean that essential relations can be straightforwardly *observed*. Marx was very far from being an empiricist. He held, specifically, that the '*phenomenal forms* of essential relations',[23] that is, the forms in which these relations empirically 'represent themselves' to observation and experience (Marx, 1867a: 537), can often obscure their true nature. In his view 'the outward appearance' and 'the essence of things' need not directly coincide (Marx, 1865a: 817). His claim, we should stress, is not that people perceive these forms wrongly but that the forms may themselves be misleading; as Godelier puts it, 'it is not the subject who deceives himself, but *reality* which deceives him . . .' (Godelier, 1964a: 337). The mechanism, like that of a mirage, is an objective one. Marx does not assume that such deception will always occur: he comments frequently, for instance, on the relative transparency of feudal as compared with capitalist exploitation,[24] and envisages a communist society being one in which 'the practical relations of every-day life offer to man none but perfectly intelligible and reasonable relations with regard to his fellowmen and to Nature' (Marx, 1867a: 79). Whether or not their phenomenal forms mislead is a function of (and must be explained by) the particular relations concerned. But clearly, where phenomenal forms are deceptive, merely to describe them will not yield adequate concepts of the essential relations at issue. For here, categories grounded in observation alone will reproduce precisely the misleading features of the forms they describe. We shall see that this is, for Marx, exactly how ideology arises. We must, therefore, go beyond observation. 'To resolve the visible, merely external movement into the true intrinsic movement' (as Marx put it) 'is a work of *science*' (Marx, 1865a: 313).

Central to Marx's science is a definite form of analysis, which he persistently referred to as a *critique*. The Kantian connotations of the concept are not irrelevant to consideration of what it meant for Marx. Kant was very careful to make clear that for him a critique was more than merely a 'criticism of books and systems'; it was, specifically, an analysis of the conditions of 'possibility or impossibility', and thereby of the 'extent and limits' of its object (Kant, 1781: 3). It goes without saying that Marx was no Kantian. But in its form, his critique is strikingly similar to that of his idealist predecessor.

The object of Marx's critique is the phenomenal, or, as he calls them elsewhere, 'social' or 'determinate economic' forms of the phenomena of material production (Marx, 1858a: 881; 1859b: 28). These phenomena assume different forms within different modes of production. The product of labour, for instance, is a phenomenon common to production in general; but only within the relations of very definite modes of production (respectively, simple commodity production and capitalist commodity production), will it display the attributes which stamp it as commodity or capital. These latter are particular social forms of the product of labour. All other productive phenomena will likewise take distinctive social forms, depending upon the mode of production. Such variations indicate, on the empirical or phenomenal plane, differences between the essential relations of these modes.

But, as we have seen, for Marx phenomenal forms may well obscure the relations of which they are the empirical manifestations. A price, for example, phenomenally defines the commodity-form of the product, a capacity to realise profit on sale its capital-form. But it is by no means apparent from simple observation of these forms themselves that the first is a manifestation of production founded upon a spontaneous division of social labour, and the second an expression of production premised in the exploitation of labour by capital. These characteristics appear, rather, to derive from inherent, natural qualities of the product as such like its utility. Essential relations, therefore, have to be *inferred* from their phenomenal forms. A critique, understood in the Kantian sense, is the kind of analysis which is most appropriate to this project. For just as in general production supposes forces and relations, so each particular set of social forms has its conditions in the essential relations specific to the mode (or modes) of production in which these forms occur. An analysis of the conditions of 'possibility or impossibility' of these forms, that is, precisely a critique, will therefore furnish Marx with the essential relations he is seeking. At the same time of course these relations, *qua* conditions of possibility, will further constitute the 'extent and limits' within which the phenomena under analysis *can* take the forms in which we observe them. The critique thus establishes the *historicity* of the phenomenal forms it analyses.

This has an important corollary. Marx held a materialist view of the world, central to which is the denial of the independence of consciousness from experience. Language, in the words of *The German Ideology*, is 'practical consciousness' (Marx and Engels, 1846a: 42); 'linguistic designation simply expresses as an image what repeated confirmation has made an experience' (Marx, 1880: 46). Economic categories are no exception to this rule: they are, so far as Marx is concerned, 'only the theoretical expressions, the abstractions, of the social relations of production' (Marx, 1847a: 109). As *Capital* clarifies (and logically enough if experience is the foundation of consciousness) the categories ordinarily grasp these relations in their phenomenal forms, which 'appear directly and spontaneously as current modes of thought' (Marx, 1867a: 542). It follows that Marx's critique, in establishing the conditions of existence of these forms, at the same time defines the 'extent and limits' within which the *categories* which apprehend them can validly be applied. Hence, Marx is now in a position to criticise the illegitimate extension of economic categories beyond their proper historical bounds; attribution, for example, of the category (and, by implication, the characteristics) of the commodity to products of circumstances where labour is not spontaneously divided. This is, we will see, central to his criticism of fetishism and ideology. Before we come to that, one or two points of elaboration are called for. They concern the sense in which Marx's critique is an empirical, and a historical, analysis.

In his draft *General Introduction* to the *Grundrisse*, Marx toyed with the idea of beginning his 'critique of the economic categories' (Marx, 1858b) not with 'the real and the concrete' (Marx, 1857: 100) but, like the classical economists before him, with abstract universal categories. But as Martin Nicolaus (1973, Part III) has shown, this was a methodological strategy he was soon to reject. Two years later he explained his omission of this *Introduction* from the 1859 *Critique* (a twice-revised version of the *Grundrisse*'s famous 'Chapter on Money') on the grounds that 'the reader who really wishes to follow me will have to decide to advance from the particular to the general' (Marx, 1859a: 19). Both the *Critique* and *Capital*, in the event, begin with the analysis of the very 'real and concrete' category of the commodity, a clearly historical economic form. That this is more than a matter of Marx's 'method of presentation' is made plain in an important (and neglected) text, his 1880 Marginal Notes to Wagner's *Lehrbuch der Politischen Oekonomie*. Talking of the analytic procedures of *Capital*, Marx is adamant that:

> De prime abord I do not start from 'concepts' . . . What I start from is the simplest social form in which the labour product is represented in contemporary society, and this is the '*commodity*'. I analyse this, and, indeed, first in *the form in which it appears*. (Marx, 1880: 50)

We could hardly wish for a clearer statement of the empirical basis of Marx's critique. The concepts of 'real historical stages' of production are, he makes clear, emphatically *a posteriori* constructs, end-products, not pre-cast tools of analysis. It should not be necessary to labour this point; but (as a glance at any Althusserian treatise will confirm), the state of contemporary views of marxist epistemology is such that it cannot be emphasised too strongly or too often.[25]

Marx's critique, then, begins with the empirical. But thereafter, we have argued, Marx goes beyond what is phenomenally evident in an endeavour to infer its conditions. He seeks to ascertain what set of forces and relations of production must exist if productive phenomena are to assume the social forms in which we observe them. Now as we have seen already, these essential relations need not, for Marx, themselves be immediately observable. Their discovery is hence essentially a matter of advancing hypotheses. Marx in fact *posits* mechanisms which, were they to exist, would give the set of phenomena with which the critique commences their observed forms. The prerequisites for the operation of these mechanisms are then taken as the conditions of existence of these forms, i.e. as essential relations of the mode (or modes) of production in which such forms occur. Profit, for instance, is in no way visibly connected with the worker's surplus labour. We cannot observe exploitation as we might in the *corvée*, for the worker's necessary and surplus labour are not phenomenally distinct. *Capital* postulates a set of putative (invisible) mechanisms via which surplus labour is enabled to take the phenomenal form of profit on capital, and argues that only if these mechanisms exist is this form possible or explicable. The key requisite for the functioning of these mechanisms, the 'severance of the conditions of production, on the one hand, from the producers, on the other', henceforth, for Marx, 'forms the *conception* of capital' (Marx, 1865a: 246).

Elsewhere (Sayer, 1975b: 170–83) we have shown that the explanatory hypotheses derived thus are susceptible to independent empirical tests of validity. Their details need not be rehearsed here. It is, however, important to grasp that for Marx the initial *proposal* of explanatory hypotheses is governed by strict criteria of empirical adequacy, as is perhaps most clearly evident from his criticisms of his classical predecessors in *Theories of Surplus Value*[26] and elsewhere. Marx praised the classicals for their attempts 'to grasp the inner connection in contrast to the multiplicity of outward forms' (Marx, 1863c: 500). But at the same time, he castigated their penchant for what he stigmatised as 'violent' (Marx, 1867a: 307) or 'formal', and therefore 'incomplete' (Marx, 1863b: 106) abstraction. To abstract 'violently' is to hypothesise explanatory mechanisms which leave an unexplained residuum at the empirical level. It involves, in Marx's words, attempting to 'rescue the law [i.e. the explanatory hypotheses] from collision with contradictory phenomena' (Marx, 1867a: 307) by the simple expedient of 'abstracting *from*' these phenomena in the sense of effectively ignoring them. Such abstraction is obviously 'incomplete' inasmuch as the irksome phenomena remain unaccounted for. The technicalities of Marx's criteria of adequacy need detain us no further here.[27] It suffices to stress only one point. We have seen that Marx regards it as imperative to penetrate 'behind' the phenomenal forms which make up our everyday experience, in order to establish what conditions make them possible. Doing so is a task for the 'force of abstraction' (Marx, 1867b: 8). But this 'force', Marx insists, must be carefully controlled. What controls its exercise, crucially, are *the forms under analysis themselves*; for so long as 'violent abstraction' *is* eschewed it is always they that define the limits of permissible theorising. In this, important, sense Marx's critique remains an empirically grounded enterprise throughout.

This latter point bears directly upon the issue to which we will now turn, that of the sense in which Marx's project can validly be described as *historical*. For many, whether disciples or critics of Marx, his work is predicated on a *general theory* of history, even a historicism. Central to this alleged theory are many of the substantive propositions attacked above, including, *inter alia*, a technologically motivated account of social change and a base/superstructure model of social organisation. In recent years, a strong challenge to historicist interpretations of Marx has been mounted by Althusser and his followers. Its outcome, however, has too frequently been the denial of *any* relation of marxism and history. Neither of these extremes in our view grasps Marx's own position.

It should be evident from all we have argued so far that Marx could not consistently advance any general theory of history, teleological or otherwise. For the critique is a method of analysis that reasons from phenomena to their conditions. The corollary is that whatever explanatory propositions this method yields are valid *only* within the domain of the phenomena from which they are inferred. A famous text of Marx's, his letter of November 1877 to the editors of *Otechestvenniye Zapiski*, makes this point very clearly. Repudiating Mikhailovsky's attempt at 'transforming my historical sketch of the genesis of capitalism in Western Europe [in *Capital* I, Part VIII][28] into an historico-philosophical theory of the general path of development prescribed by fate to all nations', he writes:

> events strikingly analogous but taking place in different historical surroundings led to totally different results. By studying each of these forms of evolution separately and then comparing them one can easily find the clue to this phenomenon, but one will never arrive there by using as one's master key a general historico-philosophical

theory, the supreme virtue of which consists in being supra-historical. (Marx, 1877)

We have argued elsewhere that Marx's work is as free from historicism in substance as it is in protestation (Sayer, 1975a: 800–6). But to say this is not to embrace that current position which asserts the study of history to be 'not only scientifically but also politically valueless' (Hindess and Hirst, 1975: 312).[29] On the contrary.

Marx's critique does not presume, and cannot produce, a 'general historico-philosophical theory'. It remains, for all that, a radically historical form of analysis; for what it does is to establish precisely the historicity of the phenomena with which it deals. It shows their existence to depend on relations which are themselves historical products; as capital, for example, supposes a class relation which 'has no natural basis, neither is its social basis one that is common to all historical periods. It is clearly the result of a past historical development' (Marx, 1867a: 169), the central feature of which is 'a Decomposition of the Original Union existing between the Labouring Man and his Instruments of Labour' (Marx, 1865b: 45). To be sure, the critique itself cannot tell us how this 'Original Expropriation' (ibid.) came about; but, as the *Grundrisse* makes clear, it is a necessary preliminary to the kind of analysis which can; for, without it, we could not know that in seeking the origins of capital we are in fact searching for the origins not of a thing, but of 'a definite social production relation, belonging to a definite historical formation of society, which is manifested in a thing and lends this thing a specific social character' (Marx, 1865a: 814):

> our method indicates the points where historical investigation must enter in . . . In order to develop the laws of bourgeois economy . . . it is not necessary to write the *real history of the relations of production.* But the correct observation and deduction of these laws . . . always leads to primary equations . . . which point towards a past lying behind this system. These indications . . . then also offer the key to the understanding of the past – a work in its own right. (Marx, 1858a: 460–1).

Even worse than the suggestion that to study history is scientifically valueless is the incredible claim that it is *politically* valueless. For to show that a set of phenomena are historical is to show that they are constructed by human beings and thus capable of being changed; while to show what conditions are historically required for their existence, as does Marx, is to show exactly *what* socialists need to change. His epigones notwithstanding, Marx, at least, had no doubts as to the political value of the denial of history, to capital, and its discovery, to labour:

> from the moment that the bourgeois mode of production and the conditions of production and distribution which correspond to it are recognised as *historical*, the delusion of regarding them as natural laws of production vanishes and the prospect opens up of a new society, [a new] economic social formation, to which capitalism is only the transition. (Marx, 1863c: 429)[30]

6 BOURGEOIS IDEOLOGY AND WORKING-CLASS CONSCIOUSNESS

For Marx and Engels, 'the ideas of the ruling class are in every epoch the ruling ideas' (Marx and Engels, 1846a: 61). Lenin was to build the political programme of *What is to be done?* on an extreme statement of this thesis: contending (in passages his contemporary followers too often rip from their context and dogmatise) that 'the *spontaneous* development of the working-class movement leads to its subordination to bourgeois ideology', he concluded that 'class political consciousness can be brought to the workers *only from without*' (Lenin, 1902: 384, 422). Such formulae, we shall see, are dangerously one-sided. The 'spontaneous' consciousness of the working class is not just ideological but *contradictory*,[31] and workers are more than the passive recipients of 'theory' donated them by 'revolutionary intellectuals'. Their experience (as this book will repeatedly confirm) is on the contrary the touchstone from whose basis it is possible to see, and overcome, the perversion of marxist theory *itself* by the ideology of capital. This ideology none the less is a threat to the workers' movement, and not just to its 'spontaneously developed' forms; how great a threat, it is part of the aims of this book to reveal. We may begin from Marx's analysis of the nature and roots of bourgeois ideology, as developed, above all, in *Capital*.[32]

There are various marxist views of bourgeois ideology, the crudest being that which takes Marx's observation that 'the class which has the means of material production at its disposal, has control at the same time over the means of mental production' (Marx and Engels, 1846a: 61)[33] as sufficient explanation of its dominance. Ideology thus becomes more or less conscious ruling-class propaganda. We do not wish to deny the existence of such deliberate attempts to manipulate working-class consciousness; but using them to explain the *dominance* of ruling-class ideology is problematic. Marx, we have seen, holds *experience* to be the base of *all* consciousness. On this supposition, we could accept the foregoing explanation only if working-class experience was itself mainly confined to exposure to the propaganda of the ruling class, which it manifestly is not. The alternative to this flagrant breach with empirical fact is to break equally decisively with a fundamental premise of historical materialism, viz. Marx's assumption of the dependence of men's consciousness on their practical experience. Conversely, a truly marxist theory of ideology must be able to explain the dominance of 'the ideas of the ruling class' in terms of *the experience of the subordinate class itself*. It is precisely such a paradigm of explanation that *Capital* offers.

Marx argues (and attempts systematically to demonstrate)[34] that the roots of ideology are to be found not in men's inaccurate perceptions of the world, 'manipulated' or otherwise, but in their *accurate* perceptions of the world as it 'represents *itself*' to experience. Ideology derives specifically from the phenomenal forms of essential relations. It is in consequence a result (or, more precisely, a facet) of these relations themselves. Phenomenal forms, we have seen, can for Marx be misleading. If experience is the foundation of consciousness, as Marx contends, then where they are misleading, experience *itself* becomes the major 'means of ideological production'. We do not, in other words, have to presume conscious deception on the part of the ruling class. On the contrary, we explain the success (and the limits) of any such ruling class endeavours by their compatibility with the totality of the working-class life-experience upon which they attempt to impose an interpretation. Empirically, it is thus the susceptibility of much working-class experience to bourgeois interpretation which accounts for the dominance of bourgeois ideology. And it is the radical *inassimilability* of other elements of working-class experience to bourgeois views of the world which explains the typically contradictory character of working-class consciousness.

We may briefly exemplify these propositions with respect to Marx's (now celebrated)[35] analysis of the ideological dimensions of the wage contract. The wage, for Marx, is not a payment for work done, but for the commodity workers sell to capitalists, the (temporary) use of their labour-power. Wage-levels are therefore a function of the value of labour-power. The value of labour-power – like that of any commodity – is determined by the labour socially necessary for its production, i.e. here, by the labour required to manufacture the labourer's means of subsistence.[36] Thus, the value of labour-power, and the value produced when the capitalist 'consumes' this commodity by setting it to work may be two completely different magnitudes. And in so far as the capitalist makes the worker work longer than the time required to reproduce the value of his labour-power – i.e. his wage – he will appropriate a surplus-value for which no equivalent has been given. The wage contract, in sum, conceals a relation of exploitation. But this relation itself is by no means phenomenally apparent. On the contrary, it all happens, 'on the surface of bourgeois society' (Marx, 1867a: 535), *as if* the wage were recompense for work performed. Marx details the (very real) appearances which sustain this illusion: they include, *inter alia*, the fact that the labourer is paid after his work is done, ostensibly for that work; that from his own point of view, it is a particular kind of useful labour he has supplied, and was contracted to supply; that it is his labour, and only his labour, that yields him his wage; and that the forms in which wages are paid, by the piece or by the hour, are such that remuneration is (apparently) a direct correllate of work done.[37] Working-class experience of capitalist social forms in this instance gives powerful support to a view of the world – 'A fair day's wage for a fair day's work!' – which objectively serves the bourgeoisie. For the wage form not only hides, but positively presents as its opposite, as the exchange of equivalents, the class relation upon which the entire edifice of capitalist production rests.

Hopefully, the general principles of Marx's analysis of ideology will by now be reasonably clear. It remains to explicate the concept of what Marx saw as the central mechanism of specifically *bourgeois* ideology, *fetishism*.

Fetishism, for Marx, 'consists in regarding *economic* categories, such as being a *commodity* or *productive* labour, as qualities inherent in the material incarnations of these formal determinations or categories' (Marx, 1866: 1046); it 'metamorphoses the social, economic character impressed on things in the process of social production into a natural character stemming from the material nature of those things' (Marx, 1878: 229). Let us elaborate.

We saw above that various phenomena were common to production in general, but took different social forms in different modes of production. What distinguishes these forms are attributes which the phenomena in question do not share with their counterparts elsewhere; as, for example, a price distinguishes the commodity-form of the product of labour, and a capacity to realise a profit its capital-form. Such singular attributes are entirely consequential upon the essential relations of the modes of production in which these forms occur; they do not, in other words, derive from their 'material side', which equivalent phenomena of 'the most disparate epochs of production may have in common' (Marx, 1858a: 881). Now, a *fetishised* discourse ascribes these eminently social characteristics just this material origin. The value-form of the commodity, say, a form products assume under the conditions of commodity production alone, is explained by its use-value, a characteristic of products of labour *per se*. A twofold reduction results. Not only is the social collapsed into the material; the historical is assimilated to the natural. For to see properties certain members of a given class of phenomena acquire only by virtue of standing in a specific network of social relations, as inherent in phenomena of that class as such, is *ipso facto* to universalise those properties. The specifically ideological implication should be obvious enough. Natural laws cannot be changed by human agency.

The political economy Marx analysed in *Capital* is not the only form of bourgeois ideology, but it may be taken as paradigmatic. Bourgeois ideology in general is powerful. It is powerful precisely because of its firm phenomenal foundation; through it, people can make some sense of much of their life-experience, most of the time. Its hold, as we have indicated above (and will substantiate below), has often extended to marxist theory itself. It is seriously worth considering, for example, the phenomenal roots of certain of the marxist dogmas criticised, on a theoretical level, in this chapter. Does not a technologistic conception of productive forces and their role in historical change betray an understanding of 'the productive forces . . . as a world for themselves, quite independent of and divorced from the individuals, alongside the individuals . . . whose forces they are' (Marx and Engels, 1846a: 83), an understanding which *The German Ideology* identifies as an effect of the division of labour, and *Theories of Surplus Value*[38] denounces as fetishistic? And does not the classical base/superstructure model, with its hermetic 'economy' and 'polity', owe something to the *apparent* independence of these spheres in the 'enchanted, perverted, topsy-turvy world' which 'Monsieur le Capital' rules?[39]

Bourgeois ideology is powerful. So powerful, in its incontrovertible obviousness, that it usually goes unchallenged because undetected. But it is not invincible. For there are experiences which it cannot frame or understand; experiences which threaten to make manifest what the obvious conceals, and provide the basis for blowing the world of capital to the winds. It is to these that we will now turn – armed, we hope, with a marxism capable of learning.

2 Bolshevism and its Critique

In 1936 J. Sen wrote to Andre Gide suggesting that 'the time is opportune for criticism to be directed against the USSR'. Amongst his reasons was one we share:

> A communist cannot refuse to examine realities, for that would be the negation of Marxism. Communists . . . have not the right, on the pretext of not discouraging the proletariat, to conceal from it the errors of a revolutionary experiment. On the contrary, their duty, their task is to examine the path followed by the Russian Revolution . . . (cit. Gide, 1937: 141–2)

Today, the obligation extends to examining the paths of all those other revolutions which have coloured one third of the world's map red. For, as Brus restated more than three decades later,

> it is neither right nor acceptable that the enemies of socialism should have the monopoly of criticising the socialist world . . . a critical but communist analysis of the experiences of socialism, the renunciation of those analyses which seek only to flatter, is essential not only for the international communist movement, but also for the future of world socialism. (Brus, 1971: 113)

It is this, very practical concern that motivates the reflections which follow. That Brus's prescription should come from an essay which bears the title 'Contradictions and ways to resolve them' is singularly germane to their theme.

1 1917

1917 was, and remains, epochal in its significance. Put most simply (and in terms the *Financial Times* understands) the October Revolution snapped the hitherto unbroken chain of imperialism. It meant that the labour-power of the former subjects of the Tsar of all the Russias ceased to be the commodity it had been, while their products would no longer be numbered among the assets of international capital. The supreme achievement of 1917, Soviet power, instead heralded a new era in the 'great contest', as Marx called it, between 'the blind rule of the supply and demand laws which form the political economy of the middle class, and social production controlled by social foresight, which forms the political economy of the working class' (Marx, 1864: 346). As Lenin stresses, Soviet power is not 'a miracle-working talisman' – but

> it does pave the way to socialism. It gives those who were formerly oppressed the chance to straighten their backs and to an ever-increasing degree to take the whole government of the country, the whole administration of the economy, the whole management of production, into their own hands. (Lenin, 1919a: 249)

Lenin was equally to stress, as did Marx before him and Mao after him,[1] that workers' power could not immediately be equated with, and did not automatically entail, the victory of socialism. It inaugurates an epoch of *transition* whose successful outcome is not pre-given, but depends upon

> a long, difficult, and stubborn *class struggle*, which, *after* the overthrow of capitalist rule, *after* the destruction of the bourgeois state, *after* the establishment of the dictatorship of the proletariat, does not disappear . . . but merely changes its forms and in many respects becomes fiercer. (Lenin, 1919b: 389)

1917 achieved this 'change of forms' in the class struggle; a change which simultaneously marked a massive shift in the respective power of its combatants. That shift (as we will argue in detail below) has *not* been reversed. Capital has yet to recover what it lost with the Winter Palace; as it has also to make good its losses since 1917, and in large part because of 1917, in the rest of that growing red third of the world. It is this revolutionary liberation from the yoke of capital, and the socialist advances, both inside and outside the USSR, it has made possible, which fully justifies our description of the Great October Socialist Revolution as epoch-making.

To say this is of course to acknowledge the immensity of the debt socialism owes to the Bolsheviks, and thus above all to Lenin. For October was a Bolshevik revolution, and Bolshevism pre-eminently Lenin's creation.

But we spoke above of the need for a 'critical but communist analysis' of the epoch 1917 inaugurated. Here, we enter a terrain mapped out by long-standing communist polemics, the debates between Trotsky and Stalin, within the Trotskyist movement, and, latterly, between the Communist Parties of China and the Soviet Union being only the most celebrated.[2] In all cases something is alleged to be rotten in what the CPSU now calls 'the State of the whole people'.[3] Diagnoses of what kind of rot it is ('state capitalism', 'bureaucratic collectivism', 'a fascist state of the Hitler type', 'degenerate workers' state'), of when it set in (1923? 1953? 1963?), and of why vary widely. But there are, none the less, congruences between the major 'critical but communist' positions, and a massive lacuna common to virtually all of them.[4] Central to most is the charge of 'betrayal' on the part of the leaders of the CPSU, following the seizure, by the alleged traitors, of State power. If it is felt necessary to explain the possibility of such coups occurring in the first place, Soviet 'backwardness' and 'isolation' are held unproblematically to account for the dominance of the social strata which sustain them. CPC, and CPC-inspired, analyses would unsurprisingly demur from this latter judgement, which is best exemplified in Trotskyist work of all persuasions. They share, however, the lacuna. *Bolshevism as such* is rarely invoked, anywhere on the Left, in the explanation of the alleged Soviet malaise. It figures solely and monotonously as that which was betrayed.

This myopia is, to say the least, curious. The Bolsheviks themselves had no difficulty in identifying as Bolshevik a coherent ensemble of theories and practices; Lenin himself did so on several notable occasions.[5] 1917, as we are the first to acknowledge, was supremely a Bolshevik achievement. The present-day 'State of the whole people' has been constructed under unbroken CPSU(B) tutelage. *Prima facie*, then, if we are to understand it, we must look amongst other things at Bolshevism itself. It is facile simply to claim that the Party has 'changed colour', that the Stalin gang or Khrushchev clique has 'usurped State power'. As we argued in Chapter 1, the conditions of such phenomena need to be elucidated; and these in turn require situating in terms of their historical genesis. We should be asking what kind of State is thus amenable to 'seizure', and how did it come to be so constructed. Here, an assessment of Bolshevism as a possible causal factor becomes unavoidable. It is at this point, in those analyses which at least attempt to penetrate behind the phenomenal forms which are held to mark the 'betrayal' of 1917, that the familiar figures of 'backwardness' and 'isolation' (the latter, we shall argue, so salient only because of the importance accorded to 'backwardness' itself) appear on the stage. But Bolshevism can no more be sidestepped here; for its theory informed judgements on the significance of such factors, and these judgements were embodied in its practices towards them. The circumstances of socialist construction in the USSR, in other words, were always mediated (and in part constituted) by what we shall term the 'social problematic' of Bolshevism itself.

Before going any further, let us clarify this latter concept and its place in our argument. Our usage of the term 'problematic' owes something to the Althusserian tradition,[6] in that we employ it to focus attention on what we regard as a definite matrix in which all variants of Bolshevism, their (important) differences notwithstanding, are rooted; a taken for granted and implicit common framework for debate, within whose confines their confrontations are articulated. But we qualify this problematic as 'social' – and this point cannot be overemphasised – because Bolshevism is not just a set of ideas but a body of *practices*. Its problematic is not only categorial, it is institutional. Unless this point is taken, our thesis is likely to be gravely misunderstood. When we attribute a causal status to the Bolshevik problematic we are not pleading the historical decisiveness of 'ideas' *simpliciter*; any such disembodied conception of 'ideas', as we have indicated in Chapter 1, is anathema to marxism. Nor are we simple-mindedly denying the pertinence of the 'objective circumstances' so central to other accounts. We simply seek to comprehend these circumstances in the ways in which they were historically pertinent; namely, within the frameworks offered by definite social practices. To approach the matter otherwise would be to fall into the errors of the 'so-called objective historiography', whose penchant for 'treating the historical conditions independent of activity' Marx castigated in *The German Ideology* (Marx and Engels, 1846a: 52fn.). The importance of these points will become graphically clear when we see, for instance, what 'backwardness' signified within the very different social problematic evident in much of the CPC's strategy for socialist construction.

But enough of preliminaries. In what follows, we will attempt to show exactly how critical is the lacuna to which we have pointed here. For, we shall argue, the historical experience of socialist construction, within and outside the USSR, cannot be understood without reference to the hegemony Bolshevism has exercised over it. In this chapter, we will set out our argument in relatively general terms; subsequent chapters will expand upon, exemplify, and document its major theses. We will begin by outlining the Bolshevik problematic itself; its initial formation, its nodal features, above all its contradictions.

2 BOLSHEVISM

Bolshevism did not emerge *ex nihilo*. And whilst, as we have already stated, we cannot provide a history here, it is as well to provide brief sketches – and they are, we stress, no more than that – of two important features of the environment of its construction: the marxism initially available to its founders; and the singular social formation that was Tsarist Russia.

Lukács, Goldmann, and Colletti, amongst others,[7] offer us valuable commentaries upon the marxism of the Second International. This marxism was formed, we should note (although this point should not be fetishised), in ignorance of many of Marx's own writings, amongst them the bulk of his 'early' work, *The German Ideology*, and the *Grundrisse*.[8] What without doubt was decisive for it was Engels's so-called 'testament', his later texts, with *Anti-Duhring*, in particular, having at least as much influence within it as Marx's *Capital*.[9] A further formative factor was the bourgeois thought of the time, against which it struggled, but much of whose dominant positivism and scientism it arguably imbibed none the less. This two-fold inheritance finds its reflection in the following features.

Most generally, the theorists of the Second International sought to elaborate marxism as a *weltanschauung*, articulating universally valid laws of both nature and society. Central to this was the development of what eventually became known as 'dialectical materialism' (a category utterly foreign to Marx),[10] conceived as providing a consistent philosophic underpinning for the marxian 'system'. This was presaged in Engels,[11] whom, revealingly, Max Adler (cit. Colletti, 1968: 62 fn.) praised for liberating marxism from the 'special economic-social form' it assumes in Marx's own work. The materialism here, for all its 'dialectical' pretensions (which amounted to little more than the *a priori* superimposition of Hegel's schema of development-through-contradiction on to a materialist ontology), was of a mechanistic variety, owing a lot more to the philosophical materialism criticised by Marx in those early writings unknown to the Second International[12] than to anything in his own work. Plekhanov, for instance, rooted Marx's epistemology in that of Helvetius and Holbach, and added, for good measure, that 'Marx and Engels, after the *materialist* turn in their development, never abandoned the standpoint of Spinoza' (cit. Colletti, 1968: 71). Marxist materialism was 'Spinozism disencumbered of its theological setting' (ibid., 72 fn.); for Spinoza's mystical single category of 'substance', with its attributes of thought and extension, Plekhanov saw Marx as substituting the (for him) less theological, but no less unitary category of 'matter'.[13] This sustained a complex series of reductions, brilliantly analysed by Colletti. The centrality to Marx's work of people's social practice (and therewith, their consciousness) was largely lost; in its stead, the theoreticians of the Second International developed a naturalistic conception of a social world whose 'laws' were strictly analogous to those of nature, and thus capable of formulation in terms of classically mechanical paradigms of causation.[14] Parallel to Plekhanov's reduction of Marx to Spinoza is Kautsky's analogy of Marx and Darwin, Marx being hailed as the discoverer of the 'laws of evolution' of human society.[15] This crude scientism, finally, concealed what was perhaps the most radical departure from Marx of all; 'science' was itself in the end divorced from social practice and historical experience. Whereas, as such texts as *The Civil War in France* eloquently testify, for Marx workers' struggles form the foundation for developing revolutionary theory, for Kautsky, unambiguously,

> The vehicles of science are not the proletariat, but the *bourgeois intelligentsia* . . . Thus, socialist consciousness is something introduced into the proletarian class struggle from without. (Cit. Lenin, 1902: 383–4 – *with approval*)[16]

The substantive theories of the Second International marxists were congruent with these general philosophical tenets. They share two features in particular which we wish to highlight here. First, Marx's 'base/superstructure' metaphor – a dubious legacy, as we have argued above – is understood as expressing a universal social law. Integral to the 'model' that eventuates is what Colletti (1968: 63) justly refers to as 'a vulgar and naive conception of the "economy" ', the key points of which he summarises thus:

> The so-called 'economic sphere' – which in Marx had embraced both the production of *things* and the production (objectification) of *ideas*; production and intersubjective communication; material production and the production of social relations (for Marx, the relation between man and nature was also a relationship between man and man, and vice versa) – was now seen as *one isolated factor*, separated from the other 'moments' and thereby emptied of any effective *socio-historical* content, representing, on the contrary, an antecedent sphere, prior to any human mediation. *Social* production is thus transformed into 'production *techniques*'; the object of political economy becomes the object of technology. (Ibid., 65)

In a footnote to the same passage Colletti notes how Engels's famous caveats (in his 1890b, 1890c, and 1894f) on the errors of naked economic determinism if anything reinforced the vulgarity of this conception. For he preserved what was fundamental to it (and, as we have argued in Chapter 1, alien to Marx): a separation of 'the economic' from 'other spheres' of social life, and an assumption of external, causal relations between them.

This impoverished conception of 'the economic' is basic to the second aspect of Second International theory to which we wish to attend: a body of related propositions dubbed by Lenin, and subsequently the

CPC, the 'theory of productive forces'. This 'theory' postulates a series of invariant stages (communal, slave, feudal, capitalist, socialist . . .) through which all social formations must necessarily pass, explaining transition between them by the development of 'the productive forces'. The latter, as we might expect, are conceived technologically. The theory asserts, crucially, that social revolution cannot successfully anticipate its technical requisites; thus the bourgeois revolution must invariably precede the proletarian, whose *sine qua non* is a mature capitalism. Socialist revolution is therefore impossible in such 'backward' social formations as Tsarist Russia; the role of the proletariat, in such a situation, is to support the 'progressive' wing of the nascent bourgeoisie. It is here, on the more obviously objectionable political implications of the theory, that criticism (not least Bolshevik criticism) has tended to focus.[17] We wish, however, to point to various implicit assumptions which lie behind the theory's overt propositions. For these, as we will see, may survive intact long after the theory itself has ostensibly been repudiated.

We should emphasise at the outset that we have no quarrel whatsoever with Marx's dictum that socialism demands maximal development of mankind's productive forces. Indeed, we see having enough to eat (being decently clothed and housed) as a defining feature of socialism, and thus expanding the production of daily necessities as absolutely basic to its construction. What is at issue is what 'the productive forces' *are*, and what is entailed in 'developing' them. Consistently with their evolutionism and that picture of 'the economic sphere' we have outlined, the theorists of the Second International had unitary answers for both questions. Productive forces were unambiguously technical, and to develop them meant to follow the trail blazed by capital. Specifically, the only adequate 'material basis' for socialism was the large-scale machine industry characteristic of 'advanced' capitalism, while creating this basis required a process of capital accumulation, paradigmatically exhibited in England's 'industrial revolution'. This process was held always and necessarily to involve radical changes in relations between rural-agricultural and urban-industrial 'sectors', the former yielding up the resources for the initial capitalisation of the latter, and a parallel shift in the 'balance of population', rural peasants becoming urban proletarians in order to provide industry with its labour force and its market. Socialism, in short, becomes theoretically and practically subordinated to the presumed exigencies of a historically unexceptionable path of 'modernisation', basic to which is the extension of the division of labour in all its forms.[18] At the same time, its distinction from capitalism comes to be understood primarily as a matter of control of an otherwise invariant technical-economic infrastructure (a perspective not unrelated to the reformism and statism into which the politics of the Second International ultimately degenerated). We shall have more to say on the errors and the consequences of this notion of 'development' in due course. For the moment it will suffice to recall two points argued in Chapter 1. First, Marx's own concept of productive forces was very much broader than the one we have just encountered. It embraced social relations of production (in the fullest sense). And second, Marx explicitly disavowed any attempt to legislate a 'general path of development prescribed by fate to all nations'. Significantly, he sharply focused both points in his prognoses for socialism in Tsarist Russia (Marx, 1877, 1881a).

We will now turn to the latter social formation; in, once more we stress, what can be no more than the barest sketch.[19] In the decades immediately preceding the October revolution, Tsarist Russia was a social formation of peculiar complexity. Capitalist production was developing rapidly[20] within it; but its dominance was doubly attenuated, in that first, it enjoyed no secure internal bases of power, and second, the majority of Russia's producers (and much of Russia's production) remained outside its ambit. Both features reflect the fact that capitalist development was imposed on Tsarism from outside and in the context of an extant world market. Russia, in sum, was in no sense straightforwardly capitalist; it was rather (to employ a formulation Mao[21] used with reference to the China of the 1920s) a 'semi-feudal, semi-colonial' formation.

In the years of which we are speaking, Russia remained an overwhelmingly agrarian society. The vast mass of its people worked the land; and they worked it, for the most part, within social relationships of a 'precapitalist' kind.[22] Feudal forms of compelling surplus labour proved tenacious, the 1861 'Emancipation' of the serfs notwithstanding; so too did the village commune, the *mir* or *obshchina*, much to the chagrin of those Tsarist modernisers who sought to build a *kulak* class of capitalist farmers out of its disintegration.[23] The ruling class was a landowning aristocracy, its Tsarist State a feudal absolutism without the slightest veneer of bourgeois democracy. But for all this Russia was in certain respects extensively 'developed'; it boasted, for instance, an industrial sector whose volume trebled in the two decades before the First World War, to stand fifth in the world rankings in 1914 (Anderson, 1974b: 353). Tsarist development, however, was by no means a simple phenomenon. It was emphatically a semi-colonial development, and internal to it was the systematic reproduction of much of Russia's feudal legacy. The expression 'semi-feudal, semi-colonial', in short, refers not to a dualism but an articulated (if contradictory) combination, in which the semi-feudalism reinforced the semi-colonialism and vice versa.

Importantly, Russia was never a colony, in the sense that it never fell under the yoke of any one national fraction of the international bourgeoisie. It was, rather, the prey of competing imperialisms. But imperialised it was, and to an extent that often goes unrealised; in 1914, for example, 47 per cent of the capital of Russian industry was held outside the country (33 per cent of this in France, 23 per cent in Britain, 20 per cent in Belgium, and just under 20 per cent in Germany).[24] Further, Tsarism's own programme of modernisation (itself largely financed via foreign loans) was precipitated by the pressures of this imperialist environment, its immediate stimulus being the Crimean debacle, and its continuing condition the military threat of the capitalist states. The development that eventuated exhibited a classically 'combined and uneven' profile. Capitalist production was overwhelmingly the creation of foreign investment under State auspices or of the State itself. It remained, economically, socially, and geographically, an 'enclave' in a largely untransformed semi-feudal hinterland; in agriculture, market-oriented cash crop production was confined to enclaves in a predominantly precapitalist milieu, and industry itself formed an enclave in its wider agrarian surrounds. Industrial production bore the typical stigmata of such enclave development, being preponderantly large-scale,[25] with a few giant (and often State-owned) enterprises dominating each sector. Their key managerial and technical personnel were frequently foreign or foreign-trained. The obverse of this was equally archetypal of semi-colonial development: that *process* of underdevelopment which many marxists still comprehend as a simple *state* of 'backwardness'. The contradictions of the Tsarist industrialisation programme are well known.[26] Briefly, the Tsarist State serviced the foreign loans which provided the initial capital for its industries by taxing the peasantry. But this level of taxation simultaneously deprived industry of the market it needed in order to become self-financing, and agriculture of resources which might otherwise be employed to improve production sufficiently to sustain such a market. The net effect was to reproduce on the one hand the dependence of industry upon the State and the State on foreign capital, and on the other the poverty, oppression and stagnation of agrarian production. This rapine (to underline once again the connectedness of Russia's semi-colonialism and semi-feudalism) was not an arbitrary depredation, the last decadent fling of an archaic Oriental Despotism. The massive capital inputs it financed were those which contemporary levels of capitalist progress *demanded* of any would-be capitalist state. The hidden hand was that of the world market.

These contradictions were to erupt, explosively, in 1905 and again in 1917. We will confine ourselves to describing the principal actors in the drama, and registering some notable absences. Overshadowing all was a Tsarist State whose social basis lay in a class anachronistic to its own modernisation programme, the feudal aristocracy.[27] State and aristocracy both ruthlessly exploited the rural masses, the aristocracy often by feudal means. These rural masses formed the vast majority of the population. Most were peasants rather than 'pure' wage-labourers; and although a *kulak* stratum was emerging, communal relations (and as 1917 would testify, collective anti-landlord and anti-*kulak* class sentiments) were still strong. There was no indigenous bourgeoisie able, or willing, to challenge Tsarism; where industry was not directly in the hands of the State, it depended upon the State for its orders, and, we might add, for 'disciplining' its increasingly recalcitrant workforce. Nor, given the enclave character of Tsarist development, was there an urban petty bourgeoisie of any significance. There was, however, a proletariat; small in numbers (three to four million in 1914 – compared to over 100 million peasants), poor in conditions, but organised and concentrated, by the logic of Tsarist development itself, in the nerve-centres of industrial Russia. It was these workers who were to bring down the edifice of Tsarism in a week.

In 1922, Lenin dated Bolshevism 'as a stream of political thought and as a political Party' from 1903 (cit. Carr, 1950: 19).[28] But Bolshevism's genesis stretches back beyond the second congress of the Russian Social-Democratic Workers' Party, at which the Mensheviks and Bolsheviks first openly split, beyond even *Iskra*. There had already been a series of struggles within the ranks of the Russian revolutionary movement which went some considerable way towards defining Bolshevism's initial contours.[29] First and foremost there was the secular, revolutionary variation of the 'great debate' between so-called 'westerners' and 'Slavophiles', in which Plekhanov ranged his émigré *groupuscule*, the Liberation of Labour, against the *narodniks*. The latter[30] envisaged a specifically Russian road to socialism through peasant revolution and the reconstruction of society on the basis of the *obshchina*, thereby avoiding a capitalist 'stage'. Against this Plekhanov's group maintained Second International orthodoxy respecting the dependence of socialism on prior capitalist development. Lenin in his early writings (especially his seminal *Development of Capitalism in Russia*) took up and extended Plekhanov's critique. Importantly, however, Lenin was equally adamant in his refusal of what many took to be a clear political implication of this thesis. Both the Legal Marxists and the Economists inferred the necessity for Russian socialists to throw their weight behind bourgeois opposition (such as it was) to Tsarist absolutism; for the former socialists had to eschew 'heaven-storming' and 'learn in the school of capitalism', while for the latter there was 'only one way out: to support the economic struggle of the proletariat and to participate in liberal opposition activity' (cit. Carr, 1950: 21, 22). Lenin denounced both tendencies in no uncertain terms in his *What is to be done?* Much of the future was anticipated in these formative battles; Lenin later lost few opportunities to point to the doctrinal debts which the Mensheviks owed to their Legal Marxist and Economist forebears. Also prefigured, however, was something else. A certain tension can be detected in Lenin's position. Basic to his critique of *narodnism* is the thoroughly orthodox Second International subordination of socialism to previous capitalist development. Rejection of what would seem politically to follow from this, though, is equally fundamental to his polemic against the Legal Marxists and Economists. In fact, as we shall shortly see, this rejection was well grounded in a superlative empirical analysis of the Tsarist social formation and its potentialities, informed by the historical experience of its class struggles; but this in no way, of itself, erases the tension. That tension, we shall argue, was eventually to develop into a raging contradiction at the very heart of Bolshevism.

After 1903, Lenin further indicates, Bolshevism underwent 'fifteen years of practical history . . . unequalled anywhere in the world in its wealth of experience' (Lenin, 1920b: 26). We unfortunately cannot detail that history, or Bolshevism's part in it or responses to it, here, important as to do so would be to any adequate account of Bolshevism's formation.[31] Suffice it to recall that amongst the historical experiences to which Lenin refers were, centrally, the 1905 revolution and its sequel, and the Great Imperialist War, the latter wreaking equal havoc in the international socialist movement as it did in the Russia of the Tsars. The shape of the Bolshevism of 1917 owes as much to this 'practical history' as it does to the prehistory we have sketched. We shall confine ourselves, however, to a discussion of what resulted. Let us begin by registering some achievements without which the October Revolution would not have been made.

Bolshevism broke, substantially, with that marxism of the Second International we have outlined above. It did so, in large part, on the basis of an acute analysis of the contradictions of Tsarist Russia; contradictions which the revolution of 1905, in particular, insistently placed on the socialist agenda. Trotsky[32] captured well the spirit of Bolshevism's break in two critical comments on the Menshevik Tscherewanin, whom he accused of 'replacing any materialist analysis of social relations by . . . formalist deduction' rather than confronting the question of the '*class dynamics* of the Russian revolution – not the "permanent revolution", not the "socialist revolution", but the one that is going on in Russia at the present time' (Trotsky, 1908: 303; 1909a: 317). In place of (to quote Trotsky again) 'that spurious

Marxism which nourishes itself on historical clichés and formal analogies and transforms historical epochs into a logical succession of inflexible social categories' (Trotsky, 1922a: 345–6) Bolshevism recovered Marx's own commitment to historical specificity in analysis. Relatedly, and just as importantly, where the Second International marxists had grounded their 'logical succession of inflexible social categories' upon a theory of productive forces, the Bolsheviks reasserted class struggle as the motor of historical progress and social change.

Bolshevism analysed Tsarist Russia not merely as a 'backward' society, but with the fullest appreciation of the complexity we have sought to indicate. It was understood not as one isolated country to be mechanically located on a pre-given and unilinear scale of 'development', but as an integral part of the world capitalist system, a part whose internal pattern of development could not properly be comprehended except with reference to the vicissitudes of that system. Lenin was among the first to explore the workings of imperialism, and to identify Russia as the 'weakest link' in its chain of dependence; Trotsky, for his part, provided a masterly exposé of just what sort of development such dependence induces. This grasp of 'the peculiarities of Russian historical development', as Trotsky phrased it, in turn sustained a sharp and realistic assessment of the balance of class forces in the Tsarist formation.

The weakness of Russia's indigenous bourgeoisie, together with its economic and political dependence upon Tsarism, and the revolutionary potential of the young, strategically concentrated, and militant working class were recognised early. So too, especially after the wave upon wave of *jacqueries* in 1905–6, was the revolutionary potential of the peasants; although here, as we shall see, Bolshevism's break with Second International positions was hesitant and ambivalent, remaining a partial one. This class analysis eventuated in a vision of (and strategy for) the revolution 'that is going on in Russia at the present time' which deviated sharply from the academic projections of Second International theory; not the national bourgeoisie, but the proletariat, backed up by the peasant masses, was to be its protagonist. Such a perspective, of course, threatened one of the most hallowed tenets of Second International dogma; the conceptual and historical separation of bourgeois and proletarian revolutions, and therewith the stages theory which underlies it. In fact the Bolsheviks were always careful to preserve a theoretical distinction between these stages; but in practice, their separation was rapidly being eroded. As early as 1898, Lenin argued that though 'the political revolution in Russia [i.e. the bourgeois-democratic revolution] must precede the socialist revolution' the two are 'indissolubly linked' (cit. Carr, 1950: 25–6). For the Bolsheviks, the class struggles of 1905 hardened this link; Lenin envisaged the next

Russian revolution yielding a 'revolutionary democratic dictatorship of the proletariat and the peasantry'. Trotsky went still further, and posited an immediate post-revolutionary transition from bourgeois tasks to socialist. If before the war Lenin polemicised against Trotsky's conception, by 1917 he had clearly accepted its substance. His April 1917 *Letters on Tactics* declare: 'Whoever, *today*, speaks only of the revolutionary democratic dictatorship of the proletariat and the peasantry is behind the times, *has*, by this fact, *gone over*, in practice, to the petty bourgeoisie, and deserves to be relegated to the museum of pre-revolutionary "Bolshevik" curiosities . . .' (Lenin, 1917j: 45). Lenin's target was Kamenev, who had found the programme of his April Theses 'unacceptable in that it starts from the assumption that the bourgeois democratic revolution has ended and counts upon an immediate transformation of this revolution into a socialist one' (*Pravda* editorial, 8 April 1917, cit. Lowy, 1976: 5), and who had accordingly denounced him, not unreasonably, as a Trotskyist. Lenin's 'Trotskyism' (and Trotsky's signal contribution to Bolshevism) were destined to receive ample confirmation a few short months later. Lenin began his first public speech following the insurrection in Petrograd with the unambiguous declaration: 'We shall now proceed to construct the Socialist order!' (cit. Reed, 1919: 129).

Implicit in this political break with Second International perspectives, and basic to the 'materialist analysis of social relations' which sustained it, is a wider philosophical critique. *Pace* Kautsky, Lenin's *Philosophical Notebooks* inveigh against 'making the concept of *law* absolute, against simplifying it, against making a fetish of it'; according to Lenin, 'laws, all laws, are narrow, incomplete, approximate' (Lenin, 1916b: 151). This rejection of mechanistic determinism is grounded in a rediscovery of what was most fundamental to Marx's materialism (and lacking in that of Helvetius or Holbach); *pace* Plekhanov, the same text celebrates 'intelligent' idealism as superior to 'metaphysical, undeveloped, dead, crude' materialism (ibid., 179) by virtue of its apprehension, albeit in mystified form, of 'the active side', the 'coincidence of the changing of circumstances and of human activity or self-change' (Marx, 1845) which Marx's *Theses on Feuerbach* identify as '*revolutionary practice*'. There is a parallel shift in epistemology, well exemplified in Lenin's insistence, in the third of his 1917 *Letters from Afar*, that 'We would be committing a great mistake if we attempted to force the complex, urgent, rapidly developing practical tasks of the revolution into the Procrustean bed of cut and dried theory . . .' (Lenin, 1917i: 33). Theory – *pace* in this case both Kautsky and the Lenin who quoted him so enthusiastically in 1902 – is recognised to have a dialectical dependence on the social practice it seeks to inform.

Importantly, as Lowy (1976) has noted, this philosophical critique has the character of a *post festum* theoretical 'reprise' of discoveries contained, 'in the practical state', in those empirical analyses upon which we have already commented. In this sense, it instantiates its own major epistemological contention. Lenin's 1908 *Materialism and Empirio-criticism*, for example – a work which postdates much of Bolshevism's empirical challenge to Second International orthodoxy – defends a materialism which differs little from Plekhanov's. *What is to be done?* likewise (as we have several times indicated) embraces Kautsky's epistemology – a point, we would think, not irrelevant to the evaluation of the mere 'theory of organisation' which many on the Left are prone to abstract from this work. In fact, Lowy argues, the 'break' at the level of philosophy was only explicitly accomplished after 1914, in Lenin's *Philosophical Notebooks*. His point is not merely a scholastic one. As the violence of the Old Bolshevik response to Lenin's April Theses testified, there were a number of fairly drastic shifts between Lenin's pre- and post-war positions on the nature and course of the Russian revolution. We have already seen that he had moved closer to Trotsky's avowal of the immediate transition from bourgeois to socialist revolution; equally importantly, during 1917 Lenin radically revised his opinion of the Paris Commune (which he had castigated in 1905 for being unable to 'distinguish between the elements of a democratic revolution and a socialist revolution' – Lenin, 1905b: 80–1) as a paradigm of proletarian dictatorship (cf. his 1917b: chapter III), and therewith went a fuller appreciation of the significance of specifically Soviet power. Lowy stresses, rightly, that these shifts were in no sense 'deduced' from Hegel's *Logic*; they resulted from 'what constitutes the very essence of the Leninist method: *concrete analysis of a concrete situation*' (Lowy, 1976: 15). Where, in Lowy's view, Lenin's September 1914 reading of Hegel was relevant, however, was in enabling him finally 'to free himself from an abstract, cut and dried theory that was *an obstacle to this concrete analysis*' (ibid.). We would place equal, if not greater emphasis on the historical experience which informed Lenin's reading of Hegel; but the road to the Finland Station was a long one and we cannot dwell further on its details here. Of one thing, however, we may be confident. By 1917 Lenin was philosophically equipped to *learn* from the struggles of the Russian masses, as his Second International forebears never had been. It was this that enabled him ultimately to lead them.

For the theoretical, methodological and philosophical advances we have sought to register here were severely practical in their implications. It was (as Lenin makes clear)[33] as an instrument attuned to precisely the 'historical peculiarities' the Bolsheviks had so acutely analysed that their Party was first created. That Party's tactical flexibility and responsiveness to mass initiatives, most devastatingly exhibited during the revolutions of 1917, are renowned. Such 'pragmatism' (as it is often simplemindedly portrayed) had its presuppositions. Not the least among them was an epistemology which predicated theory upon historical experience.

But the Bolshevik problematic also has its darker aspect. To elaborate this, one or two more general prefatory remarks are called for.

Workers' power, as we have indicated previously, must not be equated with socialism. It inaugurates an era of transition. Further, as Charles Bettelheim has reminded us, the successful socialist outcome of the transition is not assured by the simple fact of revolution; transition is a two-way corridor, and regress to capitalism is as real a possibility as progress to socialism. The outcome depends upon further struggle; the struggle to build the socialist mode of production, socialist construction, which (as Marx, Lenin and Mao unite in insisting)[34] is necessarily a class struggle. This latter notion embraces more than the mere suppression of any physical resistance to the revolution. Rather, as Marx put it in his *Critique of the Gotha Programme*:

> What we have to deal with here is a communist society, not as it has *developed* on its own foundations, but, on the contrary, just as it *emerges* from capitalist society; which is thus in every respect, economically, morally and intellectually, still stamped with the birth marks of the old society from whose womb it emerges. (Marx, 1875: 15)[35]

We stress the words: 'in every respect'. Revolution subordinates the former ruling classes to the dictatorship of the proletariat. But the extensive productive, moral, cultural and habitual bases of their power which Marx draws attention to are not therewith automatically suppressed. It is against these White bases, all of them bastions of capital, that class struggles must continue to be directed. As *The German Ideology* notes, a mode of production 'must not be considered simply as being the reproduction of the physical existence of . . . individuals. Rather it is . . . a definite *mode of life* . . .' (Marx and Engels, 1846a: 32). The struggle for socialism is appropriately extensive. And it unites, inextricably, productive and political transformations; just how inextricably we will see in due course.

This defines a post-revolutionary social formation as one in which elements of both capitalism and socialism exist, in struggle. The struggle has a different physiognomy than in capitalism itself, in so far as the capitalist class has been deprived of its monopoly of the means of production and labour power has ceased to be a commodity. This marks a *fundamental* shift in the balance of forces. But it remains the case that to socialise the means of production does not *ipso facto* do away with all the social relations upon which capitalism rests; its divisions of labour, for example, may well remain intact. And, crucially, to the extent that such relations are not equally challenged, the emancipation of labour is hampered and the advance to socialism both slowed and weakened. Now, it is in the light of this consideration that the following comments, and in particular those that talk of Bolshevism replicating certain relations and experiences akin to those of capitalist production, must be read. Let us state once and for all that we believe this claim to be both a valid and an important one because of its implications for socialism; but it does *not* amount to a claim either that the USSR is capitalist, or that Bolshevism is a programme or vehicle for capitalist restoration. Many capitalist relations, we shall argue, survive in the USSR, and they do so, amongst other reasons, because Bolshevism, not recognising them for what they are, has fostered them. But no capitalist *class* controls the means of production in the USSR, and Soviet workers are *not* commodities. To that extent (and it is, as we shall argue in Chapter 6, a very considerable extent if measured, as it should be, in terms of the material experience of the Soviet people) the USSR remains socialist. And that it does so is supremely a Bolshevik achievement; that is to say, an accomplishment of the Soviet people which the CPSU has protected, and continues to protect.

Having said this, we can move towards our criticisms. We do not deny that the Bolsheviks realised the necessity for continuing the class struggle after the revolution; indeed, we have quoted Lenin to this effect previously. What is at issue is the way in which, within the Bolshevik problematic, the linkage of the political and the productive within this struggle was conceived. We shall argue that the Bolsheviks continued to adhere to that impoverished notion of what production is, and what is entailed in developing it, which we met in the Second International's 'theory of productive forces', and that this in turn eventuated in the separation of politics from production, and thus an effective fracturing of the spiral of productive and political liberation fundamental to a socialist programme. But these are, as yet, rather abstract terms; let us be more specific.

Teodor Shanin has recently argued that

> The conception of the basic dynamics of a peasant society accepted by Russian policy makers, and, indeed, by the majority of educated Russians at the beginning of this century can be outlined in a few sentences. It was believed that in the process of inevitable economic advance, every human society necessarily headed towards an increasing division of labour, the establishment of market relations,

> the accumulation of capital, and social diversification. It was also believed that these processes were centred in towns but inevitably spread into the countryside . . . In this process – peasant farms differentiated into rich farmers who employed labour and landless agricultural labourers and ex-rural urban workers. A small middle peasantry gradually disappeared . . . This general picture of the dynamics of a peasant society was firmly established as a piece of self-evident knowledge – it had become part of the prevailing ideology, not only in the normative but also in the cognitive sense . . . (Shanin, 1972: 1–2)

Amongst those 'educated Russians' (and future Russian policy makers) who shared this cognitive (and, we stress, normative) orientation were the Bolsheviks. In E. H. Carr's words,

> Every Russian Marxist believed in the economic superiority of western capitalist society and in the backwardness of the primitive peasant Russian economy; every Russian Marxist reacted against the Slavophil myth. (Carr, 1958: 158)

He adds, revealingly: 'But Trotsky showed particular zest in dwelling on the nullity of the Russian contribution to civilisation.'[36] But if Trotsky excelled himself, he did so as *primus inter pares*; the conception of 'the process of inevitable economic advance' that Shanin summates was espoused by virtually all Russian marxists, both Menshevik and Bolshevik. It is, of course, a conception we have met before: precisely as the underpinning of the Second International's 'theory of productive forces'.

Contrary to Menshevik pedantry there was no inconsistency between Bolshevism's simultaneous rejection of this theory, and partial adherence to the model of 'development' upon which it is predicated. The Bolsheviks merely needed to argue that, in Trotsky's words:

> the conditions for the arising of a dictatorship of the proletariat and the conditions for the creation of socialism are not identical, not of like nature, in certain respects even antagonistic. (Trotsky, 1930e: 368)

Revolution, they held, depended on the conjunctures of class struggle, whose determination was by no means uniquely reducible to the level of development of 'the productive forces'. But to assert this in no way entailed denying the dependence of *socialism* on such 'development'. To put it another way (but still to use Trotsky's words), revolution was merely 'a part of the superstructure' (Trotsky, 1930a: 30), whose 'relative autonomy' allowed, in certain historic circumstances, 'anticipations'. But superstructures are 'ultimately' subject to 'the laws of world economy' (ibid.); and socialism is 'in the last instance' accordingly conditional upon building an (appropriately 'modern') 'material basis', consonant with these 'laws'. We are concerned less with the consistency of the Bolshevik position, however, than with its consequences. The language should alert us.

Evidently, the Bolshevik critique of the Second International's politics did not extend to its economics. Capitalist modernisation remained the paradigm for development of the productive forces as such, and socialism continued to be subordinated to the imperatives of development thus conceived. What we indicated above to be the essential substratum of the theory of productive forces, in other words, survived intact in Bolshevism itself. Also untouched (as the images of base and superstructure testify) was something else: that conception of material production, and of its connection with the social and political structure, upon which this model of development is premised. This conception, we have seen, is an impoverished one, central to which is precisely a separation of production from its social, political, and cultural relations. It was these relics of Second International orthodoxy, in our view, that through their practical embodiments were to fetter the spiral of political and productive emancipation we spoke of above. For the cognitive orientation they sustained was programmatic in its consequences; just as decisively as those advances which we enumerated earlier, it helped mould the social problematic through which the Bolsheviks thought about, and organised for, the future.

It is in terms of this orientation (as opposed to what is normally taken to be their unproblematic facticity) that the salience of 'backwardness and isolation' for the Bolsheviks (and *mutatis mutandis* within Bolshevik-inspired explanations of the USSR's alleged 'degeneration') need to be understood. For, clearly, if it is once assumed that socialism cannot be built except on the foundation of levels and paths of development comparable to those enforced by capitalism, Russia in 1917 presents a dismal prospect of a crippling backwardness whose obstacles isolation could only compound. But, it must be stressed, this conclusion follows if and only if we adhere to the initial assumption, and to do so is not mandatory (or, we shall argue, desirable). What matters here, however, is that for the Bolsheviks both premise and conclusion enjoyed equal (and equally self-evident) facticity; Russia's 'backwardness' was therefore for them the key problem. Isolation, it is worth noting, must itself be understood as a dimension of this problem. As we shall see in detail below in connection with Trotsky, the most ardent of internationalists, and the most vehement of critics of 'socialism in one country', Bolshevik internationalism was by no means merely a question of moral or political principle. Before Stalin mutated the problematic,[37] the

Bolsheviks predicated the success of their revolution upon its international counterpart for reasons of an emphatically productive nature. The 'material basis' of socialism, they assumed, could only be constructed internationally, employing the technical resources of what they were apt to describe as 'the advanced countries'. In short, as with 'backwardness', 'isolation' derives the particular significance it had for the Bolsheviks from their comprehension of 'the laws of world economy'.

This comprehension also informed Bolshevism's perceptions of the way forward. Central to all Bolshevik strategies for socialist construction from 1917 to the present day has been the assumption that 'modernisation' must come before socialism. Behind this lies the Second International dictum that as regards the 'base' (if not the 'superstructure', with its much vaunted 'relative autonomy') technical must precede and premise meaningful social change. And stemming from it is a further series of equally rigid priorities. Since we have dealt with these in general terms already, and document them at length in later chapters, they may be stated with extreme and polemical brevity: mechanisation before cooperation; industry before agriculture (and heavy before light industry); accumulation before daily necessities; expertise before redness. Together, these prescriptions define a programme which entails the accelerated reproduction of many of what are in fact fundamental social relations of capitalist production, above all its divisions of labour.

The Bolsheviks, of course, saw things differently but for reasons which are themselves germane to our argument. Basic to that impoverished conception of production they inherited from the Second International was a restriction of the category of social relations of production to property relations alone. It was this that enabled Trotsky unproblematically to label State industry 'the socialist sector', or Stalin to declare the USSR in 1936 'a socialist country' notwithstanding the fact (very well known to both) that what was being created, under the aegis of the Soviet State, was a set of productive forms certain of whose social relations bore a strong resemblance to those within which capital's workers produce. We will exemplify below; for the moment it should suffice to mention that amongst the latter were the production relations pioneered by Frederick Taylor, a man for whose 'scientific achievements in the field of analysing mechanical motions during work'[38] Lenin, Trotsky, and Stalin all expressed the greatest admiration. That such an irreducibly capitalist social, economic, political, moral and cultural complex as Taylorism should not merit the appellation of production relations is of course precisely the corollary of that technicism we first noted in respect of Bolshevism's forebears. For the Bolsheviks, such relations were in essence neither capitalist nor socialist, but formed part of that socially neutral, because technical, 'infrastructure' they saw as necessary to both modes of production. The reductions of production to technique and its social relations to those of ownership alone are condition and consequence of one another.

A further corollary of this technicism, likewise remarked above, was also in part at least carried over into Bolshevism. The foregoing line of reasoning, we have seen, eventuates in comprehending the distinction between capitalism and socialism as above all one of the control of this essentially common 'infrastructure', and thence, in practice, as supremely a question of whose hands wield the machinery of State. Bolshevism, as we shall have plenty of opportunity to see, did in fact go far towards endorsing this variant of the 'capture thesis', *The State and Revolution* notwithstanding; moreover, we shall argue, a form of this thesis is just as much a feature of Trotsky's (or Lenin's) criticisms of 'bureaucracy' as it is of the policies of Stalin or his successors. Nor should a renascent capture thesis surprise us; it is, after all, firmly rooted in precisely that conception of production the Bolsheviks made their own.

All Bolshevik strategies for socialist construction, from Lenin to Brezhnev, have in our view partaken of the approach to production, and thereby to politics, we have just outlined. Put rather more succinctly they combine an economistic view of production and a voluntaristic view of politics, and this combination is a recurrent one. The economism inheres in the notion of production as a set of necessary techniques governed by ineluctable laws of development, the voluntarism in the truncation of politics to matters of State this original expunging of the political from the productive entails. Of course, this couple leaves ample room for disputes within Bolshevism and, as we shall see, its dominance has never been unchallenged; but, we believe, it none the less provides the dominant common frame of reference in terms of which permissible options are formulated.

This is not the point to document this claim; later chapters do so at length. Some preliminary indications of what is to follow might none the less be pertinent, if only because those issues which were *not* in contention are conventionally overlooked by a Left in large part divided by the historical schisms of the CPSU, whereas we believe Bolshevism's convergences cannot be stressed too heavily.

In Chapter 3, we focus on Lenin, Trotsky, and Stalin. All three, we show, were united (as were Bukharin, Preobazhensky, and other Bolshevik luminaries[39]) in their acceptance of the priority of 'modernisation' and all it entailed. Of particular importance were the implications for their understanding of the worker/peasant *smychka* or 'bond' on which Soviet power was based; for, to repeat a simple fact laboured above, over 80 per cent of Russia's citizens fell into the latter category.

The congruence of views here would be striking, were these views not normally taken to be unremarkable statements of self-evident truths. At best the peasants were seen as unripe for socialism; at worst, and frequently, they were perceived as a 'sea of enemies'. The reasoning behind this was eminently economistic: mechanisation must precede cooperation, while in the meantime, in Lenin's words, 'small production *engenders* capitalism and the bourgeoisie continuously, daily, hourly, spontaneously, and on a mass scale' (Lenin, 1920b: 24). At the same time, it was equally axiomatic that agricultural production was to provide the funds and the labour force for the industrial infrastructure which was to enable its eventual mechanisation. Thus from the start socialism was something to be donated, from above and at some point in the unspecified future, to the vast mass of the Soviet people; and in the interim, they were condemned to suffer something which in at least some, non-trivial, respects replicated the experience of capitalism.

This was not the only instance of such reproduction. We have remarked Lenin's, Trotsky's and Stalin's unanimous admiration for Taylorism. This was symptomatic of the more general fascination with things American which permeates their discourse. All three, for example, were likewise enamoured of one-man management, 'material incentives' and the extensive employment of (often reactionary) 'experts' in all branches of production. Such policies were hardly unconnected with the systematic erosion of workers' power, in Trade Unions, Factory Committees, and Soviets, which characterised the first years of the Bolshevik regime.

Kronstadt symbolised one sort of consequence, the rise of the *kulak* and the NEPman another. But here, Lenin, Trotsky and Stalin had recourse to Bolshevik voluntarism; the State, they believed, was well able to keep such challenges at bay. More generally, 'our State' was considered by all three (and explicitly theorised by Stalin) as the major agency of socialist construction, in both its productive and its political facets. It was both the motor of construction and the instrument of class struggle, developing the forces and revolutionising the relations of production (as Bolshevism understood them) through its fiscal and planning machinery, whilst securing the political conditions for this stratagem through its repressive and ideological apparatuses. In this vision, we believe, much of 'Stalinism' is augured.[40]

In Chapter 5, we turn to Bolshevism after Stalin. No caesura, we argue, separates Khrushchev or Brezhnev from the fundamentals of their Bolshevik heritage; merely the context has changed. Now, it is not the industrial but the 'scientific-technical' revolution which exercises Bolshevik minds. Now, it is not the experience of capital's genesis, but that of its 'maturity' Bolshevism seeks to replicate; the debates concern the use of 'market mechanisms' as an aid to 'optimal resource allocation', of profit as a spur to 'efficiency' of enterprise performance; such 'techniques' too being checked, and where necessary (as in Czechoslovakia in 1968) curtailed by the long arm of The State of The Whole People. Stalin's machinery is more and more perceived as cumbersome, outmoded and (the term is a frequent, and in its apparent innocence an ominous one[41]) 'irrational'. But this perception is solidly grounded in the problematic modern Bolshevism shares with its classical progenitor. The economism and the voluntarism are with us still; it is only their forms which have altered.

We have argued, then, that central to Bolshevik strategies from Lenin to Brezhnev and inclusive of Oppositions both Left and Right has been a conception of what the productive forces are, and what it means to develop them which has occasioned a systematic replication of certain essential relations of capitalist production. We have already made it clear that this does not amount to claiming that capitalism as such ('State-' or otherwise) has been restored in the Soviet Union. But we do consider that such practices have gravely (and needlessly) shackled Soviet socialism. Indeed, it is in our view precisely they which are largely responsible for those distortions so many marxists habitually analyse as products of Bolshevism's 'betrayal'. For the fundamental conditions of the latter are to be found neither in a post-revolutionary coup by 'reactionary forces' nor in the supposedly immutable constraints attending 'backwardness and isolation'; to argue thus is to resuscitate the Bolsheviks' own combination of voluntarism and economism. The limitations of Soviet socialism (as well as, it should be stressed, its achievements[42]) are more readily comprehensible as effects of the mode of production sixty years of Bolshevik policies have created; a profoundly contradictory mode, which uneasily combines capitalist with socialist elements. Here, in particular, lie the roots of Soviet statism.

It should by now be evident that (to return to the notions with which we introduced this discussion) Bolshevik 'development' programmes will tend to sunder the political from the productive facets of socialist construction, and thus reproduce the phenomenal separations of economy and polity that legitimate Bolshevism's own ideology of base and superstructure. For, as we have seen, pending sufficient 'modernisation' the emancipation of labour within production was never contemplated by the Bolsheviks. Their programmes, on the contrary, without exception enforced various relations, and experiences, of production reminiscent of the dictatorship of capital; experiences that replicated capital's divisions of labour, capital's hierarchies of technical and managerial 'expertise', capital's divisive 'incentives', capital's inequalities, and, by no means least, capital's coercion of surplus labour and appropriation of its product to fuel an incessant and insatiable accumulation. This is of course not, as we shall see in Chapter 6, the whole story. But no particular acumen is needed to appreciate just how utopian were Lenin's injunctions to workers to 'take into *your* hands *all affairs* of the State' or Stalin's appeals for 'mass criticism from below' under such a productive regime. The simple fact is that to the extent that they persist, capitalist relations of production systematically erode the possibility of there being *any* genuine control (or transformation) from below. And to expand them has a clear consequence, which Bolshevism's entire history tragically confirms.

The State becomes the major bastion of an eventual socialism, and expands exponentially. The programme of 'modernisation' requires this expansion, both directly and by virtue of its enforced depoliticisation of the mass of direct producers. Administering 'modernisation' involves the creation of a massive fiscal and planning apparatus, whilst to secure its political conditions increasingly calls for just as monstrous a machinery of repression. In turn, class struggles become restricted in scope and attenuated in form; politics henceforth centres on who is in command of the State machine while the 'mobilisation from above', the Purge, and the Show Trial, become its typical and passable manifestations. In short, and unsurprisingly, to foster capitalist forms of productive activity eventuates in the reproduction of various defining relations of the bourgeois Stateform that is their condition and consequence. The Bolshevik State remains the 'supernaturalist abortion of society' denounced in Marx's *Civil War*; Bolshevism preserves that division of labour which constitutes the political as a distinct realm (apparently) 'separate of and independent from society', and sustains 'the delusion as if administration and political governing were mysteries, transcendent functions only to be trusted to the hands of a trained caste' (Marx, 1871b: 167, 169).

Here, we believe, lies the source of Bolshevism's central and most brutal contradiction. In the absence of the emancipation of labour through collective production whose possibility, for the 'backward' amongst us, is denied *a priori* by Bolshevik theory and suppressed by Bolshevik practice, the State *cannot* wither away. On the contrary, failing that emancipation, the defence of 1917's gains will continue to depend, as it has during the last sixty years, upon the bloody and brutal State machine of Bolshevism remaining intact and vigilant. This contradiction has its own depressing dynamic, which we shall trace in subsequent chapters; one in which the increased use of capitalist 'techniques' occasions greater State expansion, whose ensuing fetters on the producers, and thus on production, are 'remedied' by the introduction of further capitalist techniques, and so on *ad nauseam*.

This argument could readily be extended to other areas of Bolshevik theory and practice. We could, for example, link the practical judgements of what is objective, as opposed to ideal, utopian and subjective, embedded in Bolshevik productive programmes to the dominance of the ontology of *Materialism and Empirio-criticism* rather than Lenin's *Philosophical Notebooks* in Soviet 'diamat'; and we might likewise link the premium on expertise and the pre-eminence of the State inscribed in such programmes to the fact that *What is to be Done?* rather than the April Theses has in the main continued to provide Bolshevism with its epistemological apparatus for thinking Party/People relations. Were we thus to extend our analysis, we would find, just as we did with Bolshevik perceptions of the State, that to embrace the Second International's conception of production is perforce to rehabilitate much else that was central to its atrophied marxism. For, as we have stressed throughout, we are precisely not talking of contingent connections, base/superstructure fashion. We are pointing to a set of internal relations. But it would be churlish and in an important sense misleading to conclude our discussion of the Bolshevik problematic on this note.

Our argument is not that Bolshevism is merely a refurbished Kautskyism; we have been describing tendencies, dangers. Certainly, these tendencies are deeply etched in the Bolshevik problematic; in so far as they are anchored in its concept of production, they are absolutely basic to it. But *equally* central to Bolshevism, as we spent a long time demonstrating earlier, are many emancipatory qualities. This reminder is not prompted by a residual apologetics; it is crucial to even beginning to understand Bolshevism's history, which is in large measure the history of the struggle of classes, roads and lines that rages within it. If our discussion is taken as a whole, what emerges most forcefully is that Bolshevism is neither (as Stalin grandiloquently claimed) 'the theory and tactics of the proletarian revolution in general' nor simply a programme for 'taking the capitalist road'; it is a deeply *contradictory* body of theory and practice. By now, this should hardly surprise us. For Bolshevism is no quiet academic doctrine, polished and consistent. It is a product of class struggle; and a product, moreover, bearing the hallmarks of just that 'emergent communism' Marx wrote of in his *Critique of the Gotha Programme*. Its roots lie in the working class; but like that class, it is 'in every respect' branded with the scars of the capitalism which nurtured it.

3 SOCIALIST CONSTRUCTION

In his *Inaugural Address* to the First International Marx speaks of three 'great facts'. The first, which he documents at some length in both its particulars, is the 'great fact that the misery of the working masses has not diminished from 1848 to 1864 and yet this period is unrivalled for the development of its industry and the growth of its commerce' (Marx, 1864: 340). The second and third great facts are of a somewhat different order; they are the passage of the Ten Hours Bill, and the cooperative movement. Now it is, perhaps, difficult at first sight to see why Marx might grant so elevated a status to what are, from one viewpoint, a limited reform and a utopian experiment. But it is just Marx's reasons which interest us. Regarding the Ten Hours Bill, he first hails, as would any middle-class reformer, the 'immense physical, moral and intellectual benefits hence accruing to the factory operatives' (ibid., 346). These, as he remarks, are chronicled in the Reports of the Factory Inspectors for all to see. But not so another 'benefit', to which Marx immediately draws our attention:

> besides its practical import, there was something else to exalt the marvellous success of this working men's measure . . . it was the first time that in broad daylight the political economy of the middle class succumbed to the political economy of the working class. (Ibid.)

It is in similar terms that Marx celebrates cooperatives as a 'still greater victory of the political economy of labour over the political economy of property' (ibid.) notwithstanding his own awareness of the limitations of the cooperative movement as such. Now we interject these observations of Marx's because they superbly illustrate a point of crucial relevance to any adequate perspective on socialist construction. Marx argues it explicitly in the *Poverty of Philosophy*. Against those socialists who 'look for science and merely make systems' and who 'see in poverty nothing but poverty, without seeing in it the revolutionary, subversive side, which will overthrow the old society', he insists that

> in the measure that history moves forward, and with it the struggle of the proletariat assumes clearer outlines, they ['the theoreticians of the proletarian class'] no longer need to seek science in their minds; they have only to take note of what is happening before their eyes and become its mouthpiece. (Marx, 1847a: 125–6)

Marx's point is two-edged. On the one hand, against those who see in poverty nothing but poverty (or, *mutatis mutandis*, in 'backwardness' nothing but backwardness) he is identifying the resources of socialist construction. It is in this light that the struggle for the Ten Hours Bill and the cooperative movement are adjudged 'great facts'. On the other hand, he is making a methodological statement. Such 'great facts', he is saying, are the basis on which marxist science advances; in Stalin's words 'theory is the experience of the working-class movement in all countries taken in its general aspect' (Stalin, 1924a: 15).

Great facts of working-class historical experience likewise prompt the observations which follow; the great facts, specifically, of the socialist achievements of a quarter of humanity, the workers and peasants of People's China. Like Marx, we are concerned not only with the practical but also with the theoretical significance of these accomplishments. In particular, we shall argue, they show, as did the cooperative movement of Marx's day 'by deed, instead of by argument' (Marx, 1864: 346), where lie socialism's true resources; and in showing this, they at the same time illuminate the shackles inseparable from Bolshevism. As in our discussion of Bolshevism itself, we will merely outline our argument in general terms here, leaving its substantiation to later chapters. A few preliminary clarifications, however, are essential if we are not to be seriously misunderstood.

We are emphatically not engaged upon a geopolitical exercise whereby (socialist) China is simplistically counterposed to (capitalist or revisionist) USSR, of the kind recently indulged in by the CPC itself and its 'Friends' overseas.[43] For, first, the lessons we seek to draw from China are congruent with, and can be validated by, historical experience elsewhere; the kinds of experience grasped in Marx's Inaugural Address (or *Civil War in France*), and similarly if fitfully and in hamstrung fashion apprehended by Bolshevism. And, second, we have already made it clear that so far as we are concerned the USSR is not capitalist nor the CPSU in any simple sense revisionist. No more do we consider China the socialist Mecca. Both formations are for us in transition, and characterised by, as Lenin has it, 'in many respects . . . fiercer' class struggles than rage within capitalism itself. Neither are we engaged upon a straightforward eulogy of the CPC's theory and practice. Our concern is with the transformations of themselves and their circumstances accomplished by China's *direct producers*. Certain CPC strategies in our view foster such transformations where Bolshevism would have derided their possibility in theory, and actively suppressed it in practice. And Mao and the CPC have gone beyond Bolshevism in theorising the conditions of socialist construction. But for all that the struggle of classes, roads and lines is far from absent from the CPC; and, we should add, it must be grasped not only as a struggle between 'Maoists' and 'capitalist roaders'. It is equally a struggle internal to 'Maoism' itself; a struggle that is reflected in the hesitations and inadequacies of that generally superior theorisation of transition the CPC offers. In particular, its critique of Bolshevism remains tacit rather than overt, and the survival of various undesirable facets of the Bolshevik legacy within the PRC is a clear consequence.

These qualifications, as we have said, are crucial to our thesis, and we will develop them at greater length in Chapters 5 and 6. For the moment, however, we may lay them on one side; our object here is not to provide an adequate overall analysis of PRC or CPC. At this stage in our argument (and similarly, we might mention, in Chapter 4) we seek only to highlight certain of those respects in which the experience of the Chinese people does add up to a practical critique of Bolshevism. We will begin with the key question of socialist construction and the one to which we found the Bolsheviks' answer the most crippling: what is production, and how is it to be increased?

First, we may note a rejection, within the CPC, of the supposedly inescapable logic of 'modernisation' outlined above. This rejection is expressed most clearly in such key texts of Mao's as his celebrated speeches (both directed at what might be termed the 'Bolshevik wing' of the CPC) *On the Question of Agricultural Co-operation* (1955) and *On the Ten Great Relationships* (1956b), and is embodied in the policy of 'walking on two legs'. Jack Gray's innovative studies have set out the 'economics' of this strategy in detail. Two central axioms of Bolshevik (and bourgeois) 'modernisation' theory are effectively reversed: the socialist transformation of agriculture is seen as the prerequisite of industrial construction, while within this transformation revolution of the social relations of production (in the very broadest sense) precedes and premises technological change. Briefly, the Maoist strategy may be schematised thus. Agricultural cooperation, at first of a relatively elementary kind, enables labour (including labour which would otherwise be unused during slack phases in the agricultural cycle) to be employed more effectively than under conditions of individual peasant farming. Routine tasks can be performed more economically, and new construction projects beyond the resources of the single household (in, say, irrigation or land reclamation) become viable. The ensuing rise in agricultural output and peasant living standards supports a market for light industrial products. These allow a gradual mechanisation of agriculture, which further raises output and living standards and frees more labour for larger construction projects. Cooperation is extended *pari passu* (in China from Mutual Aid Team, to APC, to People's Commune) to provide a framework within which the latter can be undertaken, and these projects in their turn permit still further increases in output and living standards and savings of labour; ultimately, increases and savings capable of sustaining heavy industry without, crucially, diverting vital resources away from agriculture or pauperising peasant producers.

We do not instance this programme in order to set up some new 'model of development' to replace the old; indeed one of the lessons we draw from China is precisely that such models are *per se* to be rejected, as fetters on people's productive potentialities. We cite it rather in order to give substance to a point which is more fundamental and which cannot be conveyed by an abstracted account of the 'economics' of socialist construction in the PRC (an account for example which reduces what is involved to a mere 'substitution' of 'labour for capital'). To the slogan 'Take agriculture as the foundation and industry as the leading factor . . .' Mao adds the important rider 'and never forget class struggle!'. This does not bespeak an old man's outdated fondness for the revolutionary days of his youth (when the real task now is the sober one of 'development' . . .) as some within the CPC (and without) have insinuated. Nor is it in any sense a *separate* injunction. It refers, quite simply, to the means through which a programme of socialist construction can alone be accomplished.

To express the same point rather differently, what matters in the above programme is what it fosters; the collective and conscious and thus egalitarian self-emancipation of the direct producers, through their own transformation of the social relations within which they produce. For, simply, only on condition of that emancipation can it actually work; voluntary cooperation (and not imposed technology) is its major productive force, and mutual benefit, the producers' own experience of the material upshot of their cooperation, is the foundation for the gradual extensions of cooperative production which give the strategy its dynamic. It is for this reason that class struggle is central. Emancipation of labour *is* a struggle, not a donation, and cooperation is always an accomplishment: a struggle against in the first instance the capitalist and the landlord, but as much a struggle, fiercer as socialism progresses, against the division of labour that supports the fetish of 'expert' and cadre, and against the moral *ethos* and cultural *eidos* which buttress the dictatorship of capital; an accomplishment, by the direct producers, of liberation from 'all the muck of ages' (Marx and Engels, 1846a: 87) with which they are burdened. And this is likewise why politics must be 'in command'; and why to see in this prescription an opposition of politics and production (as do not only bourgeois commentators, but also, regrettably, many of Mao's 'supporters' in the West and, we suspect, in China[44]) would be fundamentally mistaken. Mao is totally orthodox (and thoroughly correct) in his insistence that

> In the last analysis, the impact, good or bad, great or small, of the policy and practice of any Chinese political party upon the people depends on whether and how much it helps to develop their productive forces, and on whether it fetters or liberates these forces. (Mao, 1945d: 301)

The point is that a socialist development of the productive forces is the task of the people whose forces they are. A Party can help liberate those forces only to the extent that it can help the people liberate themselves; otherwise, it becomes a fetter on both producers and production. Class struggle is the means of their liberation; so keeping proletarian politics in command, a profoundly *productive* requirement of socialist construction.

Other facets of CPC theory and policy – notably, for example, a political epistemology which builds on and extends the discoveries we noted equally in Lenin's *Notebooks*, and in the practices of 1917, and a 'mass line' theory of politics which embodies this epistemology – are congruent with what we have so far sought to indicate. These will be amplified in later chapters. For the moment, we have said enough to make clear where we believe the historical experience of the workers and peasants of China offers its deepest challenge to Bolshevism. Production is conceived, and practised, as an integrally social, moral, cultural, and above all political activity. And to develop it, in a socialist fashion, is accordingly conceived and practised as necessarily being a class struggle, between the producers and the entire repertoire of vestiges from capitalism which mark the transition to socialism. The CPC has, at least in part, recognised this in its theory and many of its policies – though, as we will see in Chapters 5 and 6, this judgement has to be qualified, and severely so at times. But far more importantly, the *people* of China, both in what they have achieved and how they have achieved it, ground and validate the perspectives we have sketched in the last few pages. Their class struggles likewise ground and validate our earlier criticism of Bolshevism. For it is their experience, rather than any 'theoretical acumen' on our or anybody else's part, that has shown that it is *people*, collectively and consciously transforming themselves and their circumstances, that are the key productive force of socialism, and that it is *capitalism* not 'backwardness' that is its major obstacle. In showing this they have also shown just where Bolshevism needs to be transcended; in precisely those areas where it fetters the emancipation of the people by failing to appreciate just how tenacious, pervasive and deep-rooted the stranglehold of the political economy of capital is.

3 Lenin, Trotsky, Stalin

1 LENIN

We have commented on the 'invisibility' of the social problematic of Bolshevism for most marxists. Central to their blindness is, we believe, their imprisonment within the boundaries of the Bolsheviks' own debates of the 1920s and 1930s, particularly that between Leon Trotsky and Joseph Stalin. Those debates have also left another legacy, which is of particular concern to us here. The works of *Lenin* – both practical and theoretical – are conventionally treated, by all major protagonists and their ideological heirs, merely as a resource for 'proving' the legitimacy of their respective positions. The corollary of this elevation of Lenin's work into an authoritative body of canon law is one crucial to our central theme: the *struggles* within Lenin's work, far from being examined, are suppressed in favour of an imposed and thoroughly artificial consistency.

But, we shall argue, if Lenin's work is taken as a whole, that contradiction we have sketched for Bolshevism as such will be seen thoroughly to permeate it.[1] The famous slogan concerning 'Soviets plus electrification' expresses it sharply: particularly when we know that the electrification programme involved acceleration of certain nodal features of capitalism, and displayed all the qualities of a State donation from above, while concurrently the Soviets were systematically drained of proletarian influence, and even of Party majority – where, that is, they continued to exist at all. What follows attempts to exemplify this struggle.

In January 1917, Lenin gave a 'Lecture on the 1905 Revolution'[2] which affirms his faith in the possibility of socialist revolution in Tsarist Russia. He criticises the liberal Struve, who had written two days before Bloody Sunday 1905 that there was not 'yet a revolutionary people in Russia':

> The idea that an illiterate peasant country could produce a revolutionary people seemed utterly absurd to this 'highly educated',

> supercilious and extremely stupid leader of the bourgeois reformists. (1917c: 238)

Later, Lenin provides an account of 1905 to allow us to assess a 'piece of professorial wisdom of the cowardly bourgeoisie':

> For instance, in German so-called 'scientific' literature, Herr Professor Max Weber, in his lengthy survey of Russia's political development, refers to the Moscow uprising as a 'putsch'. 'The Lenin group,' says this 'highly learned' Herr Professor, 'and a section of the Socialist-Revolutionaries had long prepared for this senseless uprising.' (Lenin, 1917c: 251)

For Lenin then, here as in many similar writings, the political power of the 'illiterate peasantry' is emphasised. This is most evident, perhaps, in the address, at the very moment of the Great October Socialist Revolution itself, 'To the people' (1917d), or in his 'Peasants and Workers' (1917e). We would argue with reference to such texts as these that what Lenin's struggles should teach us is neither a dogmatic notion of Party building nor a doctrine of socialist efficiency and organisation; but, simply, that it is people, not Parties, that transform the world and that, therefore, putting proletarian politics in command means the ending of the crucial separation of 'the political' from 'the economic' which is a necessary feature of capitalist commodity production.

On the other hand, Lenin's economic policy (and it is instructive that the term was so salient in his writings) was dominated by notions first elaborated in his *Development of Capitalism in Russia*[3] concerning what he called in 1917 'a complete material preparation for socialism'. In that year he saw, as he quoted himself in response to his left critics in 1918, 'state capitalist monopoly' as the '*threshold of socialism*'. The key text here is his *The Immediate Tasks of the Soviet Government*[4] in which he argues:

> By creating a new, Soviet type of State . . . we solved only a small part of this difficult problem. The principal difficulty lies in the economic sphere, namely, the introduction of the strictest and universal accounting and control of the production and distribution of goods, raising the productivity of labour and *socialising* production in *practice*. (Lenin, 1918b: 241)

In response to his left critics, Lenin described the path of transition from petty bourgeois capitalism thus:

> It is *one and the same road* that leads from it to both large-scale capitalism and to socialism, *through one and the same* intermediary

> station called 'national accounting and control of production and distribution'. Those who fail to understand this are committing an unpardonable error in economics. (Lenin, 1918c: 340)

He also argued in 1918 that this programme required the use of bourgeois expertise:

> Without the guidance of experts in the various fields of knowledge, technology and experience, the transition to socialism will be impossible [N.B., as Lenin might have interjected, the word used is 'impossible'] because socialism calls for a conscious mass advance to greater productivity of labour compared with capitalism and on the basis achieved by capitalism. Socialism must achieve this advance *in its own way* . . . by Soviet methods. And the specialists . . . are, in the main, inevitably bourgeois. (Lenin, 1918b: 248)[5]

The contradictory nature of this passage is part of the struggle within Lenin's work: the 'basis achieved by capitalism' denies the very possibility of 'conscious mass advance' toward greater production. A few pages further on Lenin himself denies the possibility, at that stage, of *any* 'conscious mass advance' other than one which follows *coercion* by the Party-State, and *direction* by experts.

> The Russian is a bad worker compared with people in advanced countries. It could not be otherwise under the Tsarist regime and in view of the persistence of the hangover from serfdom. The task that the Soviet government must set the people in all its scope is – learn to work. (Lenin, 1918b: 259)

Even thus far there is still the possibility of various formulations; Lenin chooses one way, one line:

> The Taylor system, the last word of capitalism in this respect, like all capitalist progress, is a combination of the refined brutality of bourgeois exploitation and a number of the greatest scientific achievements in the field of analysing mechanical motions during work . . . The possibility of building socialism depends exactly upon our success in combining the Soviet power and the Soviet organisation of administration with up-to-date achievements of capitalism. We must organise in Russia the study and teaching of the Taylor system and systematically try it out and adapt it to our ends. (Ibid.)

This illustrates the separation of 'the Soviet government' and 'the people' and the conception of combining 'Soviet' state forms with capitalist production forms. The combination of Taylorism and the use of experts reproduces very swiftly an instability in the nature of the politics that are 'in command' through the coercive Party-State apparatus. We say 'reproduces' because the same instability (in fact an inability to control) is present in all *capitalist* State forms. What is really 'going on' is a class struggle over who is to win – the bourgeoisie or the proletariat; capitalist techniques cannot be copied neutrally. To follow them is to reproduce the appropriate ideological, cultural, political and production relations which sustain them.

The above general schema can be illustrated from 1918 onwards, whether we examine Bolshevik policy toward agrarian production, the trades unions in the factories, or the Soviets. In all cases there is an attempt to marry socialist political forms to certain capitalist production 'necessities'. There are, to begin with, two invalid myths which we should dispense with. First, the fashionable notion that 'Had Lenin lived . . .' all would have been well, is doubly false. The struggle, often held to be present in Lenin's 'last' years, was there from the beginning; and, in any case, what kind of Marxist analysis is it that makes the path of a whole social formation depend on one individual? Second, the way in which the New Economic Policy is usually counterposed to War Communism ignores the continuity between them.

But we should note in passing that the NEP has a double *external* reference which is not normally associated with *Lenin's* Bolshevism, which reveals much about both the Bolshevik problematic and Lenin's adherence to it. First, as an indication of the way in which Bolshevism continues to donate the terms within which socialist construction is thought, we quote the 1969 editorial note affixed to Lenin's 21 October 1921 'Report on NEP':

> As a sum total of economic measures employed by the proletarian state, NEP is, in one or another form, a necessary policy for any state affecting the transition from capitalism to socialism.[6]

What Lenin called 'capitalism in moderation' (1921c: 49) was part of a programme which he saw as defending socialism by, for example, leasing natural resources to foreign capitalists. The relevant 1921 and 1922 discussions, focused on meetings at Cannes, Genoa and Rapallo, reveal the Bolshevik subordination to certain capitalist paradigms of production in great detail. They also make the Détente proposals of the 1970s seem quite trivial. It was after all the author of *Imperialism* who argued just before the Genoa meeting that the USSR would shortly be subject to 'the test set by the Russian and international market, to which we are subordinated, with which we are connected, and from which we cannot isolate ourselves' (cit. Day, 1973, p. 64).[7] What was argued here, regarding foreign capitalists' control of forests or railways, was only an extension of what was argued regarding capitalist techniques in general. It was claimed to be true that any country had to use these (capitalist) techniques and methods, but equally, any socialist country could *control* the techniques through powerful (and specifically socialist) State forms.

Let us now briefly examine the areas of agrarian and industrial production, before returning to the general features of this contradiction as increasingly recognised in his writings by Lenin.

Soviet agrarian policy is important for a number of reasons. Food production is basic to any successful strategy of socialist construction; Bolshevik policies here reveal much about their general perspectives; through the Comintern there was an attempt to enforce this agrarian policy beyond the USSR;[8] and its chronic failure through to the 1970s is one very significant feature of the Bolshevik legacy. As we have hinted above, Bolshevism was formed largely in ignorance of, and partly in opposition to, the mass of the Russian people – those engaged in agrarian production. This led, for example, to a failure to understand the dynamics of the peasant communes, and a marked refusal to follow the possible analyses suggested by Marx in the 1870s.[9] For Marx the *obshchina* had a collective and a private production element. He also recognised that the *miri* were differentiated, they should not be seen as homogeneously hostile to, or receptive of, socialism. In fact, Bolshevism appears to have followed the path of the Tsar's advisers. Until 1905, the *miri* were considered to be centres of rich peasant reaction. But after 1905, de Witte and Stolypin attempted to establish a class of yeoman capitalist farmers;[10] not infrequently with the explicit support of Lenin, who posed the alternatives as a Prussian-Junkers transition or an American-capitalist transition, the latter being seen as 'more progressive'. Nowhere better than here can we see the power of that 'cognitive orientation' noted by Shanin.

In 1899, at the close of his *Development* analysis, Lenin argued that one of the progressive features of capitalism was that it 'constantly diminishes the proportion of the population engaged in agriculture (in which the most backward forms of social and economic relationships always prevail) and increases the number of large industrial centres' (1899: 599).[11] In 1920, in his *Preliminary draft thesis on the agrarian question*,[12] Lenin still speaks of a 'rural sector'. The limited nature of the Bolshevik break with Kautsky's conceptions of socialism is very well displayed in its agrarian policies; readers of Kautsky's *Agrarian problem* (1899) through to his anti-Bolshevik works of 1918 and 1922, will find what were to become Bolshevik agrarian policies consistently advocated. In April 1917, a Bolshevik conference passed a resolution urging the 'proletarians and semi-proletarians' of the countryside to seek

> the formation out of every landlord's estate of a sufficiently large model farm which would be run for the social account by Soviets of deputies of agricultural workers under the direction of agricultural experts and with the application of the best technical methods. (Carr, 1952: 37; cf. Trotsky, 1930d: 19)

In the Decree on Land of October 1917, we can read the distinctions made between 'property of the whole people' and 'State Property', and note that 'Lands on which high-level scientific farming is practised . . . shall not be divided up.'[13]

But it was not simply this perspective on the necessity for capitalist forms, nor the simple fact that as late as 1920 Party work hardly existed in the Soviet countryside (Shanin, 1972: 86; Lewin, 1966: 178; Male, 1971: 87); it was that these two facets combined to create a policy, at its most severe in the Committees of the Poor grain procurement, which in one crucial respect repeated the historical experiences that agrarian producers had suffered under *Tsarism*. Peasant producers had already experienced the Tsarist grain monopoly in the War. As Owen reports:

> When requisitions were made on the basis of corn brought to bazary [the markets] and when some peasants who 'asked for more' than the stipulated price were flogged, a necessary consequence followed – one that was to haunt Russian political economy for many years afterwards – the peasants ceased to bring to market . . . (Owen, 1937: 175)

As Lenin phrased the matter in 1921: 'Hitherto, the food supply worker has known only one fundamental instruction: collect 100 per cent of the grain appropriations' (Lenin, 1921d: 353). Bolshevism's analysis of the relations of agrarian production was predicated upon a division between town and country: there was, on the one hand, 'the countryside' (*en bloc*), on the other, the needs of the towns, and, to link them, 'secure the Harvest!' So convinced was Bolshevism of this relation that the Bolshevik Party had to have campaigns in 1924 and 1925 to *Face the countryside*; in the latter there were no less than eight State agencies competing in the bringing in of the Harvest!

At the 8th Bolshevik Congress of 1919, Lenin's General Line (1919e) was adopted as the agrarian programme of the Party and elaborated in the *A.B.C. of Communism* authored by Bukharin and Preobrazhensky. This text circulated widely for ten years despite having a booklist, at the end of Chapter 2, which shows the continued dominance of the

Kautskyan problematic. In that part of the *A.B.C.* dealing with production after the revolution (in fact, written by Preobrazhensky) the Bolshevik contradiction is manifest. On the one hand, Preobrazhensky argues 'Every poor peasant should become a member of a commune. Every member of a commune should become a communist' (Bukharin and Preobrazhensky, 1920: 375). This follows Lenin's own approaches of 1919:[14]

> As long as it is possible to trade in grain and to make a profit out of it, the peasant will remain . . . a semi-working man, a semi-profiteer. As a profiteer he is hostile to us . . . But *as a working man*, the peasant is a friend of the proletarian state . . . As working men, the peasants, the vast mass of them, the peasant millions, support the state 'machine' . . . (Lenin, 1919f: 433)

> In order to abolish classes it is necessary . . . to abolish the difference between factory worker and peasant, to *make workers of all of them* . . . The proletariat must separate, demarcate the working peasant from the peasant owner . . . In this demarcation lies the *whole essence* of socialism. (Lenin, 1919d: 112, 113)

But on the other hand, the *A.B.C.* also brings forward typically Bolshevik notions of necessary techniques and expertise:

> The first requisite is that in socialist agriculture all the land of the republic should be utilized in such a way that in every district, farm, and field, that particular crop should be raised . . . which, having regard to the quality and the peculiarity of the soil, would grow most advantageously. Precisely which crop is the most suitable, is a matter for agricultural experts to determine. (Bukharin and Preobrazhensky, 1920: 352)

This encapsulated various forms of the division of labour within one technically-defined 'requisite'; we would have thought that a *first* priority might well have been taking stock of local sources of knowledge and local collective abilities.

Bolshevism continued to understand the peasantry (as an entirety) as 'petty-bourgeois'; and to see '*every* petty bourgeois' as 'an agent' of 'private capitalism', as Lenin phrased it (1918c: 337). The following year he argued:

> Peasant farming continues to be petty commodity production. Here we have an extremely broad and very sound, deep-rooted basis for capitalism . . . The forms of this struggle are private speculation and

> profiteering versus state procurement of grain . . . and state distribution. (Lenin, 1919d: 109–10)

Of course, given this framework for 'struggle', it is not surprising that the New Economic Policy could accommodate notions of wagering on the kulak, and strengthening the kulaki *vis-à-vis* the organs of the Party, which was taken to its logical and thoroughly Bolshevik conclusion, by Bukharin.[15]

The full Bolshevik commitment to 'modernisation' before socialism, and therewith accentuating the Three Great Differences, is evident in Lenin's 'Draft Theses' for the Comintern of 1920, especially when compared with the comparable theses of Kautsky (cf. his 1918: 114–19). Lenin argued:

> The victory of socialism over capitalism and the consolidation of socialism may be regarded as ensured only when the proletarian state power, having completely suppressed all resistance by the exploiters and assured itself complete subordination and stability, has reorganised the whole of industry on the lines of large-scale collective production and on a modern technical basis (founded on the electrification of the entire economy). This alone will enable the cities to render such radical assistance, technical and social, to the backward and scattered rural population as will create the material basis necessary to boost the productivity of agricultural and of farm labour in general, thereby encouraging the small farmers by the force of example and in their own interest to adopt large-scale, collective and mechanized agriculture. (Lenin, 1920a: 161–2)

Not only did these theses, and the practices which they report and engender, set the terms for the Stalin-Trotsky or the Bukharin-Preobrazhensky debates of the 1920s, they underpin the 'problem' of Soviet agriculture today. The Soviet collective farm (in contrast with the People's Communes of China) is still conceived as 'a unit of agricultural production, nothing more' (Thomson, 1973: 123–4).[16]

Were matters substantially different regarding Bolshevism and industrial production? A number of recent accounts[17] from different perspectives agree that by 1918 – and closely connected with the programme of Lenin's *Immediate Tasks* – both factory committees, and, to a lesser extent, the trades unions, had become subordinated and localised organs of workers' power. This is inevitable given the notions outlined above; how can capitalist techniques, expert supervision, and a national system of control be applied through autonomous agencies of workers' control? This is in fact the context within which the Soviet *subbotniki* (cf. Lenin, 1919f) and Stakhanovite movements must be placed: they *are* socialist emulation activities,[18] but flawed. In this they may be contrasted with the socialist transformations within China, which despite superficial similarities seek to embody a quite different politics.

This is also the context within which to situate the debates over the trades unions in 1920–1.[19] The basic disagreement between the proposals of Bukharin and Trotsky and those of Lenin (which became policy) can best be understood as a difference over timing and emphasis. The criticisms of the Workers' Opposition were more fundamental, but they failed to see how antithetical to workers' control were most trades unions by that stage. Lenin in this debate equates 'the Soviet apparatus' to what he was later to call 'the transmission belts from the Communist Party to the masses' (1922a: 382). These kinds of formulations co-exist with some startling texts which continue to feature in the polemic between the CPC and the CPSU. Lenin argued that 'every kind of democracy . . . serves production and is ultimately determined by the relations of production in a given society' (1921a: 81). That is to say:

> Politics must take precedence over economics. To argue otherwise is to forget the A.B.C. of Marxism . . . without a correct political approach to the matter the given class will be unable to stay on top, *and, consequently*, will be incapable of solving its *production problem* either. (Ibid., 83–4)

We can only make sense of this statement, understand it, that is, in terms of Lenin's practice at that time, if we carefully study those actions to provide a content for the concepts 'politics' and 'economics'. He clearly intends that proletarian politics will actually be in command; but he primarily understands by this that the Party (and the Party's State) must be ruthless, practising that 'ruthlessness which is indispensable for the success of socialism' (Lenin, 1918c: 344 fn.; cf. 1918b). We know that this is how many workers, and members of the Party, began to perceive Party and State action: fusing on the one hand the agencies of tax collection and police with the Party, and, on the other, enabling the former exploiters and their agents to become the agents for Party and State policy.

Dampening down and restricting class struggle (as with the campaigns against sabotage-by-laziness, or the abolition of intra-Party democracy) reverses the spiral which can be studied in the Border Regions of China. There accelerating class struggle and increased production (coupled with a minimal Party and a self-supporting State apparatus) spirals upwards toward greater well-being through conscious, collective and more egalitarian transformations within many different productive situations (each of which, in itself, constitutes a partial attack on the division of labour). In the case of the Soviet Union the spiral is led downwards, through notions of necessary capitalist techniques, the use of experts and Taylorism, the subordination of the Soviets to the centre and so on. What was happening in both cases were the creations of new historic blocs, to use Gramsci's significant term: in the Soviet union, especially in the Soviet countryside, these policies were forming and strengthening a new historic bloc which we might call the official-entrepreneurial bloc.

We are not arguing that Lenin, or other Bolsheviks, were not aware of these dangers; it is rather the manner of their solution which is significant. In brief, Bolshevism from the start had two kinds of policy for 'problems' of this character – technical (including policies of fiscal manipulation) and the politics of Terror. Both show that intimate and delicate relation between productive strategies and State forms which we have argued throughout. In 1922, Lenin, as Chairman of the Council of People's Commissars, wrote to Kursky of the Commisariat of Justice, declaring, as it were, to the capitalists:[20]

> Carry on your business, make money – we allow you to do it – but we shall place you under a *triple* obligation to be honest, to render truthful and accurate accounts, to observe the *spirit* as well as the letter of our communist laws, not to depart *a single inch* from our laws – this should be the first commandment of the PCJ [People's Commisariat of Justice] as far as NEP is concerned. If the PCJ is unable to cope with our capitalism by 'licking it into shape' and keeping it 'decent', if the PCJ does not prove by a number of show trials that it is capable of detecting infractions of this rule and punishing the offenders not by shamefully stupid 'communistically fatuous' fines of from 100 to 200 millions, but by the death sentence – then the PCJ is not worth a damn, and I shall consider it my duty to get the Central Committee to have all the PCJ's key personnel replaced. (Lenin, 1922b: 344)

We indicated above that Lenin, amongst others, was aware that 'something was wrong'. Before we illustrate this, we ought to remind ourselves of certain tensions within Lenin's work on the nature of the State. To begin with and not commonly stressed, the classical Leninist notion of Party-building – as established, with due reference to Kautsky, in his *What is to be done?* (1902) – clashes quite seriously with much of his polemic against Kautsky and the Second International in *The State and Revolution* (1917b; cf. 1917a).[21] It should also by now be apparent how the Bolshevik adherence to the need for certain capitalist forms and techniques would lead to a further tension. Thus, although Lenin declared to the population in November 1917:

> Remember that now *you yourselves* are at the helm of state . . . take into *your* hand *all affairs* of the State . . . Rally round your Soviets. Strengthen them. Get on with the job yourselves; begin right at the bottom, do not wait for anyone. (Lenin, 1917d: 297)

we had better pay as much attention to his 1919 lecture on the State. The ambiguities and shifts do not require extra comment.

> The proletariat casts aside the machine which was called the state and before which people bowed down in superstitious awe . . . and declares that it is a bourgeois lie. We have deprived the capitalists of this machine and have taken it over. With this machine, or bludgeon, we shall destroy all exploitation. And when the possibility of exploitation no longer exists anywhere in the world . . . only when the possibility of this no longer exists then shall we consign this machine to the scrap heap. Then there will be no state and no exploitation. Such is the view of our Communist Party. (Lenin, 1919g: 488)

By 1922, Lenin asks

> Here we have lived a year, with the State in our hands and under the New Economic Policy has it operated our way? No. We don't like to acknowledge this, but it hasn't. And how has it operated? The machine isn't going where we guide it, but where some illegal, or lawless, God-knows-whence-derived speculators or private capitalistic business, or both together, are guiding it. A machine doesn't travel just exactly the way, and it often travels just exactly not the way, that the man imagines who sits at the wheel. (Cit. Trotsky *et al.*, 1927a: 1)

The State, then, is a machine, or bludgeon, and the key question cannot therefore be its form (its inner relations) but who controls it; whose hands grasp the wheel, who brings down the bludgeon on whom?

It is in terms of the foregoing that we have to understand Lenin's long struggle against bureaucracy. This, to repeat, is not just a matter of his last years. Apart from *The State and Revolution*, Lenin's *How to organise competition?*, with its thoroughly socialist notions of workers supervising the organisational work of intellectuals and 'vigour from below' (Lenin, 1918a), shows the possibility of an alternative to the practices we have emphasised thus far. But such alternatives were in large part suppressed.

Lenin himself has provided an account of the growth of bureaucracy. Looking back in 1921 he notes

> Look at the economic aspects of the evils of bureaucracy. We see nothing of them in May 5, 1918. Six months after the October Revolution . . . A year later, the Eighth Congress of the Russian Communist Party (March 18–23, 1919) adopted a new Party Programme in which we spoke forthrightly of *'a partial revival of bureaucracy within the Soviet System . . .'*
> Two years later, in the spring of 1921, after the Eighth Congress of Soviets (December 1920) which discussed the evils of bureaucracy, and after the Tenth Congress of the Russian Communist Party (March 1921) . . . we find *them* even more distinct and sinister. (Lenin, 1921d: 351)

It is worth interrupting this narrative to indicate the State activity of Lenin himself in 1921 – his *Instructions* to local Soviets read, in part:

> Commodity exchange and freedom of trade inevitably imply the appearance of capitalists and capitalist relationships. There is no reason to fear this. The workers' state has enough resources to keep *within the proper bounds* and control those relationships which are useful and necessary in conditions of small-scale production . . .
> Today the workers' and peasants' state is the 'proprietor' and it must select the best men for economic development; it must select the best administrators and organisers on the special and general, local and national scale . . . (Lenin, 1921e: 383, 385)

But, to return to his *Tax in Kind* from which we were quoting, Lenin does not see bureaucracy as rooted in Bolshevism:

> What are their economic roots? They are mostly of a dual character: on the one hand, a developed bourgeoisie needs a bureaucratic apparatus . . . to use against the revolutionary movement of workers . . . That is something we have not got. Ours are class courts directed against the bourgeoisie . . . In our country bureaucratic practices have different economic roots, namely the atomised and scattered state of the small producer . . .
> Bureaucratic practices as a legacy of the 'siege' and the superstructure built over the isolated and downtrodden state of the small producer . . . Our bureaucratic practices prove . . . that in this respect *we still have a great deal to learn from the capitalist.* (Lenin, 1921d: 352 f.)

In February 1922, Lenin wrote to Sokolnikov, stating:

> Communists have become bureaucrats. If anything will destroy us, it is this. And for the State Bank it is the most dangerous of all to be bureaucratic . . .

> The whole essence now is practical men and practice. To find people who are *men of business* . . . (Lenin, 1922c: 549)

Lenin goes on to talk of 'replacing' 'virtuous communists' by 'people who know how to trade'.

On one of his few public speeches after his first bout of illness, Lenin said:

> We still have the old machinery, and our task now, is to remould it along new lines. We cannot do so at once, but we must see to it that the Communists we have are properly placed. What we need is that they, the Communists, should control the machinery they are assigned to, and not, as so often happens, with us, that the machinery should control them. (Lenin, 1922d: 442)

In the much more studied texts of his last year – 1923 – the criticism of bureaucracy is much more overt, but there remains the confusion between priorities. In some texts (1923a; 1923d) there is a sequence 'material base' first, 'cultural revolution' second. In others (1923b, 1923c) Lenin argues that without a cultural revolution, and politics of a new kind, there will be no secure material base for socialism at all.

We have tried to argue here[22] that Lenin's unique contribution to revolutionary theory cannot be totally sundered from Bolshevism. Despite the critical materials we have pointed to, Lenin never transcended the simultaneous and contradictory Bolshevik adherence to both capitalist productive forces and various socialist forms of political control. Already by the time of his second illness he was aware that this contradiction was 'ripening' toward a crisis, but he offered no analysis of the latter which moved beyond the restrictions of Bolshevism. We do not consider that Bolshevism was fully determined by the 'backwardness' of Tsarist Russia, or by capitalist encirclement, and certainly not by the personalities of Lenin, Trotsky or Stalin. We now have contrary historical experiences to draw from which were denied to Lenin; but he did have access to alternative potential kinds of productive forms and political control. That Bolshevism alerted him to only one kind of action follows from its own genesis and sustaining relations.

2 TROTSKY

Stalin's 'Red Professors' sought to denigrate Trotsky by instancing his deviations from the canons of 'Leninism'. This is not our intention; as Trotsky went to great lengths to demonstrate,[23] he was indeed a 'Bolshevik-Leninist'. We hope to show that both the weaknesses and the strengths of Trotsky's works derive precisely from their Bolshevism, from their 'exemplary Leninism'. We will investigate these by tracing the Bolshevik problematic through three core components of Trotskyism: Trotsky's interpretations of 1905 and his theory of permanent revolution; the Left Opposition programmes of the twenties; and the Trotskyist analysis of the 'degeneration' of the first workers' state.

Trotsky's writings on 1905[24] must be celebrated for an acute analysis of the development of capitalism in Russia, out of which Trotsky derived the 'law' of uneven and combined development and the political strategy of 'permanent revolution'. Both the analysis and the strategy broke with the Second International, and (Red Professors notwithstanding) decisively entered the Bolshevism of 1917.

The 'law' indicates that capitalism does not grow 'organically', following the classic English model. Capitalism 'creates a world after its own image' not by exporting its historical development pattern, but by imposing its current production techniques and relations, which it supports by subordinating and utilising precapitalist social, political and productive structures. Tsarist Russia is a paradigm case. Far from emerging 'naturally' from Russian soil, capitalism was forced on the Tsarist State by the (mainly military) competition of the more advanced European states. Consequently, Russian capitalism was largely created under the aegis of the State, directly through the State budget, or indirectly through State loans and foreign concessions; while the enterprises developed were amongst the largest and most advanced in Europe. This implies that the socio-economic structure is acutely 'uneven', articulating advanced capitalist 'enclaves' with the most 'primitive' agriculture in Europe, while the State inflates and takes on quasi-independent form domestically at the same time as its dependence upon imperialism increases. From this 'uneven' and contradictory 'combination' Trotsky draws the following conclusions.

The existing agrarian structure can neither support nor benefit from further development of capitalism. Expansion of industry requires a growing home market, which presupposes an increasing standard of living for the peasantry. But the latter is precluded by the financing of the industrialisation programme itself: State and imperialist super-exploitation of the peasant. The resulting pauperisation prevents the technical, cultural or educational improvements needed for any rise in agricultural production. The fact that the domestic social basis of Tsarism lies in the landowning nobility compounds the vicious circle. Consequently, the agrarian question is the key question of the revolution.

The bourgeoisie is uniquely weak. This stems from the pre-eminent role of the State and foreign capital in the Russian economy, and its consequent dependence on both. At the same time, the advanced nature of capitalist industry renders antagonisms between capital and labour more severe than in any previous comparable period of 'bourgeois revolution'. The bourgeoisie, therefore, will not lead 'their' revolution. Nor will the urban petty bourgeoisie: since capitalism did not evolve 'naturally', there is no social basis for a petty-bourgeois democracy like that of the Jacobins in the Great French Revolution. The self-same 'development', however, has produced a strong and concentrated proletariat which plays a key productive role, yet lacks the conservatism and internal differentiation of its European counterpart. It is therefore the one class able to lead the revolution: and to it fall the historical tasks of the bourgeoisie and petty bourgeoisie, including leadership over the peasantry.

The revolution, if 'bourgeois' in its circumstances and tasks, is therefore proletarian in forces and methods. The correct aim must be proletarian seizure of power. However, on winning power the proletariat will be unable to confine itself to bourgeois-democratic objectives, and will pass over to socialist ones: this is the 'permanent revolution'. It will then encounter contradictions stemming from the other side of the 'combination', Russia's backwardness, whose resolution lies only in the international revolution.[25]

Trotsky's break from Second International dogma should be evident even from this bald résumé. We should particularly note the rejection of crude 'stages theory', and the elaboration of a political strategy which expresses the 'class dynamics' (Trotsky, 1909a: 317)[26] of the revolution, both of which proceed from his understanding of capitalism as imperialism, and the ensuing uneven and contradictory character of Russian 'development'.

Having said this, let us now look at the limits of Trotsky's achievements.

Trotsky many times insisted that 'the conditions for the arising of a dictatorship of the proletariat and the conditions for the creation of socialism are not identical, not of like nature, in certain respects even antagonistic' (Trotsky, 1930e: 368). He elaborates via a quotation from Kautsky:

> Revolution in Russia could not immediately result in a socialist regime. The economic conditions of the country are not nearly mature for this purpose . . . [but the seizure of power] must lead to the political domination of the proletariat in western Europe and create for the Eastern European proletariat the possibility of contracting the stages of their development and . . . *artificially setting up socialist institutions*. Society as a whole cannot artificially skip any

> stages of its development, but it is possible for constituent parts of society to hasten their retarded development by imitating the more advanced countries. (Trotsky, 1906: 237)

These theses, which provide the theoretical underpinning for Trotsky's subsequent critique of Stalinism, rest on a definition of socialism in terms of public (State) ownership of the means of production at, crucially, a high level of technique. *A fortiori*, backwardness cannot be the basis for socialism, and precisely that unevenness which allows the establishment of proletarian dictatorship prevents the construction of socialism. This proposition underlies Trotsky's positions on both the peasantry and the international revolution.

Pace Stalin, Trotsky did not just 'forget' the peasantry. He in fact saw the proletarian need to 'organise the countryside and bind it to itself' as a 'great and simple conclusion' of 1905 (Trotsky, 1909b: 116), and was amongst the first to insist that the 'agrarian question' could only be solved through proletarian revolution. His pre-1917 polemic with Lenin concerned the degree to which the peasantry could play an independent or leading role in the revolution (on which, Trotsky held, Lenin's 'democratic dictatorship' formula ducked the issue) and the contradictions consequent upon proletarian seizure of power. But the necessity of peasant support as such was never an issue.[27] Nor did it subsequently become one: Trotsky argued for NEP-style policies a year before Lenin, against his (and the Politburo's) opposition,[28] while he consistently justified his proposed economic policies of the twenties by their benefits to poor and middle peasants, and thereby the maintenance of the *smychka*. He no more 'overlooks' the peasantry in his international writings.[29] There are, none the less, senses in which Stalin's taunt is correct.

Trotsky sees peasant support as essentially passive. The following remark is by no means untypical: 'in such a situation [proletarian dictatorship] . . . nothing remains for the peasantry to do but to rally to the regime of workers' democracy. It will not matter much even if the peasantry does this with a degree of consciousness not larger than that with which it usually rallies to the bourgeois regime' (Trotsky, 1906: 205). Conversely 'the proletariat . . . will bring all forces into play in order to raise the cultural level of the countryside and develop the political consciousness of the peasantry' (ibid.) Trotsky makes a thousand similar statements which equally clearly establish that socialism is something to be donated to the peasants from outside (the towns) and above (Party and, principally, State).[30] As recipients of revolution, 'nothing remains for the peasantry to do', least of all share in the building of socialism by transforming their own productive practices.

This perspective is grounded in that view of peasants, *en bloc*, as 'petty-bourgeois' and therefore 'an unreliable and treacherous ally' (Trotsky, 1930e: 355)[31] already noted in Lenin. Trotsky doubts peasant support for socialist construction, expecting it to evaporate with the completion of 'bourgeois-democratic tasks' (particularly land reform).[32] Whilst recognising class differentiation within the peasantry (and the theoretical possibility of proletarian dictatorship resting on poor and middle peasants through the acceleration of class struggle in the countryside), he remains pessimistic: 'the insufficient degree of class differentiation will create obstacles to the introduction among the peasantry of developed class struggle, upon which the urban proletariat could rely. The primitiveness of the peasantry turns its hostile face towards the proletariat' (Trotsky, 1906: 208–9). This will be evident in peasant hostility to internationalism and collectivism (Trotsky, 1906: 209).

All this is explained by Russia's backwardness, the low level of its productive forces. Trotsky, therefore, saw very limited scope for socialist agrarian transformation in Russia.[33] The lynchpin of his prognosis is the crucial assumption that industrialisation must precede collectivisation.[34] Just as he saw the political deficiencies of the peasantry as a result of the backwardness of Russian agriculture, so he viewed mechanisation as a cast-iron prerequisite of collectivisation. This means that industry becomes the prime instrument of agrarian revolution (which gives the latter an external and imposed quality) while industrialisation must itself be sustained through a prior capitalist development of agriculture (which pushes peasant experience of socialism into the indefinite future). This double necessity defines the politics of the workers' State as those of intervention, from outside and above, into non-transformed production practices. This, as we have argued throughout, cannot but have implications for the State-form.

Trotsky is not the only one to adhere to this doctrine. But despite its respectability, the key assumption is simply false. It generalises a narrow body of historical experience (capitalist development in Europe) and that is its limitation; for subsequent events have challenged the paradigm. Experience of agricultural cooperation in the PRC, as we have indicated in Chapter 2 and will further document below, has shown that not only is industrialisation not a precondition of successful collectivisation, but that if anything – in conditions Trotsky would call 'backward' – the relation is exactly the reverse.

Trotsky's scepticism concerning the peasant role in socialist construction was one factor which induced him to argue that the maintenance of proletarian dictatorship in Russia would depend on revolution in the West. But it would be mistaken to see in this a mere 'substitution' of the European worker for the Russian *muzhik*, as Stalin insinuated.

Trotsky's estimation of both stemmed from a coherent set of prior assumptions.[35]

For Trotsky, 'internationalism is not an abstract principle but the expression of an economic fact' (Trotsky, 1930e: 350–1): the nature of 'world economy'. The latter is 'a mighty and independent reality which has been created by the international division of labour and the world market, and which in our epoch imperiously dominates the national markets' (Trotsky, 1930a: 22). Hence 'the contemporary productive forces' are 'worldwide in their very essence' (Trotsky, 1930e: 381, 366). If we remember Trotsky's idea of socialism discussed above, which follows from his contention that 'Marxism sets out from the development of technique as the fundamental spring of progress, and constructs the communist programme upon the dynamic of the productive forces' (Trotsky, 1936: 45),[36] it is not difficult to see why he argues that:

— Socialism can only be constructed 'starting from the worldwide division of labour' and carrying 'the international exchange of goods and services to its highest development' (Trotsky, 1930e: 351), which supposes international revolution.

— Therefore isolation and backwardness are the greatest obstacles to socialist construction. The absurdity of a 'national socialist society' would entail 'an extreme reduction in the economic power of men' (ibid., 350; see also his 1930a: 22) in any circumstances. Backwardness compounds the problem. This rules out 'socialism in one country'.

— Proletarian dictatorship in one country does not exclude that country from 'the orbit of world economy' (Trotsky, 1930a: 28). State power, though of tremendous economic significance, 'is nonetheless an instrument of the superstructural order' which 'intervenes imperiously in the process of world economy, but does not abolish its deep-going laws' (ibid., 28, 30).

— It is precisely here that we must distinguish conditions for proletarian seizure of power from those of socialist construction. The law of uneven development establishes the former (for Russia): but this law 'does not replace nor . . . abolish the laws of world economy, on the contrary, it is subordinated to them' (ibid., 25).

Our general objection is that, as the Chinese people's experience in agricultural cooperation demonstrates, and as we have argued in Chapter 1, we should beware of paradigms. The undeniable growth of productive forces engendered by the world market and international division of labour gives us no grounds for assuming this is the only or even the best way of ensuring further development. Moreover, experience of that 'development', including that theorised by Trotsky, provides further objections. It is peculiar that Trotsky should distinguish 'laws of world economy' from 'the law of uneven development'. For, as we have seen him so incisively establish in his historical studies of Tsarist Russia, the former are the laws of capitalist, i.e. imperialist economy, while the latter is simply its *modus operandi*.[37] The same studies showed that the consequence of the law of unevenness was nothing so simple as 'development', but a distinctive 'combination' in which 'the contemporary productive forces' were systematically articulated with the 'backwardness' (poverty) which imperialism fed off, reproduced and exacerbated. Finally, it was precisely the 'international division of labour', revealed in Trotsky's historical studies as the division of labour of imperialism, which constituted that 'combination'. In short, Trotsky himself characterised 'unevenness' as a crushingly *unequal* distribution of 'contemporary productive forces', 'world technique' and 'the resources of world economy' (Trotsky, 1930a: 28–9). Yet here Trotsky seems to have 'forgotten' all this, arguing the international division of labour as an invariant 'infrastructure' between capitalism and socialism. 'Laws' are violently abstracted from the phenomena in which they are embodied (and as which they are experienced). The 'laws of world economy' are reified and hypostasised, whilst the 'law of uneven development' is transformed into a platitudinous abstraction devoid of any historical content.[38]

We will not seek reasons for Trotsky's failure to draw out the implications of his own historical work. The mere fact that he does not testifies to the persistence of a theory of productive forces in his work, for it is only the assumption of an (economic, if not political) 'path all peoples are fated to tread' which could prompt him to argue as he does *despite* his own analysis of what participation in 'the international division of labour' entails.

The latent economism revealed in Trotsky's theory of permanent revolution has its political corollary in his early utterances on the State. His is very much (and much more so than in Lenin) the 'capture' or 'machine' view, his theoretical vehicle being the base/superstructure model.[39]

In 1906 he argued:

> The State is not an end in itself. It is only a machine in the hands of the dominating social forces . . .
> . . . [it] is a tremendous means for organising, disorganising and reorganising social relations. It can be a powerful lever for revolution or a tool for organised stagnation, depending upon the hands that control it. (Trotsky, 1906: 194)[40]

The State is viewed as the principal agency of both political and productive transformation. State power, Trotsky contends, is not a mere prerequisite but the main instrument for 'revolutionising the masses' (Trotsky, 1906: 203) – a task whose accomplishment follows the seizure of power. The State is also the main 'stimulator' of production (Trotsky, 1936: 53). In this connection, he cites the (albeit 'unsystematic and barbaric') activity of the Tsarist State as a lesson in 'the immensely important role which state power can play in the purely economic sphere when . . . it is working in the same direction as historical development' (Trotsky, 1909b: 27; see also his 1922c: 14). The analogy of Tsarist and socialist States, taken with the notion of a general 'direction of historical development' do not merely betray once again the notion of a common 'economic' infrastructure for capitalism and socialism. They also once again establish the distinction between them, logically enough, as one of control of that infrastructure (via State power), and not one residing in production itself. Internal relations between State forms and production are thereby effectively denied. This in turn allows a voluntarism in politics and State activity which perfectly complements the economism, a voluntarism of which we will consider plenty of examples below.

But again, this is not the whole story. We saw in Lenin the contradiction between an elaborated relational theory of the State and an implicit 'capture' practice. The contradiction is also evident in Trotsky, though in his case it is his historical studies which furnish the seeds of a relational view. He is well aware, for example, of the way in which Tsarist development strategies entailed a swollen, bureaucratised, quasi-autonomous State machine, and he waxes eloquent on the massive productive fetter represented by its costs (see Trotsky, 1909b: 45–7). But, as we will see below, he failed to draw conclusions for socialist construction, clearly regarding the issue of control as the decisive one.

We have sought to show how the Bolshevik problematic and its contradictions were established in Trotsky's analysis of the first Russian revolution, its undoubted strengths notwithstanding. What follows will attempt to document this problematic and these contradictions, through succeeding years, problems and works. We will begin with the Left Opposition texts of the twenties.[41]

These are texts of struggle; against the CPSU leadership, certainly, but there is no less critical a struggle within them, between socialist and capitalist strategies in construction. It typically takes the form of a trenchant critique of the political manifestations of 'degeneration', coupled with advocacy of productive strategies which if adopted would themselves imply its acceleration.

The principal symptom and vehicle of degeneration, according to Trotsky, is the bureaucratisation of State and Party apparatuses and attendant curtailment of proletarian and Party democracy. Trotsky lists three main reasons for bureaucratisation: fusion of State and Party apparatuses; slowness of industrialisation; and delay in the international revolution. 'The first concern of the working class after the seizure of power was the creation of a state apparatus' (Trotsky, 1923b: 20). But this apparatus is also 'the most important source of bureaucratism': it 'preoccupies largely the attention of the party apparatus over which it exerts influence by its methods of administration' and it 'absorbs an enormous quantity of the most active party elements and . . . teaches the most capable of them the methods of administration of men and things' (ibid., 45). This implies 'a weakening of the factory cells' (for Trotsky the Party's backbone) 'and an increase of functionaries in the party, proletarian in their origin or not' (ibid., 20). He further envisages a 'very long period' (ibid., 21) in which the 'most active elements' of Party and proletariat will be 'taken away [from production] to be assigned to the party or the state apparatus' (ibid., 43).

Though various conjunctural factors are cited (influx of 'bad elements' after 1917, exigencies of war, etc.)[42] Trotsky stresses that bureaucratism is neither a 'survival' nor 'the aggregate of the bad habits of office holders' but a function of the circumstances, difficulties and tasks of Party and State in the USSR (ibid., 24, 45: see Trotsky, 1936, ch. 3). Predictably, backwardness – numerical paucity and low cultural level of the proletariat, 'lack of culture of the broad masses', the requirements of rapid industrialisation and its harmonisation with 'peasant economy' (Trotsky, 1923b: 45–6) – dominate the explanation. Hence the paradox that Trotsky, while recognising the source of bureaucratism in the Soviet State-form, assumes the necessity to retain its apparatus and argues for extension of its sphere of activity. For him bureaucratism is ultimately contingent on backwardness, elimination of which demands the pre-eminent role of the State. In 1923 he argued that Party awareness would suffice to cope with any short-term dangers of an industrialisation programme which (with the international revolution) would provide the ultimate answer to bureaucratic degeneration (ibid., 18–19). Voluntaristic optimism later succumbed, predictably, to fatalistic (and economistic) pessimism; by 1936 he was writing that degeneration had been 'inevitable' (Trotsky, 1936: 89; also 55–6).

Trotsky (1923b: 18, 45) quite correctly identifies the danger of bureaucratism as the divorce of the Party and State machinery from the masses, and counterposes 'political leadership of the masses' to 'the administration of men and things' (ibid., 45). He is similarly correct to link this two-line struggle to class struggle, regarding bureaucratic degeneration as a possible road of capitalist restoration (ibid., 39–41). We should therefore particularly note what sustains his refusal to draw the implication that the 'machine' must be smashed: the assumption, on the one hand, of industrial development as an absolute prerequisite of socialist construction,[43] and on the other hand, of the sufficiency of 'Bolshevik-Leninist' control of the State to deal with the relational and political implications[44] – in brief, the characteristically Bolshevik combination of economism in production and voluntarism in politics.

Opposition productive strategies, as such, are worthy of more detailed attention.

The grounds on which Trotsky was the first to argue for NEP underlie all his productive announcements of the twenties: the paramount need simultaneously to develop the productive forces and maintain the *smychka*. It need hardly be reiterated that for Trotsky developing the productive forces is synonymous with industrialisation, nor that this is the only road to the agrarian socialist collective. In the meantime, 'the personal interest of the producers themselves in the system of socialist economy', and thus the *smychka*, can only be sustained, Trotsky assumes, by encouraging a capitalist peasant agriculture (Trotsky, 1925: 26).

From this it follows that the direction of development is the crucial question. The 'national economy' (nationalised industry, transport and credit) must outstrip the 'peasant economy' and private (NEPman) capital if proletarian dictatorship is to survive (ibid., 29).[45] But since these economies are mutually dependent (industry for capital generated in agriculture, agriculture for industrial products) correct proportions must be sustained. Concretely, then, direction is a matter of scale and tempo of development of each sector. Most of the twenties polemics focus on this issue: prior to 1929 Trotsky argued that industry was developing too slowly, which resulted in the scissors crisis.[46] With Stalin's abrupt 'leftward turn' industrial expansion became too fast, and took too many resources from agriculture.[47] Either strategy, for Trotsky, had disastrous repercussions for both the productive forces and the *smychka*: productive, in so far as the balance between the sectors was upset, and political, in so far as in either case the mass of the peasantry would be alienated from the Workers' State and tend to solidify round the *kulak*.

Trotsky was well aware of the political dangers that attended NEP, but argued that 'our state is too firmly at the helm' for these to become serious (ibid., 26);[48] always assuming, of course, that leadership pursues correct policies in respect of the direction of development. 'Our state', indeed, plays a key part. The Opposition proposals envisaged it as acting through three channels (Trotsky *et al.*, 1927a): production (as planner in the nationalised sector); distribution (redirecting resources between sectors and classes, largely through the fiscal machinery);[49] and the legal-coercive apparatus (protecting workers and poor peasants, penalising kulaks and NEPmen).

Trotsky is explicit on the relational consequences of his argument. Beyond the 'controlled' encouragement of purely capitalist relations in agriculture he urges, in the 'national' industry, the maintenance and extension of all the social relations typical of capitalism other than its property relations, which latter, characteristically, he sees as sufficient to define the 'national industry' as socialist. These include inequality of income – often conceived, via a theory of 'material incentives', as a stimulus to production (see, *inter alia*, Trotsky, 1932: 157; 1933: 21; 1936: 54–6, 58–9 and ch. VI); a strict hierarchy of technical and managerial expertise (Trotsky, 1925: 38; 1936: ch. III); and, in general, utilisation of 'the best' in capitalist technique (see e.g. Trotsky, 1921c: 14–15; 1922c: 7–8; 1925: 41–4 and *passim*).[50] Technique here, as for Lenin and Stalin, includes that set of productive relations known as Taylorism (Trotsky, 1920a: 121), and Trotsky soundly berates those who complain of monotony at work as 'Tolstoyan reactionaries' (Trotsky, 1925: 42). He is also fully aware that experience of working for 'primitive socialist accumulation' differs little from that of work under capitalism, and explicitly concludes that work experience *cannot* show the worker that the USSR is his State.

Addressing young workers in 1922, he observes:

> Now he [the worker] must understand the nature of the Soviet state in order to gain a correct understanding of the conditions of his working life. Now he must become aware of the building of the whole of Soviet society in order to grasp his position in the factory and the workshop.
>
> Before it was sufficient to *grasp his position in the workshop by feel* and then he would in essence *correct his position in society*. But now on the contrary he must become aware of the building of all Soviet society in order *not to lose his way in the workshop*. (Trotsky, 1922c: 11)

There could be no more eloquent testimony to the Bolshevik divorce of politics and production than this.

Much of this is Bolshevik stock in trade. Where Trotsky is relatively distinctive is in his wish to harness primitive socialist accumulation to the accelerator of the world market.[51] We have dealt with his premises above, though in that case it was in the context of the role of the international revolution, rather than international capital, in socialist construction. From the assumption, 'retardation is far more dangerous to us than the importation of foreign machines or of any necessary foreign commodities in general' (Trotsky, 1925: 40; cf. Day, 1973: 137), Trotsky argues for widespread import of capital goods, raising of foreign loans, leasing of concessions, etc.[52] We could have no surer testimony to the hierarchical aspects of his programme than his proposal that the 'shock troops of our production leaders', i.e. 'managers . . . directors . . . technical students . . . foremen, mechanics and specialists', should avail themselves of foreign tours to enable them to judge 'the comparison coefficients of world economy' (Trotsky, 1925: 38). Nor could we emphasise the relational consequences more than does Trotsky himself, who in 1925 jubilantly celebrated the restoration of 'the old relations' between industry and agriculture: to wit 'exports of grain and raw materials, imports of machinery and manufactured articles' (ibid., 39: cf. Day, 1973: 113–14).

Opposition programmes, then, advocate a development that is either purely capitalist (agriculture) or capitalist in most matters other than ownership. This goes beyond mere imitation, for Trotsky (to a greater extent than any other leading Bolshevik) wished the world market to have direct influence on the construction possibilities of the USSR. The clear implication is that the State becomes the major bastion of (an eventual) socialism. We should again stress both that Trotsky himself draws out the relational and experiential correlates of this strategy, and that he assumes they can be handled through an extension of State activity, despite his awareness of the dangers of 'degeneration' attending this. What emerges once more is the deep-rootedness of the capitalist paradigm of development, and thus the hegemony of the theory of productive forces, in Trotsky's marxism.

Trotsky's work culminates in that centrepiece of his legacy, his historical account of the 'Soviet Thermidor' and careful characterisation of Stalin's USSR as a 'degenerate Workers' State'.[53] On the former we may be brief, since it recapitulates themes and rests on premises already examined.

The dominant motifs of Trotsky's account should by now be familiar: backwardness and isolation.[54] Backwardness is adduced to explain the vagaries of peasantry, proletariat and politburo, not to mention the character, views and policies of Djugashvili himself.[55] The exigencies of its conceptual partner also play their part: as we saw in the 1923 critique of bureaucratisation, Trotsky recognises certain of the anti-socialist implications of the modernisation strategy, and this is held to have solidified the social basis for Stalin's triumph (Trotsky, 1936: ch. 5). But in so far as Trotsky never queries the necessity for 'modernisation' *per se* this too is understood simply as an effect of backwardness. Trotsky finally identifies the failure of the international revolution as the precipitate cause, and continuing condition, for 'bureaucratic domination'. In short, he sees events in the USSR after 1917 as the supreme vindication of those perspectives he first elaborated in 1906 (ibid.).

For Trotsky, the notion of the 'degenerate Workers' State' is not a propagandistic description of convenience, but a precise, historically grounded concept which enables us to grasp the nature and contradictions of the USSR.[56] In his view, Stalinists abstract from the content of social relationships and trumpet the socialist nature of the USSR on the exclusive basis of its juridical (property) forms (ibid., 60–1). But the errors of the 'petty-bourgeois opposition' are equally grave; they define the USSR as 'State capitalist' (Urbahns) or 'a social formation of a new type' (Laurat and Rizzi; Burnham and Shachtman) only by way of an analysis which abstracts from social relations entirely, and is typically bourgeois in its focus on externals and failure to situate these in terms of their historical conditions – in our terms, a purely phenomenal analysis.[57] Neither of these approaches can grasp the specificity of the USSR.

On Trotsky's account, the October revolution established Russia as a transitional formation, neither socialist nor capitalist but in struggle between the two. October achieved the overturn of bourgeois property relations and the dictatorship of the proletariat. Since neither have been reversed by the bourgeoisie, the USSR remains a Workers' State despite the (for him) obvious fact that it is not the proletariat, but the Stalinist bureaucracy, which is in power. This latter fact, however, defines the Soviet Workers' State as 'degenerate'.

The bureaucratic nature of the State, therefore, does not follow from the property relations established by the revolution; it is rather to be explained by the specific historical conditions in which the revolution took place (backwardness) and the USSR developed (isolation). This implies that the bureaucracy is not a ruling class in the strict sense, its economic and political privileges notwithstanding; for its basis lies precisely in the socialist property relations established by October, which under different conditions would have supported a socialist dictatorship. The bureaucracy therefore must be conceptualised as an essentially parasitic excrescence on socialism.

From this follows the peculiar contradiction of the USSR: the survival of the bureaucracy depends upon its defence of the gains of the revolution, since these constitute its sole foundation and *raison d'être*. This explains the considerable achievements of the USSR and indicates that these retain, and are made possible by, irreducibly socialist features, however deformed. It has the further implication that bureaucratic rule remains unstable, in that its parasitic nature becomes evident with each advance in socialist construction. From this Trotsky draws two key conclusions: a political, rather than a 'social' revolution is required to unseat the ruling caste; and, pending this, the USSR must be defended against imperialism in so far as it remains a Workers' State.[58]

As with Trotsky's early writings, certain of the enduring strengths of marxism, *and* Bolshevism, are evident here.[59] Those who argue that class struggle is over in 'The State of the Whole People' are very much with us, as are the political heirs of those who saw the Molotov-Ribbentrop pact as 'proof' of the essential similarities of socialism and fascism. Such 'radicalism' has served the Cold Warriors well. Trotsky also emphasised the massive achievements of the Soviet people, the fetters on their socialism notwithstanding (see his 1936: ch. 1). All this is to Trotsky's credit, as is his insistence on the need for both socialist defence of, and the extension of socialist revolution in, the USSR, and it is not difficult to see why many socialists have been seduced by Trotskyism in the face of the doctrines of the Kremlin. But this is precisely why the inadequacies of Trotsky's account must be highlighted. Its emphases are typically Bolshevik. The USSR's property relations suffice to define it as a 'Workers' State', and degeneration, by implication, is purely a 'political' phenomenon. To say this is not to deny that Trotsky recognised 'economic' causes, but to stress that his diagnosis centres on who is in command of the State machine, while his programme is a narrowly 'political' one for its recapture. The machine, suitably stripped of its bureaucratic features, would presumably then be used to effect the Opposition programme of the twenties. We have sought to suggest, however, that such a programme would not resolve but could only perpetuate the Bolshevik contradictions. For these are contradictions of productive strategies, and relations, in a wider sense than Trotsky ever fully recognises. Here – in Trotsky's last word on socialist construction – we return to the nub of the question. We once more face, in Trotsky's final strategy for the capture and utilisation of State power, the typically Bolshevik conception of production as economics plus technique, and productive as technical problems; and of politics as control over and utilisation of an extant machine, and political problems as problems of capturing State power. The internal relation of productive and political forms still fails to emerge.

While Trotsky is absolutely correct to point to Soviet property relations as an indication that the gains of 1917 have not yet been lost, the analysis cannot stop there. If it does it remains, to use one of Trotsky's own expressions, 'algebraic'.[60] Socialisation of the means of production is indeed a moment and prerequisite of socialist construction, but it is the *content* of these 'juridical forms', as Trotsky recognises, which matters. Consistently with his overall conception of socialism, Trotsky seeks to define this content technologically: his criticism of Stalin's claim that the USSR is socialist is that the content does not match the forms because the productive forces are insufficiently developed. This ignores that it is *how* these forces are developed which establishes the content of the social relations of production. And in Stalin's USSR – as in Trotsky's – this entailed simultaneous acceleration both of certain nodal relational features (and experiences) reminiscent of the capitalist mode of production, *and* of the State machine which, through its monopoly of precisely ownership and political power, was to contain the capitalism of those features until the requisite 'level of development' had been achieved. It is here that the politics and economics of what Trotsky analyses as 'degeneration' are indissolubly linked. It follows that no purely 'political' revolution, in Trotsky's sense of the word, and still less his productive strategies, will break that link or resolve the contradiction. What is required is a profoundly social, and cultural, revolution: a revolution in the social relations of production in the fullest sense. For, *pace* Trotsky, the content of juridical forms is not a technical question, but a question of whose politics are in command.

3 STALIN

For many years now, the so-called 'question of Stalin' has paralysed marxist analyses of the social formation of the USSR and, more generally, of Bolshevism. The historical experience of the years 1923 to 1953 is rarely[61] comprehended otherwise than as an effect either of the personality of Joseph Stalin *simpliciter*, or of the irreducibly 'objective' data of 'backwardness' and 'isolation'. Sometimes, as for Trotsky, the two approaches coexist, if rather uneasily: the immutability of the latter explaining the salience of the former, a 'bad man with yellow eyes' (Ratcliffe, 1974),[62] and, it seems, the power to change everything. The unease finds an indication in the kind of bridges built to connect the two; an isolated quotation from Engels on leaders 'in advance' of their class (as in Colletti, 1970: 66; a use criticised elsewhere by Lenin as 'doctrinaire'),[63] or, more often, especially in Trotskyist work,[64] Marx's caricatures of Napoleon III. These latter, which Marx himself criticised at some length in his 1871 drafts and texts,[65] are plundered in order (violently) to abstract a notion of 'Bonapartism' which has been used to explain *both* Stalin *and* Hitler; an historical methodology, as we have argued in Chapter 1, which is singularly inimical to marxism. In short, in marxist treatments of Stalin, caricature and analogy have usually replaced materialist analysis. We can neither substantiate these charges nor provide that analysis here. We can, however, attempt to *pose* the problem of Stalin anew; precisely *not* as a problem of *Stalin*, the individual, but as a problem of Stalin as, in the words of the CPC, 'a phenomenon of the international communist movement'; and therefore, we would add, as a phenomenon of *Bolshevism*, whose problematic dominated that movement.

In 1930 Trotsky described 'the theory of socialism in one country' as 'the only theory that consistently and to the very end opposes the theory of permanent revolution'. He added, characteristically, that

> The world division of labour, the dependence of the productive forces of the advanced countries of Europe upon Asiatic raw materials, etc., etc., make the construction of an independent socialist society in any single country in the world impossible. (Trotsky, 1930a: 156; cf. his 1930e)

We have argued against Trotsky's perspective previously. But in seeing 'socialism in one country' as fundamentally opposed to his 'theory of permanent revolution', Trotsky is correct. For how *does* Bolshevism support socialist construction in the least optimal conditions? By waiting for these conditions to change (although, for Trotsky, it would appear that some social relations, like the 'world division of labour', are simply natural facts)? Or by working against the restrictions they temporarily impose? Does Bolshevism, in other words, celebrate and defend 1917 as part of a revolution which will eventually be worldwide? Or does it cringe before the 'etc., etc.' of Trotsky's formulations? It is as a response to this, very *practical* dilemma, that we must begin to understand 'the theory of socialism in one country'.

As Carr (1959: 56f.) recognises, 'socialism in one country' marks a shift to self-reliance accompanied by the 'Bolshevisation' of world revolution. In the face of the failures (and defeats) of those revolutions in the 'advanced countries' on which the Bolsheviks had originally predicated their analysis and pinned their hopes, these jointly form an *international* strategy, self-reliance to defend and the Bolshevisation of the Comintern eventually to extend what 1917 had won. These gains, it must be stressed, were for Stalin victories *for* the international working class, in a double sense. First, he sees the USSR as a 'mighty base' for world revolution (Stalin, 1924b: 116; 1927c: 201), the Five Year Plans as international beacons (Stalin, 1933: Pt. I; 1934; 1939; 1952b). In his own words, 'the working class of the U.S.S.R. is part of the world proletariat, its vanguard; and our republic is the cherished child of the world proletariat' (Stalin, 1934: 538–9).[66] This recalls his insistence of ten years previously that

> The victory of socialism in one country is not a self-sufficient task. The revolution which has been victorious in one country must regard

itself not as a self-sufficient entity, but as an aid, a means *for* hastening the victory of the proletariat in all countries . . . (Stalin, 1924b: 113)

Second, consistently with his postulate that 'theory is the experience of the working class movement in all countries taken in its general aspect' (Stalin, 1924a: 15), Stalin seeks to generalise the theoretical gains of the experience of 1917. Largely through his work, Leninism, canonised as the 'theory and tactics of the proletarian revolution in general' (Stalin, 1924a: 2), becomes the dominant theory in Bolshevism, which is henceforth regarded as 'the Marxism of the era of imperialism . . .'.[67] For Stalin, then, 'socialism in one country' is *not* to be counterposed to world revolution. On the contrary, especially given the failure of revolutions elsewhere, preserving 1917's victories, and extending the Bolshevism that made them possible, are seen as fundamental *to* the advancement of international socialism.

If 'socialism in one country' responds to unfavourable world conditions, many other of the policies held to be specifically 'Stalinist' follow from an analysis of internal problems. The weakness of Soviet power, as we have several times stressed, was most evident in the countryside. Carr's studies of the Harvests are exemplary here.[68] What was taking place throughout the twenties, in the absence both of Soviets in the countryside and of an agrarian policy which reflected the collective enthusiasm of agrarian producers, was the consolidation of that 'official-entrepreneurial bloc' to which we have referred. This rested upon old power relations partially revived by Bolshevik policy, into which Party members were themselves absorbed. This group politically and productively sealed the countryside from the towns. And until that blockade was broken – by the unleashing of class struggle from below which would sweep away cadres living on the backs of the people and abolish the princes, priests, and petty intellectuals lording it over the peasants – the agrarian problem would remain the dominant internal problem of Soviet life; especially when (and here Stalin was a good Leninist) that countryside was seen as yielding up extra funds, labour and resources to fuel the necessary industrialisation of the urban economy. When, as by the late twenties,[69] a political party finds itself increasingly dependent upon those it fears most and knows least the historical stage is set for a clash. The Five Year Plans, Collectivisation, and the Terror and Purges are a series of clashes resulting from contradictions internal to Bolshevism, which had ripened explosively by 1929. These are, we have indicated, contradictions which would have had to be faced whether Lenin had lived, or Trotsky, rather than Stalin, had triumphed in 1923. In what follows, we shall examine Stalin's handling of these contradictions; not as a historian might, but by example, simply to show, as we have for Lenin and Trotsky, Stalin's Bolshevism. We will begin, in 1929, with some texts which at first sight promise the transcendence of the limitations of the Bolshevik problematic; a promise, we shall see, which was not fulfilled. Stalin's achievement – and that it *is* an achievement needs to be acknowledged – was not to transcend Bolshevism. It was to preserve it, and with it, much that is socialist in the USSR.

The approval and discussion of the first Five Year Plan exactly coincided with Politburo, Party Conference, and Soviet Congresses' approval of Kalinin's April 1929 theses on agrarian production. These posed the central issue as '*Who will direct economic development, the kulak or the socialist state?*' (cit. Carr, 1969: 274). When he presented his theses to the Conference and Congresses, Kalinin linked 'class struggle' to the 'limitation of capitalism', and stressed that 'the socialist way of development is the only way to free poor and middle peasants from poverty and ruin' (cit. Carr, 1969: 266–7). Stalin's text *The Right Deviation in the C.P.S.U.* (*B*) (1929a), which was first adumbrated at the Central Committee to which Kalinin presented his theses, argues that this Right wing constantly underestimates class struggle. We have here the possibility of seeing political and ideological powers as a means of overcoming what had previously been regarded as a technical problem. In this criticism, moreover, through a variety of shifts of level and concept, Stalin identifies what are in fact constituents of Bolshevism: he comments unfavourably, for instance, on Bukharin's view of the peasantry:

> In his description of the peasantry the differentiation is lacking, the existence of social groups disappears, and there remains but a single drab patch which is called the countryside. (Stalin, 1929a: 260)

Further, through the ambiguous use of the notion of 'scale', he poses socialist productive forms against 'scientific knowledge and modern technique'.

Stalin's speech of 27 December 1929 extends these points via a refutation of six major 'bourgeois prejudices', in which he argues the need to pose socialist against capitalist ways of advancing. In this text, which deserves close study, the shifts we have indicated in Stalin's Bolshevism are brought to theoretical visibility. First, he rejects a 'theory of equilibrium', since the Soviet Union can either go '*back* – to capitalism, or *forward* – to Socialism. There is no third way . . .' (Stalin, 1929c: 309). Second, the 'theory of spontaneity' (which argues the inevitability of socialism in the countryside, since socialism, like capitalism, flows automatically to the countryside from the towns) is dismissed because it, like the former, overlooks class struggle and the need for specifically socialist forms of organisation. Third, he rejects the 'theory of stability' in terms we will consider shortly. Fourth, he argues that only with a change in the contradictory relations between town and countryside can poor and middle peasants really be aided. Fifth, the notion that the *kolkhozi* are not Socialist is rejected by reference to the (correct) question:

> What determines the type of an economic enterprise? Obviously, the relations between people in the process of production . . . Of course there are [also] contradictions in the collective farms . . . (Ibid., 319f.)

Finally, Stalin directly relates class struggle to novel forms of production: the elimination of the *kulaki*, as a class, is linked to replacing their output with the 'output of the collective farms and state farms' (ibid., 325; cf. his 1930a: 332).

Stalin's refutation of the 'theory of stability' (which argues an inherent stability in small peasant farms), like several features of his 'Dizzy with Success' (1930b), has particular theoretical significance. For with his implicit recognition that social *relations* of production can be *forces* of production, we come close to seeing both what the nature of the resources for socialist construction are, and, concurrently, how such capitalist social relations as are reproduced by the modernisation strategies integral to Bolshevism batten them down. Stalin acknowledges both the peasants' power in cooperation, and their power*less*ness 'under the conditions of individual labour'. It is worth quoting him at length:

> In my recent article, *A Year of Great Change*, I advanced certain arguments in support of the superiority of large-scale farming over small farming; in this case I had in mind big state farms. It is self-evident that all these arguments fully and entirely apply to the collective farms, which are also large economic units. I am speaking not only of developed collective farms . . . but also of collective farms in their embryonic stage . . . Outwardly, the technique of these collective farms scarcely differs from that of the small peasant farm . . . And yet the simple pooling of the peasant implements of production within the collective farm has produced results of which our practical workers never dreamed . . . the peasants who were powerless under the conditions of individual labour, have been transformed into a mighty force once they pooled their implements and became united in collective farms. (Stalin, 1929c: 314–15)[70]

'Dizzy with Success' complements this with a recognition of the importance of whose politics are in command:

> Collective farms cannot be set up by force. To do so would be stupid and reactionary. The collective farm movement must rely on the active support of the great bulk of the peasantry. Methods of collective farm construction in developed districts cannot be mechanically transferred to backward districts. To do so would be stupid and reactionary. Such a 'policy' would discredit the idea of collectivisation at one blow. (Stalin, 1930b: 334)

It would be wrong, we believe, simply to dismiss these insights as mere rhetoric. They testify, rather, to the contradictions within Bolshevism. But collective farms *were* for the most part set up by force (with precisely the result that Stalin predicted). To an extent this was because Bolshevik policies since 1917 had cumulatively both sharpened the crisis and suppressed the basis for a socialist way out; collectivisation was carried out on the ruins of a thousand initiatives from below which go back to just those peasant collectives stigmatised *en avant* by Bolshevik ignorance and dogma.[71] But equally to the point of our argument, alternatives continued to be formulated through the Bolshevik problematic. However much Stalin spoke of the need for 'mass criticism from below' or saw the *smychka* between workers and poor and middle peasants as the key to Soviet power (cf. his 1925), Bolshevism (and the USSR) was preserved through a series of revolutions from above. The innovations we have discussed, in other words, may have stretched Bolshevism to its limits. But they did not transcend them.

Thus within, or contemporaneously with, the above-quoted texts, we find the familiar Bolshevik emphases. We have, for example, remarked the ambiguities present in Stalin's call for 'large-scale' productive units, noting how this occasions a (partial) recognition of cooperation as a socialist force of production and a (similarly partial) shift away from reliance on 'scientific knowledge and modern technique' *simpliciter*. But equally, Stalin's notion of 'bigness', like Lenin's, was grounded in inter-country comparisons which evince a unitary conception of 'development'.[72] In July 1928, for instance, he lavishly praised a report on large-scale grain farms in the USA, urging their construction as large-scale *sovkhozi*, with machinery and tractors, within five years (Carr, 1969: 200f.). The priority of heavy industry likewise remained unchallenged: in 1929, Stalin quoted approvingly from Lenin (and echoed Trotsky) to the effect that 'without heavy industry we shall be doomed as an independent country . . .' (Stalin, 1929b: 297); while his *The Right Deviation* poses the historical alternatives as a 'Bolshevik plan' ('the key to the reconstruction of agriculture is the speedy rate of development of our industry') versus a 'Bukharin plan' ('the key to the reconstruction of agriculture is the development of individual peasant farming')[73] (Stalin, 1929a: 271, 272). Commitment to 'heavy industry' here means, once more as for Lenin and Trotsky, commitment to those paradigms capitalism had bequeathed for building it. In the event, the USSR *was* industrialised via 'primitive socialist accumulation'; on a scale (and with a ruthlessness) greater than any proposed by the Left Opposition in the twenties. Through the thirties, payments to MTSs and the State absorbed 50–60 per cent of *kolkhoz* produce, while the 'scissors' (between industrial and agricultural prices) widened. Peasants understandably tended to work less for the collective and more on their private plots; which in turn elicited the typically Bolshevik response of increased State control and coercion. The 1935 *Kolkhoz* Model Statute declared the collective farm a 'voluntary association of producers'; but *kolkhozi* remained subject to the instruction of local State and Party organs on all questions of production and procurement, while both the MTSs and the local Party Secretaries had effective power of dismissal over elected *kolkhoz* officials. By 1939, it was deemed necessary to legislate a compulsory minimum of work-days for *kolkhoz* members. Industry tells a similar story. Stalin's enthusiasm for 'American efficiency' (which, following Lenin, he saw as a *defining* feature of Bolshevism)[74] was reflected in the systematic extension of such capitalistically-inspired 'techniques' as one-man management, wide wage differentials, and 'material incentives'. Here, too, direct State control of production (through centralised and detailed planning) was backed up by the apparatus of coercion, whether through penalties on management for non-fulfilment of targets, or the draconian labour legislation of 1938 and 1940; the latter, incidentally, being proposed by those 'transmission belts' from the Party to the masses, the Trade Unions.[75]

Stalin's Bolshevism, then, was distinctive and revolutionary (by comparison – importantly – with *both* Trotsky's *and* Bukharin's) inasmuch as, rather than capitulating before the brute facticity of 'backwardness and isolation', it asserted the viability (and value *to* the international working class – a value recently, and yet again, proved in Angola) of socialist construction in the USSR, and recognised class struggle as basic to that construction. But, we have argued, Stalin's understanding of socialist construction remained Bolshevik in its subordination to capitalist paradigms of 'development'. It is this, we believe, rather than the supposed interests of 'bureaucracy' or Stalin's 'Asiatic' character, which explains the unreal quality of the calls for 'mass criticism from below' with which we commenced this discussion. For, quite simply, Stalin's modernisation programme involved the systematic imposition on peasants and workers of social relations whose conditions and consequence were, by and large, the suppression of *any* independent transformation from below. This same Bolshevik orthodoxy, in our view, also goes far towards explaining the massive inflation of the apparatus of the Soviet State which *par excellence* defines the Stalin Years. The modernisation programme entailed such inflation: manifestly, through the increasingly monolithic apparatus of Planning; and covertly, but no less directly, through the machinery of coercion increasingly required to secure the political conditions and to stem the political consequences of that programme. Amongst the latter were both widespread mass disaffection, and (this group being, significantly, prominent among the victims of Stalin's Terror)[76] the growth of a 'caste' of technocrats and *apparatchiks*. Within this context, Stalin indeed (successfully) continued to wage class struggle to defend the conquests of 1917. But unsurprisingly, given the continued hegemony of the unreconstructed theory of productive forces within Stalin's Bolshevism, it remained severed from production and statist in form. Stalin saw not mass action from below (as displayed, for example, in the myriad local accomplishments of the Chinese people which – by instructive contrast – the CPC *itself* highlights as exemplary)[77] but State action from above, as the motor of productive transformation, while the replication of many of the defining social relations of capitalism, conceived as those of 'modernity', was envisaged as essential to that transformation. In such a perspective, the State becomes the *sole* guarantor of an eventual socialist outcome. It need not surprise us then, if we find that what Stalin's Party supremely required of the Soviet People was their obedience, that the ideological purity of Party and State personnel became of critical import, or that notions like 'infiltrator', 'saboteur' and 'traitor' increasingly emerged as passable concepts through which to think, and the Terror and the Purge appropriate weapons with which to wage the class struggle Stalin (rightly) saw as fundamental to socialist construction.

Stalin's own texts are in fact revealingly explicit on much of what we have just been attempting to indicate. In his seminal *Foundations of Leninism*, Stalin argued that

> The state is a machine in the hands of the ruling class for suppressing the resistance of its class enemies. *In this respect* the dictatorship of the proletariat does not differ essentially from the dictatorship of any other class, for the proletarian state is a machine for the use of the suppression of the bourgeoisie. (Stalin, 1924a: 32)

It is noteworthy here that Stalin (in a definition with which Lenin, Trotsky, Bukharin or Preobrazhensky would concur) makes an emphasis that he drew, five years later, from the NEP experience when he accused Bukharin of forgetting the 'role of the State as the regulator' (Stalin, 1929a: 363) during that policy. Ten years later, Stalin closed his *Report* to the 18th Congress of the CPSU with a discussion of 'Some Questions of Theory', most of which is devoted to consideration of the role of the State in socialist construction. 'Certain of the general propositions in the Marxist doctrine of the State', he argues, 'are incompletely worked out and inadequate' (Stalin, 1939: 657). He has in mind Marx's and Engels's views on the withering away of the State. The 'clarification' Stalin goes on to develop is doubly revealing: first, he advances an analysis which is succinctly encapsulated in what is, regrettably, a *contemporary* Soviet definition, viz., that throughout the transition to socialism the State is 'the basic instrument in effecting economic, political, social and cultural transformation' (Chernilovsky, 1970: 474); second, he explains the power of such 'saboteurs' and 'traitors' as Trotsky and Bukharin by Bolshevism's failure, due to what he sees as dogmatic adherence to the utterances of Marx and Engels, to appreciate that the Soviet State has such a key part to play. Finally, we may cite one of Stalin's last major texts, *Marxism and Linguistics*, which (apart from denying the theses of Marx and Engels on language as practical consciousness) has as much to do with a theory of State power as with linguistic competence. In it, the whole base/superstructure metaphor is celebrated as a universal law, as an anonymous *Pravda* article (5 October 1950) accompanying Stalin's text makes very clear. This latter argues that 'the special creative role of the new Socialist superstructure and in particular of the Socialist State' results from this superstructure having been created in order to serve the economic base. Above all, 'the Socialist State . . . represents the principal instrument in the creation of the economic base for socialism' (cit. Mehnert, 1952: 66).[78] The following year, Kedrov in the *Bolshevik* wrote, *à propos* collectivisation:

> The transition to the Socialist *kolkhoz* regime in the village was a revolution that removed the old bourgeois system in the village and created a new Socialist system. But this revolution did not take place through an explosion, that is to say not by means of the destruction of the existing machinery of state, but by means of the gradual transition from the old bourgeois regime to a new one. This was possible because it was a revolution from above. (*Bolshevik*, 15, 1951; cit. Mehnert, 1952: 70f.)

Concerning the mechanics of the 'revolution', he was substantially correct. Stalin himself explicitly conceived collectivisation as a matter of *pacification* of the villages (Carr, 1969: 36f.; Lewin, 1966: 184f.).

Thus, Stalin too matched his Bolshevik conception of 'development' with the Bolshevik severance of politics from production, and ensuing statism, which we have indicated as its inevitable corollary. His distinctiveness, therefore, is a distinctiveness *within* the Bolshevik problematic; a matter finally of emphasis, though of important emphasis. Like Trotsky, for example, Stalin believed it 'profoundly mistaken' and 'absolutely untrue' that 'the Soviet state and its leaders can abolish existing laws of political economy and can "form", "create" new laws' (Stalin, 1952a: 2); indeed, he considered the existence of commodity production and the law of value 'not a bad thing' because 'it teaches our executives to count production magnitudes . . . and to make their enterprises pay' (ibid., 19). Conversely, as we have seen, Trotsky too (at times) held an incredibly optimistic opinion of what 'our State' can do. Where Stalin in the end differed was in taking the voluntarism we have seen to be one option inscribed in Bolshevism's divorce of production and politics to its ultimate, but still very Bolshevik, conclusion. The resultant expansion, and activities, of the Soviet State machine were both brutal and bloody. But this should not obscure the fact that other Bolsheviks all shared both the image (and politics) of that machine, and the understanding of what it is to develop the productive forces which we have argued was basic to its inflation.[79] Stalin used the machine to defend the gains of October, just as Trotsky and Preobrazhensky would have used it control price levels between town and country, or Bukharin would have used it to protect the rich peasant, or Lenin almost used it to lease large amounts of Soviet resources and capital via the Genoa and Rapallo conferences – *all* in the interests of 'development'. Conversely, it must be faced that – in the absence of that genuinely socialist construction from below which, we have tried to show, Bolshevism in large measure systematically suppressed – much of what the Soviet working class enjoys to this day (in terms of having enough to eat, being well clothed and housed) was constructed through, and relies precisely and identifiably on, that very machine which so horrifies so many marxists. The text from which we were just quoting, Stalin's *Economic Problems of Socialism in the USSR*, makes a further (and critical) observation on the law of value. It is that *because* of the Soviet state this law does *not* govern the distribution of the Soviet people's labour. It is to this degree, measurable in the conditions of life of the Soviet workers, that socialism and capitalism remain in tension within the social formation that is the USSR. This defence of October's gains in the face of the ravages of domestic and international capital, culminating in the bloody cataclysm of the Great Patriotic War,[80] was Stalinism's great achievement. But it was a limited achievement, and its costs were astronomical. The achievement belongs to Bolshevism. But so, too, we believe, do the limits and the costs. For what 'Stalinism' cumulatively represents, we have sought to argue, is thoroughly Bolshevik. It was a distinctive Bolshevism, certainly, as was Trotsky's and Bukharin's, and one massively scarred by the circumstances of its development, including those resulting from prior Bolshevik policies – but it was a Bolshevism none the less.

In 1939 Victor Serge wrote:

> It is often said that 'the germ of all Stalinism was in Bolshevism from its beginning'. Well, I have no objection. Only, Bolshevism also contained many other germs – a mass of other germs – and those who lived through the enthusiasm of the first years of the first victorious revolution ought not to forget it. To judge the living man by the death germs which the autopsy reveals in a corpse – and which he may have carried in him since his birth – is this very sensible? (*New International*, Feb 1939, cit. Sedgewick, 1963: xv–xvi)

We have no wish to deny the 'other germs' which Serge speaks of, or the enthusiasm of the first years of the revolution; *or* the well-documented socialist enthusiasm, come to that, of those who built, say, the Magnitogorsk metallurgical centre.[81] But we believe it is not only sensible, but imperative, for socialists to consider the extent to which Serge's 'death germs' *were* in Bolshevism from the beginning. Not to do so risks spreading them.

4 Mao

It is the aim of this and the following chapter to illuminate much of the foregoing in terms of available but contrary historical experiences of socialist construction. We shall argue that the class struggles within the People's Republic of China, and between the CPC and the CPSU, illuminate Bolshevism's social problematic in a unique manner; not least because those struggles – over two lines, two roads, two paths – present and represent the supposedly *impossible*, or *utopian*, alternatives denied *a priori* by both Bolshevism and many contemporary marxist analyses of socialist construction. Here, we shall concentrate on presenting a theoretical account of events within China in the years after the Long March up until the early 1950s.[1]

1 THE IMPORTANT THING IS TO BE GOOD AT LEARNING[2]

In 1908, in his *Philosophical Notebooks*, Lenin argued that experience

> needs only to be explained. To explain it means simply to formulate the relations it involves, and which it itself brings to our attention, if we know how to grasp its lessons. And science is beginning to concern itself with them. But, being all reality, experience is not in need of justification: it exists. (Lenin, 1908a: 475)[3]

Much of Mao's work, and the wider practices of the CPC, have been concerned with formulating the relations involved in *socialist* construction, by trying to learn how to grasp the lessons of *historical* experience, including errors of judgement and policy. Above all, perhaps, Mao has been concerned to indicate the particular conditions that encourage collective, and therefore both more egalitarian and more conscious, learning-by-transformation. Socialist construction is, of course, centrally concerned with a complete transformation of social reality. Transformation of this character always requires a prior judgement about what is to be changed and what is to effect change.

Mao agrees with Marx that there are a number of false steps possible here. In a critique of early materialism, in his *Theses on Feuerbach*, Marx argued (Thesis III) that materialist notions that people 'are products of circumstances and upbringing', and that, therefore, 'changed' people are 'products of other circumstances' forget that *circumstances are changed by people.*[4]

> Hence, this doctrine necessarily arrives at dividing society into two parts, one of which is superior to society (Robert Owen, for example). The coincidence of the changing circumstances and of human activity can be conceived and rationally understood only as *revolutionary practice.* (Marx, 1845)

If you want to be good at learning you must admit first of all the *possibility of learning* itself; that is to say, you must acknowledge the possibility of error, for it is the latter that records the phenomenal forms of new possibilities, whether it be an improved accomplishment of an old practice or a new practice. Changing reality involves self-knowing and self-changing. As Mao argued in 1937

> If you want to know a certain thing or class of things directly, you must personally participate in the practical struggle to change reality. (Mao, 1937b: 300)

For

> Idealism and mechanical materialism, opportunism and adventurism, are all characterised by the breach between the subjective and the objective, by the separation of knowledge from practice. (Ibid., 307)

Freedom or liberation, within this framework, cannot be merely an end state (Mao, 1957a: 438). 'Freedom is won by the people through struggle, it is not bestowed by anyone as a favour' (Mao, 1945d: 293). Twenty years later, taking up a text frequently used to represent a working definition of socialist construction, Mao has argued

> Engels spoke only of moving from the realm of necessity to the realm of freedom, and said that freedom is the understanding of necessity. This sentence is not complete, it only says one half and leaves the rest unsaid. Does merely understanding it make you free? Freedom is the understanding of necessity *and* the transformation of necessity – one has some work to do. If you merely eat without having any work to do, if you merely understand, is that sufficient? . . . only by

> transformation can freedom be obtained . . . New things are to be found in reality, we must grasp reality. (Mao, 1964b: 229)

Freedom, liberation, are relative states of increased well-being accomplished by the collective efforts of particular communities through more conscious and more egalitarian transformation, itself involving knowing-through-changing simultaneously people and things.

Congruent with this theory of learning is Mao's refusal of any rigid separation between the political and the economic, or between Party/Army and people. Cultural images and political practices were discovered to have as much productive potential as machinery and sources of energy. We have emphasised the extremely basic and objective nature of the constraints accomplished by certain ideas (facts and values). The power of ideas and images is most acute when institutionalised into an intellectualist image of the Party, celebrating and articulating a more and more consistent dogma which entails an apparatus of enforcement and evaluation. The Party develops a knowledge of 'what is best' for the People, whom it increasingly feels surround it as a 'sea of enemies'. Mao's notions of the struggles involved in genuine (or 'solid') knowing-and-changing reality, by contrast, stress that what is at issue is struggles over the defining or negotiation of social reality. In turn, therefore, such struggles entail conflicts over whom shall be told (and by whom) how things shall be defined and carried out.

Mao argued in 1943

> As rent reduction is a mass struggle by the peasants, Party directives and government decrees should guide and help it instead of trying to bestow favours on the masses. To bestow rent reduction as a favour instead of arousing the masses to achieve it by their own action is wrong, and the results will not be solid. (Mao, 1943b: 131)

Or in 1942

> Another mistake is 'draining the pond to catch the fish', that is, making endless demands on the people, disregarding their hardships and considering only the needs of the government and the army. That is a Kuomintang mode of thinking which we must never adopt. (Mao, 1942d: 114)

What is entailed in these prescriptions is a recognition and reconceptualisation of many of the key terms of Bolshevism's problematic. 'Social relations' (in the broadest sense) are seen to confer meaning and significance on machinery and production processes. The resources of socialism are seen to be *existing* human beings,[5] but not considered abstractly (or reduced to some homogeneous reserve of labour power) so much as viewed as many overlapping and interlocking productive collectivities. Socialist construction consists in a subordination of the Party's vanguardism (although we shall argue that this too was qualified significantly in China) to the myriad exemplary transformations carried out by those productive communities. This conception of exemplary transformations pervades Mao's empirical investigations from the 1930s until the present day and is a constituent of his theory of social organisation which we examine below.

We can best counterpose what we have argued thus far to Bolshevism, by providing a quotation from Mao's 1945 speech arguing that 'We [that is, we emphasise, *the Party*] must learn to do economic work':

> If instead of coercion and commandism, which are self-defeating because of their quest for quick results, we adopt a policy of patiently persuading people by setting them good examples, then it will be possible for the majority of peasants to be organised into mutual aid groups for agricultural and handicraft production in the next few years. Once such production groups become the usual practice, not only will output increase and all kinds of innovations emerge, but there will also be political progress, a higher educational level, progress in hygiene, a remoulding of loafers and a change in social customs, and it will not be long before the implements of production will be improved too. (Mao, 1945a: 241–2)

2 GET ORGANISED![6]

Mao's short 1930 pamphlet, *Oppose book worship!* opens with the words 'No investigation, no right to speak!' (Mao, 1930: 40). We now know that Mao himself had to learn that the role of a good communist is to investigate:

> Formerly, I was principal of a primary school [Mao explained to his nephew in 1966], and a teacher in a middle school. I am also a member of the Central Committee, and was once a department chief for the Kuomintang. But when I went to the rural areas and spent some time with the peasants, I was deeply struck by how many things they knew. I realised their knowledge was wide, and I was no match for them, but should learn from them. (Mao, 1966a: 251)

Mao's own learning of the need for new forms of organisation is clearly exposed in his own investigations,[7] beginning with the remarkable

Hunan documents of 1927, where he first urged the Party to *get organised* (Mao, 1927: 24f.). By 1934, in an important text of implicit criticism of much of Bolshevism called 'Be concerned with the well-being of the masses, pay attention to methods of work', Mao provides a sketch of new Party-People relations:

> In short, all the practical problems in the masses' everyday life should claim our attention. If we attend to these problems, solve them and satisfy the needs of the masses, we shall really become organisers of the well-being of the masses. (Mao, 1934b: 147–8)

These investigations had to be informed by theory, but

> Our comrades in the Party School should not regard Marxist theory as lifeless dogma. It is necessary to master Marxist theory and apply it, master it for the sole purpose of applying it . . . we all know there are many intellectuals who fancy themselves very learned and assume airs of erudition without realising that such airs are bad and harmful and hinder their own progress. They ought to be aware of the truth that actually many so-called intellectuals are, relatively speaking, most ignorant and the workers and peasants sometimes know more than they do. (Mao, 1942a: 38, 39)

Hence the mass-line, first systematically presented in 1943 in Mao's 'Some questions concerning methods of leadership', but implicit in many earlier analyses. In 'Get Organised!' itself Mao states:

> The gist of this policy is to organise the masses, to mobilise and organise into a great army of labour all the available forces without exception – the people, the army, the government and other organisations and the schools – all men and women, young and old, who can contribute their labour-power on a part-time or full-time basis. [. . .]
>
> To organise the strength of the masses is one policy. Is there a contrary policy? Yes, there is. It is one that lacks the mass view-point, fails to rely on the masses or organise them, and gives exclusive attention to organising the small number of people working in the financial, supply or trading organisations, while paying no attention to organising the masses in the villages, the army, the government and other organisations, the schools and the factories; it treats economic work not as a broad movement or as an extensive front, but only as an expedient for meeting financial deficits. (Mao, 1943c: 153, 155)

The previous year, Mao had argued that

> Financial difficulties can be overcome only by down-to-earth and effective economic development. To neglect economic development and opening of sources of finance, and instead to hope for the solution of financial difficulties by curtailing indispensable expenditures, is a conservative notion which cannot solve any problem. (Mao, 1942d: 111–12)

A month before 'Get Organised!', he urged in a Party directive:

> In the financial and economic field, the Party and government personnel at the county and district levels should devote nine-tenths of their energy to helping the peasant increase production, and only one-tenth to collecting taxes from them. If pains are taken with the first task, the second will be easy. (Mao, 1943b: 132)

Production is thus conceived culturally and politically. Rather than an emphasis on either specialisation (the army for fighting, the schools for education and the countryside/farms for food production), or upon the single instruction 'Bring in the Harvest!', the purpose of Party and Government (in conditions, it is worth interjecting, of encirclement in an impoverished terrain) is to make it possible for differing communities to support themselves from their own efforts at production. Production *precedes* procurement; living standards of the collectivity are raised in order to make accumulation of capital possible; through the increased demands for daily necessities, the demand for the light engineering that makes *their* production possible is also increased; more effective communal production produces demands for the technological resources that the new social relations can sustain. Here is a set of production relations that offer a programme for the increased well-being of the masses. Indeed we are close to grasping the truth of the Chinese revolution in its most significant form: production is increasingly understood to be equivalent to the well-being of the masses, and thus automatically entails *both* raising the production of daily necessities so that everyone may be better clothed, housed and fed; *and*, to make this possible, the control of production by workers themselves. In short, socialism must be *experienced* as a greater freedom than capitalism.

Jack Gray[8] has indicated the theoretical importance of the Border Region years in a recent comment:

> The border region experience gave the Chinese very low expectations from centralised planning . . . I'm quite sure that one of the most

> important things to have been built into the Maoist economic tradition is the experience of the Chinese industrial cooperatives . . . The border regions were in the poorest parts of China, so the Chinese became experts at substituting labour for capital, in organising large masses of people, more or less voluntarily, to undertake cooperative production.
> These choices are not politically neutral . . . (Gray, 1973a: 16–17)

For Mao, by 1943, 'The cooperatives are now the most important form of mass organisation in the economic field' (Mao, 1943c: 155). In their *Outline for Cooperative Development*, published in Shensi in 1935, the CPC defined the cooperative as 'an instrument of resisting private capitalism and developing a new economic system'. Edgar Snow (who summarises this document in his 1937: 232f.; 1961: 227f.) provides the fullest account of the industrial cooperatives.[9] Many of the visitors to China in those years (Snow, Belden, Gelder, Epstein and Smedley) recognised that these cooperatives, along with the self-supporting economy, were far more than temporary pragmatic expedients forced upon the CPC by war. But it is as well to remember (particularly when considering the 'backwardness and isolation' of the USSR) that the Border Region years *are* defined by those wars – whether against the external imperialism of the Japanese or the equally brutal attacks of the KMT forces. And it is also as well to note, even if only *en passant*, that this entailed an equally thorough transformation of Bolshevik notions of strategy and tactics for military warfare, and, equally important, the relations between a 'popular army' and the people. In his stress upon the productive potential of the army (as opposed to the normal practices of compulsory procurement by the army and the Party from the villages and farms of the area) Mao is drawing attention to two significant facets of socialist construction. First, the army must be truly popular; as with the State apparatuses in general, it must not be a drain or fetter upon production. The army must feed itself as far as is possible. Second, fighting a war involves being good at production as much as firing a gun or organising an army. Pervading both points is the subordination of the army to the Party.[10]

3 LEANING TO ONE SIDE[11]

As is well known, Bolshevism did not merely represent a possible historic example for the CPC to follow; through the Comintern, the CPSU attempted to encourage the CPC in replicating and expanding Bolshevism. It is also widely known that Mao's own theories and practices were criticised precisely because of their anti-Bolshevik character. We did not begin our examination of Mao and Bolshevism with this material because it seems far more important to us to stress how his notions of socialist construction are themselves implicitly subversive of what we have outlined as the social problematic of Bolshevism, as we must if we are to situate the open polemic between the CPSU and the CPC in terms of the fundamental questions which we discuss in this book. But let us now consider it.

'De-Stalinisation' begins for Mao in the mid-1930s.[12]

> Even before the dissolution of the Third International, we did not obey the orders of the Third International. At the Tsunyi Conference [1935] we didn't obey, and afterwards for a period of ten years, including the Rectification campaign and down to the Seventh Congress, when we finally adopted a resolution ('Resolution on certain questions in the history of our Party'), and corrected 'leftism', we didn't obey them at all. Those dogmatists failed utterly to study China's peculiarities . . . (Mao, 1964b: 218)

In 1936, Mao criticised the dogmatists who thought it was enough

> merely to follow the laws by which the civil war in the Soviet Union was directed and the military manuals published by the Soviet military organisations.
>
> They do not see that these laws and manuals embody the specific characteristics of the civil war and the Red Army in the Soviet Union, and that if we copy and apply them without allowing any change, we shall also be 'cutting the feet to fit the shoes' and be defeated. (Mao, 1936: 181)

This general criticism of 'Blind Faith'[13] is congruent with what we have tried to emphasise in this chapter, and it is, moreover, as well to emphasise the last two words of the above quotation. Recalling these years in 1956, Mao said that

> We have already suffered politically from dogmatism. Everything we copied from abroad was adopted rigidly, and this ended in a great defeat . . . and the victory of the revolution being delayed for many years. (Mao, 1956d: 87)

In 1964 Mao argued that Soviet 'products are heavy, high-priced, crude, and they always keep something back' (Mao, 1964c: 199). Speaking of 1945–9, Mao suggested in 1962 a more dynamic policy of obstruction by Stalin personally.

> Stalin wanted to prevent China from making revolution, saying that we should not have a civil war, and should cooperate with Chiang Kai-shek, otherwise the Chinese nation would perish. But we did not do what he said. The Revolution was victorious. After the victory of the Revolution he next suspected China of being Yugoslavia and that I would become a second Tito. Later when I went to sign the Sino-Soviet Treaty of Alliance and Mutual Assistance, we had to go through another struggle. He was not willing to sign a treaty. After two months of negotiation[14] he at last signed. When did Stalin begin to have confidence in us? It was at the time of the Resist America, Aid Korea campaign, from the winter of 1950. (Mao, 1962b: 191)

As Rice (1972: 119) has noted, in 1949, the last ambassador to take leave of Chiang Kai-shek was that of the Soviet Union. Nevertheless (and equally important as critical concepts to investigate many of the less socialist practices *of the CPC*) Mao did not reduce the international Communist Movement to an epiphenomenon of that one individual, Joseph Stalin; rather he saw him as a product of a whole politico-ideological formation, or what we have called a social problematic. In 1944, in 'Our Study and the Current Situation', Mao stated:

> 1. On the question of what attitude to adopt in studying our historical experience . . . in dealing with questions of Party history we should lay the stress not on the responsibility of certain individual comrades but on the analysis of the circumstances in which the errors were committed, on the content of the errors, and on their social, historical and ideological roots, and this should be done in the spirit of 'learning from past mistakes to avoid future ones' and 'curing the sickness in order to save the patient', in order to achieve the twofold objective of clarity in ideology and unity among comrades . . .
> 2. Treat all questions analytically; do not negate everything. (Mao, 1944: 163–4)[15]

4 FROM IMPLICIT CRITICISM TO INTER-PARTY POLEMIC

Marxism, in China as in Tsarist Russia, was formed in the contexts of particular disputes and discussions; for example, over land-holding or historical periodisation. In that sense the frequently repeated claims that Mao has 'Sinified' marxism are true but trivial: in learning marxism we change ourselves and our views of social reality, we learn in order to change. If marxism itself did not change in these practices it would not be a guide to action at all, but a set of mystical commands, requiring a caste of interpreting scholars and a rigid authoritarian social apparatus of enforcement. It would also be a curiously unempirical, ahistorical body of thought, about as scientific as Tarot cards or croquet.

It would be wrong to suggest that Mao *knew* what we can now know of Bolshevism, or that he had a detailed plan of socialist construction in his head in, say, 1927 or 1936. We have explicit evidence that he has had to learn through errors, that he has changed his mind. What has remained constant, indeed, has been the openness of the marxism-leninism. If there has been a continuity it resides at the level of a methodology which can be elucidated through reading the works we have available from the mid-1920s. There is, first, the refusal to accept marxism as universal history in a future tense. Second, Mao is concerned to point up the consequences of analyses which differ from his own, depicting 'opportunism' as all unity and no struggle, failing to remember that it is a full social *system* that socialists are opposed to. He similarly describes 'adventurism' as all struggle and no unity, failing to take various enemies seriously over particular issues. Third, Mao recognises the double significance of agrarian production and the poor and middle peasant producers. As early as 1927 Mao was clear on the tremendous resources for revolution in China:

> altogether 70 per cent of the rural population . . . the backbone of the peasant associations, the vanguard in the overthrow of the feudal forces . . . the heroes who have performed the great revolutionary task which for long years was left undone. Without the poor peasant class (the 'riffraff', as the gentry call them), it would have been impossible to bring about the present revolutionary situation . . . (Mao, 1927: 32–3)

Fourth, and finally, Mao's exemplary marxism is evident not least in his ability to show the connectedness of apparently discrete and unrelated phenomena, thereby showing the error of those who argue for a fixed order of priorities (fighting the war or establishing cooperatives), an invariant sequence, or a rigid time scale.

These aspects are clear in his analyses of the significance of the Long March:

> What we say is that in one respect the Red Army has failed (i.e. failed to maintain its original positions), but in another respect it has won a victory (i.e. in executing the plan of the Long March) . . . Speaking of the Long March, one may ask, 'What is its significance?' We answer that the Long March is the first of its kind in the annals

> of history, that it is a manifesto, a propaganda force, a seeding-machine . . . It has announced to 200 million people in eleven provinces that the road of the Red Army is their only road to liberation . . . In the eleven provinces it has sown many seeds which will sprout, leaf, blossom, and bear fruit, and will yield a harvest in the future. (Mao, 1935: 159, 160)

Chesneaux has noted that Mao brought to the Border Region a consciousness of a need for a movement which 'aimed first of all at the political and moral liberation of the peasants without which it would have been fruitless to propose a radical reform of the system of economic exploitation' (Chesneaux, 1973: 160). He has also argued (ibid., 130f.) the very extensive changes in political consciousness which were in fact achieved during what some have stigmatised as reformist economic programmes. As Schurmann notes

> The military victories of Chinese communism took place at the same time that a revolutionary struggle was waged on the land against the rural gentry. A whole class was destroyed not only physically but psychologically. Every act of land reform was climaxed by a drama where the landlord literally lowered his head . . . (Schurmann, 1966: xxxi)

Madian comments on this specific passage:

> The process of conceptual change is far more complicated than Schurmann indicates. He has captured the symbolic importance of the lowering of heads but he views it from the point of view of the landlord, as an expression of his acceptance of defeat by the people. But it was far more than that . . . the drama is ultimately an acting out of a conceptual innovation; the meaning of landlordism is radically altered; from a highly respectable position it becomes a status deserving of opprobrium. (Madian, 1967: 100)

The same should be said for the contrast between the Japanese and KMT armies' relation to the peasantry and that of the Red Army; or a similar contrast regarding KMT agrarian policy and that practised, especially in the mutual aid teams, by the CPC.

Nevertheless, possibly because Mao took a position in what he called the 'second line' (Mao, 1966f: 266), the economic programme of the reconstruction years after 1949 was largely that of orthodox Bolshevism.[16] But, as we know now from a range of texts, there was a fairly open intra-Party struggle raging specifically over agrarian production by the middle of 1951 which was to lead through the *High*

Tide documents of 1955 and 1956, the Great Leap Forward, the Socialist Education Movement and other struggles to the Great Proletarian Cultural Revolution. The dimensions of recent struggles are best appreciated in terms of the campaigns of the Border Region years. In July 1951 Liu Shao-ch'i attacked those (which clearly included Mao) who sought to 'shake the foundations of private ownership' through enlarging and politicising the cooperative movement in agrarian production. In June 1953 Mao counterattacked through a speech critical of those who sought to maintain 'New Democracy'.[17] In 1964 Mao recalled his long struggle against the Rural Work Department of the Central Committee in the following terms:

> To consolidate New Democracy, and to go on consolidating it for ever, is to engage in capitalism. New Democracy is a bourgeois-democratic revolution under the leadership of the proletariat. It touches only the landlords and the comprador bourgeoisie, it does not touch the national bourgeoisie at all. To divide up the land and to give it to the peasants is to transform the property of the feudal landlords into the individual property of the peasants, and this still remains within the limits of the bourgeois revolution. To divide up the land is nothing remarkable – MacArthur did it in Japan. Napoleon divided up the land too; land reform cannot abolish capitalism, nor can it lead to socialism. (Mao, 1964b: 216)

The crucial point to be grasped is that these class struggles within the CPC *and* the struggles against the Comintern, Stalin and Bolshevism, and, recently, against Krushchev, Brezhnev and the CPSU are increasingly conceptualised as struggles against the persistence of capitalist relations (productive, political, fiscal, personal, cultural and ideological). Like Lenin, Mao has grasped that the greatest and most fierce class struggles follow a socialist revolution. Perhaps a better formulation would be that socialist construction begins long *before* a socialist revolution and, equally, that these beginnings exercise a serious constraint upon or facilitate a useful flexibility for policies *after* the revolution.

The materials of the much more explicit break with Bolshevism – the documents of 1955 and 1956 onwards, especially the texts 'On the question of Agricultural Co-operation' (1955), and the 'Speech on the Ten Great Relationships' (1956b), taken with Mao's editorial introductions to the case studies in the *High Tide* materials (1956a) – belong properly in the discussion of Bolshevism since Stalin. We mention them here simply to stress two points: first, their serious neglect as works of Marxist *theory* (indeed the general neglect of Mao's total output is marked, not least in contrast to the attention lavished upon Lukacs or Gramsci); secondly, because of their link with the experiences of class struggle and learning of the years since the Long March and before. Mao himself has argued an equivalence between social science and class struggle (Mao, 1964b: 213), adding:

> To get some experience of class struggle – that's what I call a university. (Ibid., p. 213)

Because, he stresses,

> You can't understand the countryside just by going there, you must study the relations between all the classes and strata in the countryside. I devoted more than ten years to these problems before I clarified them for myself . . . In 1925 I was active in the Peasant Movement Training Institute, and carried out rural surveys. (Ibid., p. 219)

We began with Mao's epistemology as basic to his whole perspective, whether on organisation, on production relations, or on cultural activity. We could equally have stressed that this epistemology is methodological, its critical cutting edge carries forward precisely the qualities we attempted to draw from Marx in our first chapter. But Mao also recognises that the struggles which we depicted within Bolshevism, not least within the thought and writings of Lenin, are indeed internal to all those human beings who are stamped and scarred by capitalism. In his frequent stress on the significance of the political (the pervasiveness of the struggle to establish socialist relations) in the era, which he correctly suggests will extend for one or more centuries, of socialist construction in the world, Mao is reminding us of this internal reference of the notion of class struggle. He excludes no one from the injunction to become more conscious through collective, increasingly egalitarian attempts to know-by-changing the social world. He thereby most significantly erases that convenient division, criticised by Marx in his Third Thesis, which we quoted above, and revived within the notion of Party building within Bolshevism, between Party persons and others (and within the Party between Godhead and Priests). This, like all such separations, is an essential relation of capitalist production and reproduces capitalist relations.

In a speech in 1965, Mao argued:

> Marx's *Capital* started with the analysis of the dual nature of commodities. Our commodities also have a dual nature. In a hundred years' time commodities will still have a dual nature. Things which

> are not commodities have a dual nature too. Our comrades likewise have a dual nature, correct and incorrect. Don't you have a dual nature? I know I have; young people easily make the mistake of being metaphysical: they cannot bear to talk about their shortcomings. People improve with experience. (Mao, 1965: 239)

In the same speech he argued that there are no laws of dialectics other than 'the law of contradiction' (ibid., p. 240) which pervades all social formations, classes, parties and individuals. This law extends into the era of socialism and that of communism. That perspective, taken with Mao's similar insistence upon social practice in his epistemology, and his emphasis upon politics as the key (or, to use a different formulation, on 'class struggle as the key link') eventuates in a theory of socialist construction which places emphasis upon the potential of particular kinds of human communities, rather than machines, on the one hand, or dogmatic notions of economic laws on the other.

As such, of course, Mao, or the CPC, could only act in a militantly negative way – they held back the enemies of the people; they guarded the frontiers of the Border Regions and, eventually, the People's Republic. The actual transformations which have been so much in evidence in China are the result of the people themselves demonstrating, as Marx suggested, that once correct ideas are seized by the masses they become a material force. Mao's implicit critique of Bolshevism is also a correct theory of socialist construction, but, as he would be the first to stress, a theory articulates (realises at a cognitive level) the actions and accomplishments, the organised learning, of the peasants and workers who validate it. Read properly, the historical experience of China will provide us with the conditions under which the phenomenal forms of socialism (simply phrased as having enough to eat, adequate housing, clothing, and actual control of work procedures) are possible. Such a reading is one constituent of how we are ourselves enabled to make a fuller sense of both the positive and the negative lessons of Bolshevism, and, importantly, to grasp the core of proletarian experience transmitted in the work of Karl Marx.

BIBLIOGRAPHICAL APPENDIX

Two useful collections of documents are those of Schurmann, 1967, and Gittings, 1973. The best contemporary sources are the two journals produced in the PRC, *Peking Review* (weekly) and *China Reconstructs* (monthly), plus the HSINHUA News Agency daily and weekly translation bulletins from the press.

(a) Before 1936

B. Moore, 1966; L. Heren *et al.*; K. Buchanan; Treadgold, 1973: Vol. 2; Krymov, 1971; Schwartz, 1954; Yakhontoff, 1934; Lowe, 1966; Bianco, 1971; Snow, 1937/61.

For Bolshevik perspectives: Carr, 1953: 485–540, covering 1917–23; Carr, 1964: ch. 40, covering 1923–6. Contrast Deutscher, 1959: 316f. For Bolshevism within China: cf. Brandt, 1958; Isaacs, 1961. On Chen Tu-hsiu's Trotskyism see Deutscher's analysis of Trotsky's papers in Deutscher, 1963: 32f. and 422f. Cf. Rue, 1966; Thornton, 1969; Snow, 1937: 376f.; 1961: 422f. On Li Li-san see Schram, 1973b: 10f.; on Wang Ming, see ibid., 14f., Mao's own writings, his interviews with Snow, are essential sources: the best starting point is 1945c and the first of his Chengtu talks, 1958b; but cf. the political reports to the 9th and 10th Party Congress and Mavrakis, 1973. On the CPC see J. P. Harrison; F. W. Houn.

(b) People

On Mao: Han Suyin, 1972, 1976; Gray, 1973c; Snow; Yung, 1966. On Liu: Han Suyin, 1972: 484f.; Yung, 1966; Hinton, 1969. Others: biographical notes to Snow, 1961; Who's Who section in Rice, 1972; Elegant, 1951, and Helen Snow, 1972. Theoretical introductions to Mao: Thomson, 1971, 1973; Rossanda, 1970; S. Mauger, 1973; Maccio, 1970; Mavrakis, 1973; and all the texts of Gray and Hinton.

(c) 1936 to 1949

Chesneaux, 1973; Snow, 1941, 1961; Gelder, 1946; Belden, 1949; Hofheinz, 1969; Hinton, 1966; M. Meisner, 1970; M. Selden, 1969, 1970, 1971; Stein; Smedley; plus the survey by Gurley, 1975a.

(d) 1950s

Gray, 1965; Gurley, 1975b; Myrdal, 1963; Hinton, 1966; Liu Ching; plus the notes to Mao, 1955; 1956a, in Li Chien, and in Chih Heng's exceptionally important articles.

5 Bolshevism Now

1 THE BOLSHEVIK HEGEMONY

It is conventional to picture the death of Stalin in 1953 as marking a scission in Soviet history. Before, lie tyranny and purge. After, lie (relatively) greater humanism and liberalism, gradual moves towards détente with the West, and the acceptance of certain modes of organisation and policy formulation previously labelled as capitalist. For some interpreters, of course, these changes do indeed mark the victory of capitalism over Leninism in the Soviet Union. Bourgeois interpreters, preferring discretion, more often speak of an inevitable surrender by Soviet leaders to the universal imperatives of Development, kept distinct from any reference to the political system. There is a general belief on the part of these latter observers that the break with the past is characterised by a growth of pragmatism which has generated a series of forms of 'de-Stalinisation' and a consequent departure from Bolshevism.

Both these analyses we reject. The Bolshevik problematic, far from being defunct, retains its dominance today. Contemporary policies powerfully testify to the continuity of the Bolshevism which they embody. Just as Lenin, Trotsky and Stalin, so Krushchev and Brezhnev have responded to the possibilities and constraints inherent in the structure of their position in ways which form variants solidly within the boundaries of that problematic. They are testimonies to the tenacity of Bolshevism as much as to its failings.

Two themes dominate the 20th through to the 25th Congresses of the CPSU. Peaceful coexistence, embodied in the policy of détente, is one; the second theme, quoted here from the 21st Congress, can be recognised as a line well-established even before 1923:

> . . . The historic task of catching up with and surpassing the most developed capitalist countries in per-capita output must be carried out.[1]

This tragic irony, the effort to outstrip capitalism on terms and priorities which are essentially capitalist, has repeatedly been used to justify policies in the name of socialism. Given the overriding goal of output, the problem since Stalin has been to combine such economistic progress with the maintenance of 'political' control by the Party through the use of the State machine.

The view of production as 'economics', as a matter of technology plus a particular 'socialist' form of organisation (the Plan) is a tradition which has been reinforced and refined in the practices of Bolshevism since Stalin. Thus by the 17th Komsomol Congress in 1974 Brezhnev was able to present Komsomol successes as entirely 'labour-achievements' wherein commitment to communism had become measurable solely as a plan fulfilment. He was unequivocal:

> If we are to single out the main thing in the Party's economic policy at the present stage of our development, then it is the sharp turn towards raising the effectiveness of the country's economy on the basis of accelerated scientific-technological progress . . . All these measures and all our efforts will not produce the desired effect if we do not drastically improve the quality of work done in all sections of our economy, at each place of work. The quality of work is a very capacious concept. It is composed of many production-economic factors and at the same time it embraces a broad range of moral problems. (Brezhnev, 1974: 3)[2]

Production-economic factors on the one hand, 'moral problems' on the other: the separation is as instructive as the order of priorities.

Yet this adoption of supposedly rational pragmatism has been associated with a flagging rate of growth of production and a consequent repeated postponement of catching up. Having once accepted a diagnosis of problems akin to that of bourgeois economics, however, Soviet leaders became limited to seeing the only solution as more of the same therapy. When Kosygin presented his report on the shortcomings of industrial organisation and his recommendations for change to the plenum of September 1965, then, he offered a picture of defects 'remarkably similar to Western analysis of the same subject'.[3] The emphasis was on increasing complexity and sophistication with which the existing planning system, far from being the expected spur to advance, was completely unable to cope. This, coupled with inattention to consumer goods and agriculture, was seen as the cause of failing growth rates in productivity and of the allied problems of unemployment and underemployment in some areas.

The 1965 economic reforms, proposed as the solution, often read like a modified bourgeois text on the decentralised, competitive basis of economic rationality. Khrushchev had accepted some of these arguments, but had reacted only by devolving decision-making powers to regional planning authorities. However, once the economist's frame of reference is accepted it becomes difficult to stop part-way. The 1965 reforms thus gave enterprises far greater independence and shifted the emphasis of performance indicators strongly towards profitability. The intention was to increase responsiveness to consumer demand. Only the term 'market' itself remained forbidden fruit.

However, Kosygin's acceptance of the logic of bourgeois rationality, with its massive political consequences, was not a new departure for Bolshevism:

> By state trusts are meant state industrial enterprises to which the state accords independence . . . and which act on principles of commercial calculation with the objective of making profit.[4]

This is not, despite appearances, a quote from the 1965 reforms, but comes from the period of NEP, and forms part of the 1923 decree defining the legal position of enterprises. Compare its descendant:

> Normally functioning enterprises must obtain profits from the sale of their products at wholesale prices; they must gain the opportunity to set up incentive funds and to have the necessary means for expanding their activities, for paying for fixed capital and for making other contributions to the state budget.[5]

Thus whilst Liberman and his associates may find much of their inspiration from their Western counterparts, ample justification for their proposals is available (and is actively sought) in classic Bolshevik texts, particularly those of Lenin.

The solution of the difficulties faced in securing socialism is seen as simply the development of production. This stark theory of productive forces was similarly conceptualised by Bukharin and Preobrazhensky:

> The foundation of our whole policy must be the widest possible development of productivity. (Bukharin and Preobrazhensky, 1920: 315)

Lenin's formulations were often similar,[6] speaking also of the need for a period of 'state capitalism' to achieve this end.[7] Again, it is in the light of this that Brezhnev's or Kosygin's statements of policy should be read. In 1971, Brezhnev announced that for building communism 'scientific and technical progress' constitutes the 'main level'.[8] The reason for this ordering of priorities is repeatedly clarified by use of the term 'rational' and is emphatically finalised in the following passage:

> The experience that has been accumulated has made it more obvious where effort has to be concentrated. This is the creation of economic conditions, which would, first, induce enterprises to undertake optimal commitments, i.e. adopt maximum plans and make more rational use of capital investments and labour resources, second, ensure the maximum acceleration of scientific and technical progress and the growth of labour productivity, and third, facilitate a constant drive for a higher quality in production.
> The consistent implementation of the principles of operation on a profit-and-loss basis remains an urgent task . . . The role of the economic contracts and the responsibility for honouring them must be enhanced . . . It would be expedient to provide enterprises with broader possibilities for giving incentives to those workers and collectives of workers who make the largest contribution to the development of production . . . (CPSU, 1971: 83–4)

Five years on, we find Brezhnev describing the 25th Congress as 'keynoted by realism and efficiency'.[9]

In order to vanquish this understanding of how socialist construction has to operate, however, it is necessary first to acknowledge that the Soviet planning system has indeed been unable to cope with the direction of economic activity. Shortages, unwanted output and other distortions are all too common. Yet only a severely impoverished notion of socialism would present it as embodied in institutions of planning and Party control of the State machine. A relational conception of socialism encourages attention not to the success or failure of planning *per se*, but to the political content of the way planning has proceeded in the particular instance. Such an approach also leads to immediate recognition that to promote market relationships is to promote capitalism. As production is a political problem in this view, it comes as no surprise to find that the introduction of supposedly rational methods of incentive and allocation, after a short-term effect, have failed to produce the expected sustained output growth.

Let us consider a moment longer the logic behind the introduction of the market mechanism. We are told that it will ensure that information will reach producers (via the price mechanism) to enable them to meet consumer demand instead of being burdened by the clumsy ill-detailed plan quotas. It is thus a politically neutral resource for coping with irrationalities such as these:

> When output is measured by the number of complete machines produced, there is a shortage of spare parts . . . When chandeliers are measured in tons, they are unnecessarily heavy. Because geological surveying units receive plans in linear metres of drilling, they

> undertake work they know to be useless . . . (Ellman, 1968: 26)[10]

The last phrase gives the game away. All of these are acts born not of ignorance of social needs but of a conflict between producer and planner wherein the former seeks personal advantage. The market is a tool which attempts to compel or induce the producer to act in accordance with the authorities' requirements. A right-wing British trade union leader expresses the implied view of society perfectly:

> There has to be an enforcement agency in a country. If it isn't the market, it has to be the police force.[11]

In short, it is useless to rely on the people.

An alternative perspective is possible, however; people cannot be relied on precisely because, as a legacy of Bolshevik policy over six decades, they have never been relied on. Instead they have been told to be obedient, stimulated by competition between themselves and fellow-workers organised from above in the name of 'socialist emulation', or prompted by bonuses. These relations of production replace self-transformation through the transformation of the world by the experience of repressive demands. Capitalism is the epitome of such experience, so the 'economic' solution employing capitalist incentives can and does only worsen the problem. By going beyond appearances we thus find ourselves with proposals entailing a complete inversion of the analysis on which present-day Bolshevik strategy is based.

The Bolshevik understanding of socialist construction as the creation of a material 'base' on which to build socialist relations has continually pursued a quasi-capitalist programme in its struggle against capitalism. One crucial aspect of this to be expected from Marx's analysis is an exacerbation of the Three Great Differences which again socialism is aimed at abolishing. The division between mental and manual labour has certainly grown in the course of Soviet history, and the current worship of scientific and technical advance can only intensify this. Yet Bukharin and Preobrazhensky again provide an impeccable reference for such policy, having spoken of the unavoidable requirement that 'bourgeois experts' be used, and paid better than other workers as an inducement, if the prime goal, production, was to be achieved: 'there is nothing else for us to do'.[12] Ultimately they foresee the transcendence of the 'two great divisions of those who labour, the mental and manual workers, kept asunder by capitalism',[13] yet their own proposals make this a pipe-dream.

The principle of concentrating authority in the hands of one man, the factory director, is a related outcome of the expert fetish. This principle was first affirmed by Lenin in 1918, reinforced by NEP and by Stalin, and was simply re-emphasised in the 1965 legislation. Thus the decentralisation of decisions to the enterprise provides autonomy not for the workforce but for the director.[14] For labour the emphasis is on passive, disciplined effort as epitomised by Stakhanovism. Once the politics of such policies is recognised, it becomes easy to follow why efforts to involve workers via participation schemes (Permanent Production Conferences) begun under NEP and re-emphasised in a joint Government/trade union decree in 1958 and in 1970 and 1971 legislation have faltered in the face of apathy and passivity by worker representatives. However, just as with 'economic' policy the Bolshevik disbelief in the reliability of the people in constructing socialism leads them instead to search for techniques of inducing motivation. Once again this turns them in a disturbing direction for inspiration. The following passage comes from a book which the Soviet authorities were proud enough to translate and issue in the West:

> Study and critical use of everything positive contained in the concepts of the bourgeois theory of organisation and management which, notwithstanding all their contradictions, to some extent reflect the objective requirements of modern large-scale social production, are thus one of the important tasks facing Soviet scientists.[15]

The other major potential divisions, between town and country, industry and agriculture, are also nurtured rather than overcome by the policies of modern Bolshevism. The Bolshevik conceptualisation of peasants and rural production is another unbroken strand from the past. It follows from the picture of development based on the building of heavy industry by leeching resources from agriculture. This is accompanied by a belief that the peasantry are innately antagonistic to socialism, and must be turned into an industrial working class as soon as possible. This politics explains the problems of agrarian production today as surely as those of the past. Within Bolshevik practice, however, the failure of policies based on false premises only serves to intensify the grip of those premises. If peasants don't respond to these 'socialist' policies or to exhortations in the name of socialism, they can only be anti-socialist.

Khrushchev committed himself to reinvigorating farm policy. From 1953 to 1958 he seemed blessed with success as output rose 51 per cent.[16] He then undertook a series of reforms which had the institutional appearance of socialism, but which, given the nature of pre-existing relations in the countryside and the mechanical means by which the changes were imposed, were devoid of socialist content. He transformed many *kolkhozi* into state farms; amalgamated others; wound up the infamous Machine Tractor Stations, selling the equipment to the *kolkhozi*; and taxed and otherwise discouraged the private sector. A production increase of 70 per cent was thus projected for 1958–65. The actual rise was only 14 per cent;[17] Khrushchev fell. The bourgeois interpretation of this failure has been that the reforms were socialist dogma exerting a disincentive pressure, remediable only by greater private enterprise. Given the importance of private plots in Soviet agriculture this has a veneer of accuracy. The existence of an alternative attachment to collective production exemplified by the PRC forces us to dismiss the implied explanation in terms of the inherent nature of peasants, however. The question then becomes: why were private plots so important, and why did Bolshevik policy only seem to reinforce this? A steady glance at the content and implementation of that policy provides the answer.

Had administrators felt able to rely on socialist commitment in the countryside, they need only have issued broad guidelines as to the socially required crops. Instead they felt, under Khrushchev as before, compelled to issue strict and detailed directives. The Party constantly interfered and undertook authoritarian campaigns in favour of crops which, worse still, were all too often unsuitable to local conditions. In other words they acted as arrogant and poorly-informed 'experts' and gave increasing justification in the experience of producers for the withholding of initiative and effort for application to their work on the private plots over which they had control.[18]

The post-Khrushchev response to these production problems was familiar. The 1965 reforms sought to treat state farms as industrial enterprises, subjecting them to the new profit indicators. The results are a testimony to the failure of economics. State farm gross profits increased astronomically,[19] yet there has been evidence only of decline in productive effectiveness and resilience to climate. Hence the USSR was forced to resort to the machinations of Nikolai Belusov on the US grain market in 1972, and to further massive grain purchases in 1975. The reaction to failure was to increase bonuses and other incentives offered to peasants achieving plan quotas in 1973. In 1974 the emphasis turned to 'practical business efficiency', with increasing use of factory centres for livestock and farm specialisation (Development and division of labour). This 'farm industrialisation' campaign, apparently pushed hard by Brezhnev, was intensified in 1975 and 1976.[20] Another innovation is the 'Link Brigade', previously experimented with by Khudenko in the 1960s, but condemned then as too akin to private farming.[21] This system involves the allocation of an area of land to the responsibility of a brigade of peasants who are paid by production results. (Although Western commentators see in this merely a pursuit of private farming, a knowledge of China leads to a suspicion that a distorted attempt to copy their brigade system may also be involved. Bolshevism perceives only the institution, however, and not the politics which give it life.) Finally, 1976 saw the greatest stress yet on material incentives, with special credits being granted to farms to finance the payments.[22]

Again, then, Soviet and Western accounts embody remarkably similar analyses of the problem of and answer to poor performance. It is related to the need for rural 'modernisation', entailing the use of 'expertise' in management and technique, coupled with increasing rewards to those who best meet the imposed models of efficiency; technical economics has lain at the heart of all the brutal modernisation programmes, wedded to a still burgeoning oppression by a bureaucracy with paltry knowledge of local needs;[23] managers of collective farms themselves seem to conceptualise consciousness in the manner of economists. They too turn to fiscal manipulation to induce more production from the workforce. Several bourgeois writers[24] have unknowingly accurately sketched the struggle between two lines in the Soviet countryside by linking the continuities of the 'fundamental mode', command farming (shadowy socialism), with the growth of the market mode linked to private plots (mounting capitalism). The division of labour related to expertise is deeply embedded in the social structure of the collective farm, just as surely as it operated through the State terrorism of the Machine Tractor Stations. In formal terms the collective farm is a cooperative organisation, but in practice it is an edifice of enforcement. Less than 5 per cent of managers come from the 10–15 million workers of the *kolkhozi*.[25] On a purely phenomenal level, given these facts, bourgeois economics can grasp the character of real production relations in the Soviet countryside, though they cannot discern the fundamentally political nature of the problem or the alternatives. Nor can Bolshevism. Thus Kosygin echoes the past in 1976:

> The most important element characterising the peasant situation in our agriculture is the continued process of far-reaching economic changes planned by the Party 10 years ago. Vladimir Ilyich Lenin pointed out that the main thing in the socialist restructuring of the entire way of life in the countryside was the 'material basis, technical equipment, the extensive use of tractors and other farm machinery and electrification on a mass scale'. (Kosygin, 1976: 17–18)

A comparison of the important charters of the *kolkhozi* of 1935 and 1969 reveals[26] a firm continuity, but with a trend to the weakening of socialism and the strengthening of capitalism and concomitant managerialism. Massive forms of corruption, extending and never eradicating the parasites of NEP, are an inevitable further consequence. The policies of the 1970s will no more solve these problems than capitalism will overcome its own innate putrefaction.

Besides the internal 'economic' policies with which we have dealt, two related shifts in relations with the capitalist world are often claimed to mark a qualitative change of Soviet policy in the last two decades. The first of these is the goal of détente. Its companion is the acceptance and encouragement of trade with the West. Yet these policies, too, follow from the premises of Bolshevism concerning the nature of socialist revolution, construction and class struggle. The separation of Party control of the State (politics) from the organisation, stimulation and modernisation of production (economics) explains, for instance, the belief that following Trotsky's advice, on participation in the international division of labour, cannot affect the political colour of the Soviet Union. Hence Kosygin's view of the pressing need:

> . . . to develop foreign economic relations with the object of using to the maximum the advantages of the international division of labour. (CPSU, 1971: 198)

One pillar of this belief is a further matter of Bolshevik faith: that socialism in the USSR has already been attained and made secure. This achievement was heralded at the 21st Congress of the CPSU,[27] and has frequently been proclaimed since. The same perception was encysted in Khrushchev's advocation of 'a state of the entire people, expressing the interests and will of the people as a whole'.[28] Class struggle thus retains a minimal place in the Soviet conception of internal social relations, whilst socialism is apprehended as something which cannot be touched by any production policy. Consider the resulting congruity of the views of Lenin, Stalin, and the eminent Academician Rumyantsev writing in 1969:

> The proletarian state may, without changing its own nature, permit freedom to trade and the development of capitalism only within certain bounds, and only on the condition that the state regulates (supervises, controls, determines, the forms and methods of, etc.) private trade and private capitalism. (Lenin, 1922a: 375)
>
> Commodity production leads to capitalism only *if* there is private ownership of the means of production, *if* labour power appears in the market as a commodity which can be bought by the capitalist and exploited by him . . . *our* commodity production . . . is a special kind of commodity production, commodity production without capitalists, which is concerned mainly with the goods of associated socialist producers . . . (Stalin, 1952a: 455)

> As we see, the product in socialist society, even though it is a commodity – that is, a thing produced for exchange – is a thing produced for *socialist* exchange. Even though the commodity mediates certain relations of socialist producers and in this sense 'materialises' them, it does not dominate them, but on the contrary, producers dominate things. (Rumyantsev, 1969: 224)

The attitude of Soviet leaders to détente and trade follows naturally from this sense of security, particularly when that security is felt to be threatened only by a failure of production whose potential causes are also conceptualised within the Bolshevik problematic. An obvious consequence is the trading deficit with the West of $3·3 thousand million in 1975 alone, with an accumulated deficit by the end of that year of $13 thousand million.[29] Yet this debt itself, for all the leverage it gives the capitalist countries in demanding concessions of various sorts in return for continued credit and supplies of sophisticated technology, is far less significant than the future of relations of production at the workplace which the size and form of this trade signals and reinforces. A further trend which follows inexorably from the logic which sees no threat in trade is a nascent readiness to hire out disciplined, obedient Soviet labour to foreign firms prepared to invest in the USSR.[30] The 'new era' of trade relations trumpeted since the 1972 trade accord signed by Brezhnev with Nixon is not so new after all, however. Even the bourgeois press has caught on to parallels with the past:

> 'We have a great need for technical aid . . . If the Americans keep their promises, the advantage for us will be gigantic. The agreement, and the concessions to the Americans, have exceptional importance . . . I consider it crucial to attract United States capital for the construction of the oil pipeline.'
>
> It sounds like a Brezhnev directive for his détente-through-trade meeting with President Nixon in Russia. In fact, it's a secret memo from Lenin to his associates dating back to October 1921.[31]

The policies which cause despair (or delight) for many on the Left are therefore not the product of some mystical 'de-Stalinisation', or of the capture of power by an anti-Bolshevik group of 'new Tsars', 'Hitlerite fascists' or 'bourgeois agents'. They emanate from the very core of Bolshevism itself. It is this which creates the seeming blindness to the fact that détente, and the bourgeois proposals for efficiency, rationality, and management reforms constitute a form of warfare none the less effective for being non-military.

Analyses of the Right speak of 'vested interests' and 'habits' as the key to understanding the USSR.[32] Others on the Left cite waste and queues as the basis of Soviet political economy.[33] Both operate purely at the level of the phenomenal as if this were the end of analysis rather than just the beginning. Neither can penetrate the essential nature of the situation, and their 'alternatives' remain trapped within the same political cul-de-sac as those they purport to analyse and criticise. The criticisms of the Left are those which must, however, be taken the more seriously. If the USSR is not to be dismissively classed as 'state capitalist', 'degenerate workers' state' or even 'fascist', then it is necessary to analyse in what way there remains a struggle between the two roads, lines and classes, notwithstanding the defeats suffered by socialism.

That the bourgeoisie continue to regard the USSR as a threat to the rationale of their very existence is evidenced by the continued virulence of the familiar attacks on the Soviet people. It is strange how some of the most accurate comments can come from the Right, from the clarity with which they recognise their enemy.

> . . . the Soviet Union must not be allowed to think that it can put trade and aid into a quite separate compartment from its various commitments to ideological and class struggle. (*Times* editorial, 26 April 1976)

Bourgeois intellectuals continue to see the CPSU as a major obstacle to the implementation of their rationality. And in a sense, it is, for 1917 is not so easily erased, and the roots of the Party are still nourished by the political economy of a different class. Certain instincts of socialism survive, however eroded. There is still often a certain apologetic note when the use of what are half-recognised to be capitalist methods are mooted. The commitments of which *The Times* speaks survive, as evidenced (for all the scoffing of the merely cynical) by the support for Angola.

The speeches of Soviet leaders, in justifying their policies, remain doggedly in favour of the furthering of socialist construction, however misguidedly the latter is conceived. Their appeals are invariably to the tradition of Marx, Lenin and the proletarian revolution, whatever the limits on their understanding of that tradition. Thus even amidst the exhortations for efficiency and discipline are found the legitimations of the advancement of socialist consciousness and communal planning. Occasionally a standard Soviet text will pronounce more convincingly something like this:

> Naturally things did not always go smoothly, for it was a question of establishment and development of a new form of creative activity of the masses on a gigantic scale. (Borisova, 1973: 334)

The struggle between lines marks a profound contradiction in the policies of Soviet leaders. Détente and the reforms threaten the very rationale of the Party whose control they are seeking to reinforce. At the point of production, meantime, where the new rational economic system should have encouraged enterprise directors to dispose of labour surplus to requirements, the expected change has not occurred. The explanation lies not in unfathomable managerial calculations but in the political economy of the working class (which has always been the stumbling-block for supposedly neutral bourgeois rationality). Enterprise directors are generally powerful, but they operate in a system where the working man retains far greater prestige than in any non-socialist state. His own socialisation and the consciousness of those he commands, whilst condoning many of the policies we have surveyed, continues to compel the acceptance that a man is more than mere labour-power subservient to the whims of capital. The struggle continues, and if it is the antithesis of secured socialism, then the restoration of capitalism is never ensured either.

It would be a simple matter to verify our analysis of the hegemony of Bolshevism by examining any of the other People's Democracies. However, one society in particular has been presented as an alternative model of socialism to the Soviet Union in recent years. That this country's policies have also experienced problems is not denied, but they are nevertheless seen as a qualitative break with the politics of Lenin and Stalin. The society in question is Yugoslavia, characterised by 'market socialism' and 'worker self-management'. Yet there is, in spite of these surface contrasts, a great deal of reason to comprehend the difficulties of Yugoslav socialism as stemming from the same constraints and burdens that we have called the Bolshevik problematic.

The Yugoslavs certainly make the claim of having advanced socialist practice through their split with the USSR. This is presented chiefly as a fracture with Stalinism, however, and heavy use is made of Lenin in the justification of policy. Nevertheless, that policy seems to offer an implicit criticism of Lenin's own views on the administration of factories, as evidenced by the following two quotations from Tito:

> Under state ownership . . . the worker's attitude towards his job was that of a wage labourer and he was not directly interested in higher efficiency or better performance of his enterprise. He continued to be alienated from the means of production and could not change the conditions of production. (Tito, 1968a: 95)
>
> . . . awareness grew in this country of the need to put into practice Marx's idea that the factories should be turned over to the workers to manage . . . the subject of Socialist development could not be the

> state apparatus, but rather the working class and all the working people, associated in their management of the socialised means of production. (Tito, 1968b: in his 1970: 183)

The justification is sought in Marx, and its form (except for a foreboding reference to 'efficiency and better performance') seems quite distinct from Bolshevik pronouncements on organisation and democratic centralism. The reliance on people is, sadly, illusory. The incentive to work, and work 'efficiently', is to be ensured by the market. But the same arguments apply here as to the 1965 Soviet economic reforms: the market is not merely a device for ensuring the availability of information and correct allocation of resources. It is a mechanism of monetary coercion. As such its implications for the conception of the masses are clear. The market also operates by rendering the relations between people calculative and divisive, and impels the division of labour between experts and ordinary workers. In short, it is a form of capitalist politics, and can never act as a neutral 'economic' device.

Clearly, were self-management to create a genuine, deep involvement in the running of their factories by workers, unimpeded by the market, then the analysis offered here would be rendered suspect. One could indeed decentralise control by using the market as coordinator and regulator. The evidence on social relations in factories set up on this basis, unfortunately, sustains our account of the market's effect. It reveals not the Yugoslav-predicted gradual increase in involvement of workers in self-management as competence grows, but a *growing* control by professional managers[34] and a *decreasing* preoccupation of workers with self-management.[35] Changing practice and consciousness crystallise this:

> With obvious sorrow in their voices, several workers told the researcher of the era of festivity (dancing, embracing, etc.) when the company's siren would announce that a production plan had not only been realised but surpassed. People no longer felt pride in such accomplishment or in their production heroes.
>
> Those individuals who began to gain status were technocrats . . . the shift in status stripped the worker from the potential glory to be derived from hard work on the line, a glory that, earlier, was part of the culture and a symbol of workers' dominance . . . As one of the interviewed directors said:
>
> 'We are being freed from dogmas . . . Now working is not enough . . . It has to be profitable work. Those that are not good, whose work is unacceptable by the market should disappear. Thus maximum employment lost its importance and maximum efficiency took its place.' (Adizes, 1971: 214)

The Yugoslav leadership were prepared to admit that their experiment was facing difficulties by 1974. Tito spoke of 'tendencies and manifestations running counter to self-management' (1974: 33), and further decentralisation of control to Basic Organisations of Associated Labour was instituted in an effort to stir up worker interest once more. There is little grasp, however, of the need to grapple with decay on a relational level.

Yet is this Bolshevism at work or merely a failed alternative? The affinity with the history of Bolshevism in the Soviet Union suggests emphatically the former. The goals which are set out for Yugoslavia are dominated by the prime requirement of Development, conceived as modernisation, output growth, and the conquering of backwardness. This, it is argued, must *precede* and will *bring about* the possibility of cultural advance and socialism. Thus Tito in 1950, commenting on the recent enactment of workers' management, argued:

> . . . there are tremendous difficulties in the way of building communism in a backward country . . . the transfer, sooner or later, of all the functions of management in the economy depends in our country on the higher or lower rate of development of the productive forces. (Tito, 1950, in his 1970: 82–3, 80)

Nearly a quarter of a century on:

> It will be one of the fundamental tasks in the period ahead to raise production and labour productivity faster . . . this will pave the way . . . to lever further advancement in socialist production relations on the grounds of self-management. (Tito, 1974: 23)

It is on these grounds that the market is judged acceptable. The conceptions are familiarly Bolshevik, adapted to a differing immediate strategy, but none the less bound by the same problematic. If the self-managing system is recognised as a potential source of productive energy in itself, this is presented in a manner destined to strangle any such political possibility.

> Now our forces are trained on the construction of such a self-managing system as will be capable of solving effectively the most highly complex problems of modern economy, by integration, by adopting the most modern technology and, on that basis, by incorporating successfully into the international division of labour. (Tito, 1968b: in his 1970: 185)

Confronted with the growth of capitalist relations, embodied in increasingly calculative attitudes and practices and a growing feeling on the part of workers of being mere wage labour, once more the Yugoslav explanation echoes the sundering of politics and production. Zukin summarises their analysis:

> Yugoslavs argue that these forms are related to norms of selfishness and greed, which are in turn related to the objective conditions of economic development and peasant society. (Zukin, 1975: 25)

Another account of the series of steps by which the Yugoslavs progressively turned their society over to the untender mercies of the market is worth quoting for its wider significance. It illustrates what we have said before, that once the logic of bourgeois economics has a hold it is hard to stop part-way. The resulting deterioration of socialist politics makes stopping still harder. And this is the very path on which the Soviet Union has ventured since the 1965 reforms:

> . . . starting from the intellectual heritage of Marx and from the Soviet interpretations . . . the Yugoslavs liberated themselves from Soviet tutelage and developed a system based on market relations in the area of current production decisions. In the process the Yugoslavs defined a new Marxist relation between plan and market. Yet investment planning within the market framework proved unsatisfactory and centrally planned investment came under attack. The choice to abandon central planning had important consequences. Entrepreneurship, both existing and potential, proved necessary to organise the factors of production, and capital had to be allocated amongst users. Decentralisation of the supply of capital and its allocation expanded effective group and individual property rights over social property and raises doubts about whether socialism still exists in Yugoslavia. (Milenkovitch, 1971)

How, then, do Yugoslav theorists feel the revolution can be protected, given the apparent threat that the market will resurrect capitalist relations? The isolation of Yugoslavia from Comecon and their subsequent acceptance of forcign aid and investment are unconcealable menaces. The answer lies in a familiar conception of politics and the State:

> . . . we have a completely new state machinery, which is a vital condition for further development in the direction of socialism, that is to say, the political conditions for development have been created. (Tito, 1948, in his 1970: 60)

The State, under the control of the Party, patrols the ideological frontiers of socialism whilst the inevitable if unfortunate process of

Development is undertaken. The view of peasants has already been inferred in an earlier quote: by nature backward and anti-socialist, remediable only by education and the discipline of industrial work. Tito himself quotes Lenin to depict the peasantry as a constant reservoir of capitalist habits within socialism.[36]

The historical experience of the Yugoslav system can, therefore, be understood readily within the analytic framework offered here. It does not make sense in terms of any 'sell-out' theory from the Left, naïve humanistic enthusiasm from liberal intellectuals, or sterile economic analyses from the bourgeois pragmatist. Its strengths and weaknesses remain in large measure those of Bolshevism. Hence there is a two-line struggle. There is a genuine effort to discover a means to real worker involvement as revealed by repeated and strong criticism of elitism and managerial domination, and the attendant (if fruitless and misguided) reforms in the participative institutions. Thus Tito has officially faced up to the existence of:

> . . . bourgeois ideological conceptions engendered by the growth of technocratic tendencies in society. As the reflection of forces which strive to restore class relations and reduce workers to labour power, technocracy generates tendencies towards monopolising knowledge and expertise, thus transforming science, education and culture exclusively into instruments of such development of technology as would consolidate the role of top technocratic and managerial circles. That is why the technocracy spreads distrust in the goals and values of the revolution, giving impetus to bourgeois and petty-bourgeois ideas, commercialism and unbridled licence. (Tito, 1974: 29)

Yet the comprehension remains stunted by Bolshevik elements, as evidenced most clearly by the idea here that class relations might be restored, as if they had ever ceased. An ingenuous description by one commentator evokes for us the irony of this, displaying as it does the division rather than unity of the pressures for production and the politics of revolution:

> The two great efforts of [Yugoslav adults'] lives have taken – and continue to take – the forms of a struggle for socialism [*borba za socijalizam*] and the struggle to make a buck [*trka za dinarom*]. (Zukin, 1975: 27)

2 BOLSHEVISM CHALLENGED?

At the end of Chapter 4 we suggested that the ongoing transformations in the People's Republic of China are a function of the socialist consciousness of its people, of their grasp and practical application of correct ideas. In their battle against the restoration of capitalist relations they have created the conditions making possible a marxist critique of Bolshevism based on an effective understanding of socialist construction. But where do these 'correct ideas' appear from? Are they merely the product of an unusually gifted group of intellectuals buried in some Peking propaganda factory?

> Do they drop from the skies? No. Are they innate in the mind? No. They come from social practice and from it alone; they come from three kinds of social practice, the struggle for production, the class struggle, and scientific experiment. (Mao, 1963a: 502)

These words themselves form part of a struggle against revisionism in the CPC, and their bite is made direct later in the same introduction:

> Among our comrades there are many who do not yet understand this theory of knowledge. When asked the source of their ideas, opinions, policies, methods, plans and conclusions, eloquent speeches and long articles they consider the question strange and cannot answer it. Nor do they comprehend that *matter can be transformed into consciousness and consciousness into matter*, although such leaps are phenomena of everyday life. (Mao, 1963a: 503, emphasis added)

By 1965 these comrades had become 'those within the Party who are in authority and taking the capitalist road'.[37]

The key strand of the socialist line is thus struggle. The three struggles identified in the first quote above are not discrete, rather the first and third are aspects of the second, the driving force of any society in transition, class struggle. For the proletariat this takes the form of the battle against capitalism. A correct understanding of socialist production not only emerges in struggle, then, but requires the realisation that production itself is part of the struggle. To separate the two would be to sunder politics and production, and as Mao insisted:

> Political work is the lifeblood of all economic work. (Mao, 1956a: 302)

This statement precedes a discussion not of abstract theory but of the inevitability of constant struggles in the establishment of agricultural cooperatives if a relapse is to be avoided. The GPCR brought still more explicit statements of this relation between politics and production. 'Grasp revolution and promote production' became an enduring slogan:

> We must not make revolution in isolation from production. *The conservative faction do not grasp production.* This is class struggle. (Mao, 1967: 276 – emphasis added)

Note the insistence that conservatives fail to grasp production. This contrasts with the Western assumption that 'moderation' is the key to efficiency. These radical themes have been universally taken up by discussion groups of Chinese workers and peasants in factory and commune, and articulately given concrete context and application. When building roads or bridges or tackling earthquake relief is tied to this theme it is no hollow ideological echo of the Little Red Book; it is a recognition that these things are made possible by the advance of socialism and the repression of capitalist politics.

An awareness of the constant vulnerability of socialism to capitalist restoration thus evokes still more forcefully its *raison d'être*, its force and resilience, in the minds of the people. One workers' theoretical study group, considering the production problems of the USSR, and Brezhnev's proposal (at the 25th Congress of the CPSU) to increase efficiency by raising labour productivity through a combination of sanctions and material incentives, commented as follows:

> The low production efficiency in the Soviet Union today is an outcome of its social system. It can never be changed by Brezhnev and company's ruble-and-stick policy.
>
> What makes for production efficiency? Man's labour has always proceeded in certain social relations. Where social production relations are different, the social character of labour is different too. Under the system of exploitation, labour is compulsory and the working people's initiative is limited and impaired. It is only under the socialist system of public ownership that the working people, now the masters of the means of production, change from working under compulsion to working for themselves and bring their production initiative into full play. (A study group at Kweilin Steel Plant, Kwangsi Chuang Autonomous Region, *Peking Review*, (29) 1976: 29)

The range of policy possibilities is seen quite differently by Mao and the Bolsheviks (including those of the PRC such as Liu Shao-chi or Teng Hsiao-ping). The gulf is opened by elementally opposed conceptions of human nature. To Mao (as to Marx) man is capable of vast achievements if released from the bonds of social slavery, including those left in his consciousness by past experience. Hence Mao's belief that 'the masses have a potentially inexhaustible enthusiasm for socialism',[38] that people are the chief productive force, and so the conviction that politics is the basis of economics. The alternative perspective is that people require inducement, individual incentives, and clear guidance through rules formulated by those with greater knowledge. In judging Liu's proposals, or those which the Western press describe as 'moderate' and 'pragmatic' economics, this implicit assumption must not be forgotten. Bourgeois accounts naturally treat any other view from this as 'ideological', sustainable only in short bursts of propaganda and political frenzy. Offered conclusive disproof by the Chinese masses, they recoil in bewilderment, then tentatively seek to ignore it or elide certain elements to render it soluble by the reagents of their own models. To a Bolshevik also, reliance on the people feels inherently unstable, uncontrollable, in need of displacement by more natural order at the earliest opportunity. The conflict between these two conceptions of people forms the struggle between two lines and two roads in the PRC today. When, in the face of a coal shortage, an 'active' rather than 'passive' planning balance had been struck by calling on the people for aid, resulting in huge economies of use and sharply increased production, a member of the Liaoning revolutionary committee observed:

> This shows that it is better to rely on the initiative of the masses than on slide rules. (Bettleheim, 1973: 61)

The political content of work thus becomes of dominant importance;

> What is meant by doing a good job of production? This in *no* way refers to increased output. Rather it depends on whether or not we have developed production according to socialist principles, whether or not we have promoted the superiority of the commune system, and whether or not we have aroused the revolutionary activity of the masses. (Canton newspaper, 9 November 1965)

This is not an idealistic rejection of the pressing need to produce more; it is a recognition of the *imperative* ordering of priorities if there is going to be enough to eat. A particularly popular quotation from Lenin in China comes from his criticisms of Trotsky and Bukharin, where he insists: 'Politics are the concentrated expression of economics' and so 'without a proper political approach . . . the given class cannot maintain its rule, and *consequently* cannot *solve its own production* problems'.[39]

This is the basis for the fierce rejection of the theory of productive forces in the PRC. Putting production first will actually retard production in the long run. To argue that people must have machines before they can achieve socialist cooperation is to stand the truth on its head (and if you do that, everything falls out). Socialist cooperation enables people to produce and make good use of machines. People will never become invested with the power to dominate things through being told that their existence must be subjugated to the availability of material objects to be brought to them. This is a capitalist form.

> Classes must be abolished. A scientific socialist guiding thought is needed to attain this goal. Once this thought is grasped by the masses, spiritual force will turn into material force; and they will transform the objective world, and at the same time, their own subjective world. (Chou En-lai, 1973)

This lesson emerges most transparently from accounts of the way people feel they have, through the change to cooperative relations with one another and with the State, metamorphosed their whole existence. It may be expressed in having halted the periodic ruin and starvation brought by drought or flood, or simply as having enough to eat, but in-depth accounts from communes[40] bring out a constant awareness of the *political* basis of their achievement on the part of almost all Chinese peasants. Hinton's description of his period of work in a locomotive works where the GPCR had sparked innovations, the removal of supervisors and clocking-on, and rapidly increasing production, offers the same message:

> This all comes from the consciousness of the people and the system they have set up to operate this plant. It puts technique in the hands of the rank and file and, really, responsibility in the hands of the rank and file, and does away with the bonus and incentive system that tended to divide and dismay people. (1973: 36)

Hinton is emphatic on the commanding role of politics; in Long Bow (the village which was the subject of his classic *Fanshen*) he found on his return in the early 1970s that political problems remained – and consequently production was relatively poor. The recognition that capitalist methods for goading on production such as piece-rates and other forms of material incentive result in capitalist relations between people is also a common feature of workers' reminiscences. They recall most recently (in most cases) the period 1961–5, when Liuist policies held their greatest sway:

> We used to say 'the more prizes we allocate, the more bitter become relations among workers'. (A member of the Revolutionary Committee at the 555 Clock Factory, in Wheelwright and McFarlane, 1970: 74)[41]

Mao's own analysis of this matter is made clear in his critical notes on a Soviet textbook on Political Economy:

> The personal material interests stressed by the Soviets are in reality short-sighted individualism. This kind of tendency is economism from the period of the struggle between the proletariat and the bourgeoisie, manifested in the period of socialist construction.[42]

There is little doubt, however, that in many factories the rehabilitation in the early 1970s of Teng and others originally disgraced in the GPCR was accompanied by a revival of forms of material incentive.[43] This provoked a wave of Tatsebao[44] in 1974 critical of such policies, many of which probed to the very core of what the officials who justified them on pragmatic grounds were implying. For instance, the following reaction to the publication by the Party committee of a league table of production teams within a commune, based on output:

> Superficially the purpose of the table is to support the advanced and stimulate the backward . . . In effect it tells us that if a place has high grain output then it is advanced in its own right . . . The suggestion is that if we have output and income then we have everything, and we can cover up a hundred shameful things with just one good thing. To use high output and income to cover up the struggle between two classes, two roads and two lines in the countryside will lead to a situation in which we would have eyes only for money and grain, and no consideration for the key link and the line. (Chayuan Production Team, Tienmen Commune, Hangshan County, Hunan Province, March 1974)

The rejection of the theory of productive forces does *not*, however, mean that production is unwanted. Mao has made this clear in a statement which is remarkably pointed in the light of our own arguments:

> We do not propose the slogans 'cadres decide everything' or 'technology decides everything' or that 'communism is the Soviet Union plus electrification'. But does it mean we do not want electrification? We want it just the same, and even more urgently. The first two slogans were Stalin's way and rather one-sided. If 'technology decides everything', then what about politics? If 'cadres decide everything' then what about the masses? Dialectics is missing here. Stalin sometimes understood dialectics and sometimes not.[45]

Reliance on the mass line as the basis for developing production constitutes a basic tenet on which the break with Bolshevism is founded. The success of Chinese production testifies to its validity. In exploring other facets of the challenge to Bolshevik orthodoxy below, we will find ourselves constantly back to this central point.

The orthodox development model was expressed in the slogan

'bigness/modernity/completeness/newness' by those who opposed Mao's line in the GPCR. The alternative was encapsulated in the slogan 'more/faster/better/more economically', which had been forged in the 1950s criticisms of Stalin and the USSR, where Mao acknowledged it as based on Soviet mistakes: 'the pupil should be more intelligent than the teacher'. This reflects further a distinctive view of learning consanguine with that of learning from the people, investigated in Chapter 4 above. It charts again the need to absorb the Soviet lessons with care:

> . . . There are two methods of learning; one is merely to imitate, the other is to apply the creative spirit. Learning should be combined with creativity; to import Soviet codes and conventions inflexibly is to lack the creative spirit. (Mao, 1958b: 96)[46]

One reason for this is obviously the specific nature of Chinese conditions differing from those elsewhere. When this notion of learning is considered with the criticisms of Bolshevism in the USSR, however, it becomes apparent that something far more significant than mere Sinification is involved.

The relationship between town and country, and that between industry and agriculture which accompanies it, have always provoked massive rifts under the strain of the capitalist development model, wherein resources are leeched from agriculture to supply industry. These are two of the Three Great Differences which the Chinese, following Marx, have recognised and have fought to dissolve. The lynchpin here is the guiding theme: 'Take agriculture as the foundation and industry as the leading factor, and never forget class struggle.'[47] This is an encapsulation of the thesis advanced by Mao in a talk in 1956, known by the title *On The Ten Great Relationships* (1956b). The argument is simple and yet enormously potent, given the world-wide failure of the capitalist model. If you really want heavy industry you have to take resources from there to nourish the growth of light industry and above all agriculture in the first instance. That way, when it comes to promoting heavy industry it will have a basis of supply and a market to serve; choose the other way and your chief achievement will be long-term misery and starvation for most of the people (who will have little attachment to your grandiose schemes for progress[48]). In 1966, then, Mao repeated his 1942 judgement of Soviet agricultural policy in rejecting Liu Shao-chi's policies:

> The agricultural policy of the Soviet Union has always been wrong in that it 'drains the pond to catch the fish', and is divorced from the masses, thus resulting in the present dilemma. (Mao, quoted Gray, 1969a: 46)[49]

In the 1960s this view was put into practice through a growing emphasis on commune self-sufficiency. This included encouragement of a strategy to create industry on a 'backyard' local basis. Without this, many aids to production could not have been provided for decades while urban industry grew. If the results were often crude and less effective than mechanical aids available in the West this is irrelevant. Those models could not be supplied, and to take the short-cut of pouring all effort into industrial centres would have generated a politics of expropriation of peasants which would have rendered such centres useless. Instead of being oppressed by manufacturing, the people were controlling it, learning to create it themselves. Embedded in this logic, of course, was a view of peasants as fully qualified participants in revolution, rather than harbours of capitalism to be regimented, suspiciously patrolled and rendered magically socialist by proletarianisation as rapidly as possible.

The Ten Great Relationships perspective followed from a particularly severe inversion of Bolshevik theory. It implied rejection of that aspect of the theory of productive forces which argues that social relations can only change once 'material preconditions' are satisfied. A Soviet commentator, for instance, disregarding the great strides of Chinese agriculture following collectivisation, expends a great deal of energy in attacking the imbecility of the Socialist Upsurge, Hundred Flowers, and Great Leap Forward movements. His chief complaint, it seems, is that they blasphemed against Bolshevik orthodoxy:

> An attempt was being made to effect radical reforms in the farmers' way of life, in a matter of months and without any serious change in the character of productive forces. (Korbash, 1974: 16–17)

Mao was highly sceptical of the official interpretation of their own history used to back this type of argument by Soviet theorists. In his 'Reading Notes' he observes that at the time of collectivisation the Soviet Union itself was at a very low level of agricultural mechanisation.[50] By contrast, Mao's own view was that the transmutation of producers' way of life was *itself* the change in the character of productive forces required:

> . . . socialist industrialisation cannot be carried out in isolation from agricultural co-operation . . . In agriculture, with things as they are in this country, co-operation must precede the use of big machinery (in capitalist countries, agriculture develops in a capitalist way). (Mao, 1955: 405–6)

Here we also find the recognition of two roads, capitalist or socialist development. But socialism is not identified merely by whether or not the capitalist entrepreneur or the State under the aegis of a communist party provides machines. It represents a specific *relation* of peasant to peasant, and collective to State:

> . . . the experience of some socialist countries proves that even where agriculture is collectivised, where collectivisation is mismanaged it is still not possible to increase production. The root cause of the failure . . . is that the state's policy towards the peasants is questionable. (Mao, 1956b: 64)

For reasons connected with the historical experience of the revolution before 1949, then, agrarian production has attained a place in socialist construction quite alien to that allotted it by Bolshevism. Collectivisation was largely achieved on a voluntary basis during the movements of 1955–7, Mao himself citing 1955 as the decisive year in the struggle for the application of the correct line. Inevitably, when the Great Leap Forward foundered under the impact of climactic disaster and too rapid an inception, it was represented by the opponents of Mao as a vindication of the Bolshevik strategy and of the need for scepticism when it comes to reliance on the masses. Yet there is strong evidence that the main way in which the Great Leap was too precipitate lay in the ill-preparedness of the Party, an anaemic appreciation of the correct line by those who were to implement and encourage it.[51] All too often the policy was actually imposed as a directive from above by local activists versed in orthodox Bolshevism. As such it revealed an imprudence of tactics which, on closer examination, serve to vindicate Mao's strategy by exemplifying the consequences of not following the injunctions of the mass line.

Even in the face of peasant hoarding and resistance to requisitions after the collapse of the Great Leap, Mao kept his confidence in the dependability of the people. Thus he argued that if they reacted thus, the Party was being seen as an oppressor and exploiter, and if so this was a failing of the Party not the peasant. The peasant was merely defending the produce of his own labour, and a socialist State could not imitate a capitalist one by expropriating what the producer was unwilling to give without re-creating the relations between peasant and landlord's or Emperor's tax collectors. In 1957 Mao had argued that 'persuasion, not compulsion is the only way to convince . . .' (1957b: 494). Now he insisted that 'our policy is not Stalin's policy'.[52]

Characteristically, rather than condoning accusation and punishment of individuals Mao, throughout the years in which collectivisation fell into disfavour in parts of the country, called for encouragement of reform from within, not its enforcement from without. He called for an appeal to the poor peasants to consider their own position under private farming as compared with collectivisation, so that they would themselves exert pressure for a return to production for the welfare of the majority instead of the few.

Nevertheless, the period 1961–5 saw a revival, under the direction of Liu Shao-chi and his colleagues, of markets and private farming, impelled above all by the *San Zi Yi Bao* (Three Freedoms and One Guarantee) policy based on the Soviet management of the *Kolkhozi*. This was bolstered by methods of clandestine investigation and witch-hunting of those who committed mistakes; officially this approach was aimed at the protection of socialism.

In fact this persecution was largely carried out under the banner of the Socialist Education Movement of the early 1960s. It was a reproduction of the distortion of a policy originally aimed by the Maoists at explaining and discussing with the people the nature and benefits of socialism once more, re-enlisting trust and cooperation in the process. It became increasingly apparent that the Party itself would have to be tempered afresh in the fires of the mass line ignited by a large-scale upheaval in the interests of class struggle. That eruption was to be the GPCR. Mao initiated a 'four clean-ups' campaign in May 1963 with his Ten Points directive, prefaced by *Where Do Correct Ideas Come From?* His caustic warnings fell on deaf ideas, and his Ten Points were realigned from an emphasis on raising peasant consciousness to the pursuit of control and the allotting of blame in two revisions, the first by Teng Hsiao-ping, the second by Liu Shao-chi. In January 1965 Mao's Twenty-Three Points revoked these fraudulent revisions, but it was the GPCR, spreading the message, particularly by the medium of the itinerant Red Guards, which animated the wind of change in the countryside. The right to rebel and criticise, and at the same time the call not to negate everything but to accept self-criticism if genuine, brought release from the shackles hindering socialist construction.[53] This has been combined with a rigorous curb on commune taxation to promote self-sufficiency, made possible by unprecedented restriction on the growth of State apparatuses (in turn possible through the politics of reliance rather than of control), and, of course, the Ten Great Relationships strategy.

After the final declaration of the People's Republic in 1949, a period of 'New Democracy' had been accepted. This entailed elements of a machine view of the State. It involved an alliance against the imperialist powers of rural and urban proletariat with petty and national capitalists under CPC leadership. After a keen fight, however, in 1953 Mao began to make ground with his view that the socialisation of agriculture must proceed, and that the 'alliance' could only block socialist construction.[54] Liu's opposition to this was later cited by Chou En-lai as one of his five major errors.[55]

After this period, as will be apparent from the above accounts, a conception of the role of State and Party quite different from that proposed by the Bolsheviks (including Lenin) emerged. A basic reason for the divergence between Mao and Liu in this and other respects emanated from their different understanding of the democratic centralist principle. Liu stood solidly in the Bolshevik (and bourgeois) tradition in his belief that a form of democracy involving a large degree of local autonomy was inherently irreconcilable with centralism. This perspective stands out, for instance, in the Soviet and Yugoslav models. The contrast conventionally made between the two relies on the assumption of a need to choose, i.e. they are bound within the same problematic. Mao, on the other hand, argued with increasing conviction (and experience proved him right) that these two, democracy and centralism, were not only compatible but positively complementary. Thus while, like Liu, he advocated central control, his view of the form of centralism and the part to be played by the Party (the relation of State to workers and peasants) was quite different. The fulcrum of the break is Mao's abandonment of a Leninist definition of centralism in terms of organisational principles alone, to one based on 'the centralisation of correct ideas' (1962a: 163). The reasoning is straightforward:

> Without democracy you have no understanding of what is happening down below . . . it will be impossible to achieve unity of understanding and unity of action, and impossible to achieve true centralism . . . (p. 164).[56] Without a high degree of democracy, it is impossible to achieve a high degree of centralism, and without a high degree of centralism, it is impossible to establish a socialist economy . . . We shall become a country like Yugoslavia [i.e. bourgeois]. (p. 167)

This demands a Party responsive to, and ready to learn from, as well as educate the masses. Mao thus cajoled a certain kind of Party member:

> They are afraid of the masses, afraid of the masses talking about them, afraid of the masses criticising them. What sense does it make for Marxist-Leninists to be afraid of the masses? (p. 160)

Clearly all this continues to presume the dependability of the masses if the mass line is followed. Politics, the correct line, thus determines organisation, and the line is derived by the Party from the experience of the masses themselves. If mass approval is withheld, then mishandling has taken place, but by following the correct line this can be put right. The method is alien to those who believe the Party should be the fount of wisdom, that this is what centralism means:

> Criticism and self-criticism is a kind of method. It is a method of resolving contradictions among the people, and it is the only method . . . But if we do not have a full democratic life and do not truly implement democratic centralism, then this method of criticism and self-criticism cannot be applied. (p. 163)

Politics in command thus rejects the orthodox machine idea of the State whereby the problem becomes one of democratising preformed vertical organisational authority structures.[57] Socialism instead becomes a matter of relations and consciousness. Liu Shao-chi, in contrast, argued ever in his classic work *How To Be a Good Communist* (long a standard manual for CPC members) that there must be primarily a fight against the 'backward state of the masses'.[58] Rejection of this perspective alone makes possible the transcendence of the old democracy v. centralism dilemma.

Development according to the gospel of the theory of productive forces is internally related, we have argued, to capitalist State apparatuses and relations. As such it could only be inimical to the Maoist principles of democratic centralism. For a socialist State to exist, then, there must be a total rejection of capitalist forms. Some of these we have discussed already, such as the fight against divisions between town and country or industry and agriculture. The third Great Difference and the most intractable of all is that between mental and manual labour, between 'expert' or cadre and worker.

The right and duty to rebel against and criticise any person in authority whom the people felt to be adopting a style contravening the socialist line established in the GPCR, lies at the heart of this (class) struggle to prevent the rise of new mandarins or technocratic elites. From this arose the slogan 'Red v. expert'. An expert is not simply someone with skills in this context, but one who regards his knowledge as entitling him to instruct others or decide his own style of work without needing to learn from or attend to the expressed requests of 'ordinary' workers. The result can only be the reinstatement of rigid hierarchy, degradation of the working man, and a goal for cadres of serving themselves instead of the people first.

In the battle to prevent this eventuality, the Chinese principles of democratic centralism have been extended to planning and to factory and commune management. The planning system, known as 'unified planning', thus rejects the model of issuing directives and conducting supervisory inspection from above. Instead it adopts the role of information centre on social needs and coordinator of country-wide production to achieve the necessary balance (e.g. availability of inputs for manufacture of more complex goods, etc.). This balancing function explains the term 'unified'. Enterprises are assumed to be committed to the same social purposes as the planners, and thus willing of their own volition to ascertain and do their best to meet society's needs. Certainly this is something which neither commandism nor profit-orientation can ever achieve. It will be recalled that the problems of Soviet planning can be traced at the phenomenal level to the purposely distorted information supplied to planners by enterprises, and to deliberately misinterpreted directives to benefit the director at the expense of society. This emphasises even more powerfully the greater productive potential of a system founded on political commitment to a correct line. Thus, for example, Chinese factories commonly send representatives to work in retail organisations or to interview directly those using their products. The result is a far greater responsiveness than even the trial and error of the illusory 'perfect market' of the bourgeois economist could ever achieve,[59] and an enhancement of socialist relations in the process. Planning, too, operates upward from the people rather than downward from the State.

Within the factories themselves the basis for transforming relations has been the constitution proposed by the workers at the Anshan Iron and Steel Works, in 1960. This received Mao's endorsement at the time, but was submerged by the managerialism of the early 1960s, and only gained widespread acceptance as a result of the GPCR towards the end of the decade. Chou En-lai in 1975 confirmed its status as the officially encouraged institutional basis for factory administration.[60] It is often contrasted in China with the 'Magnitogorsk constitution', said to be the rule-book-oriented and managerialist-based system by which a large steel plant in the USSR not far from the Chinese border is run.

The Anshan Constitution has five basic principles:

1. Keep politics firmly in command.
2. Strengthen party leadership.
3. Launch effective mass movements.
4. Institute the two participations and three-in-one systems fully and alter as necessary any existing rules which might obstruct this.
5. Go all out for technical innovation and technological revolution.

The fourth point contains two of the most basic components, both first emergent in the GLF. The 'triple combination' or 'three-in-one' system entails the replacement of the old one-man management structure with jointly elected representatives from technical, administrative and manual workers who constitute the decision-making bodies of the enterprise. The second component, the two participations – not only participation of workers in management, but also of cadres in manual labour – is directly aimed at the decomposition of the 'expert' aura.

> The cadres of our Party and state are ordinary workers and not overlords sitting on the backs of the people . . . (10th thesis on socialist construction in Mao, 1964a)

This thesis called for the need to continue cadre participation in labour. This has the practical effect, of course, of orienting cadres towards practical production problems, and to finding ways of resolving them whereby technology serves rather than oppresses people. Equally significant, it fractures the preconception that 'participation' is no more than a matter of allowing the lower ranks to feel represented in higher councils. Similarly, it belies the assumption that experts and managers are a universal imperative of effective production.[61] In this way, in combination with the unified plan, it shatters the problematic of workers' control that so haunts the Left.

The eleventh thesis on socialist construction, meanwhile, opposes the inegalitarianism supported by Bolsheviks from Lenin and Stalin to Dubcek:

> . . . the system of high salaries for a small number of people should never be applied. The gap between the incomes of the working personnel of the Party, the enterprises and the people's communes, on the one hand, and the incomes of the mass of the people, on the other, should be rationally and gradually narrowed, and not widened.

This is a natural accompaniment not only to the egalitarianism of the socialist tradition but also to the rejection of material incentives and all aspects of the division of labour. Nevertheless, the available evidence[62] suggests that progress in this sphere has been pretty limited, especially perhaps during the mid-1970s under the supervision of Teng Hsiao-ping. The two-line struggle remains strongly in evidence.

The dissolution of elitism necessitates the removal of the barriers erected to maintain a distance between workers and those capable of intellectual application and creativity. To this end there has been a growing stress of the accessibility and practical relevance of traditionally academic matters to all:

> According to Liu Shao-chi's line, workers are naive to think that we are capable of studying philosophy, which is a science only intellectuals can master. Mao's line tells us that we all can study it to good advantage by applying theory to running our own factories.

These words were spoken to Maria Macciocchi[63] by a forty-six-year-old textile worker, one of 128 workers in her factory who have elected to join a study group, the 'philosophy brigade'. The same woman puts the fundamental reason for this innovation thus:

> . . . our studies taught us that the study of philosophy helps you to understand things better and to solve all kinds of problems, and that an understanding of philosophy would help us to become a force capable of changing society. Its study is not for study's sake but for the revolution and to develop class consciousness. Philosophy is participating in the class struggle on the level of production. (In Macciocchi, 1971: 142)[64]

There is no good in only the Party cadre grasping the meaning of socialist ideas if the motive force of the revolution must come from the masses.

No explanation of the circumstances in which a political strategy for socialist construction offering a major departure from the fetters of Bolshevism would be complete without reference to the struggles, internal and external, in which the new line has been forged. The conflict with Liu Shao-chi and his fellow 'capitalist roaders' is already familiar, but both Sinologists and anti-Maoists on the Left are liable to assign this and other upheavals the label merely of disembodied power struggles. In this view Mao invents errors of his rivals and follows a line dictated not by principle, but expediency. Such commentaries envision politics merely in the form of political intrigue. From the Left this is a subordination of marxism which, we have argued, provides the resources to explain historical experience in both the USSR and the PRC (as it must to validate itself). In fact the disruptions in the PRC have followed not an extemporised political line, but one of remarkable consistency. To argue otherwise is to ignore the *content* of the criticisms advanced against both Lin Piao and Teng Hsiao-ping, and their isomorphism with those levelled against Liu.

Lin Piao, it has been claimed, presented to the Ninth Congress of the CPC in 1969 a draft plan advocating that the development of production should in future be given precedence over class struggle. The plan was rejected, and he was compelled to accept a different strategy. Such proposals are not merely a reversal of priorities, as the Western press (eagerly supporting Lin, and later Teng) would have one believe. It is a rejection of the entire Maoist theory of revolution and human nature.

Teng trod a similar path. This has been made clear by documents on future policy drawn up at his bidding in 1975 and released openly to the Chinese people after his fall for them to judge him themselves. In retrospect it becomes clear that even before open criticism of Teng began, the seeds of a counter-attack by the Maoists against his revisionism were being sown. The spearhead was a New Year's Day 1976 editorial in *Renmin Ribao*, *Hongqi* and *Jiefangjun Bao*, quoting as its centrepiece a statement by Mao of the essence of his policy; this was in effect a riposte to the speech by Teng on 1 October 1975, the 26th anniversary of the PRC's foundation, in which he put unity/stability and class struggle on the same level.[65] Behind the scenes he argued for a quietening of struggle so that stability could reign for the sake of developing the national economy. He proposed the slogan 'take the three directives as the key link',[66] which openly placed development of production and unity on a par with the third, combating revisionism and studying the theory of proletarian dictatorship. In this context the significance of Mao's words become clear:

> Stability and struggle do not mean writing off class struggle; class struggle is the key link, and everything else hinges on it. (*Peking Review*, (1) 1976: 9)

The New Year editorial employs the favourite quote from Lenin on the precedence of politics over economics in support, and another quote from Mao proclaims: 'The capitalist roaders are still on the capitalist road.' Articles by Chih Heng and Cheng Yueh[67] shortly after this restated with unequivocal emphasis the theory of class struggle as the basis of socialist construction and the bankruptcy of the theory of productive forces.

Teng's policy has been to call for greater expertise (in his view hindered by the emphasis on worker participation), for accelerated importation of 'advanced' technology from outside China, and for the reinstatement of material incentives. Teng himself is clear evidence for the continuing strength of the forces for capitalist restoration in China, and so ironically for the primacy of class struggle that he himself denied:

> Historical experience shows that both the old and new revisionists often make a fuss about economy in order to oppose the proletarian revolution and the proletarian dictatorship. Following in their footsteps and wearing the mask of an 'expert' in developing economy, Teng Hsiao-ping pretended to be most concerned about production . . . He vigorously peddled bourgeois ideas about economy and preached giving the priority to science and technology . . . But he never mentioned people and revolution as the most important factors . . . (Mass Criticism Group of Peking and Tsinghua Universities, *Peking Review*, (28) 1976: 12)

Yet if internal struggles have represented a concretisation of the two roads, lines and classes theory of the dynamics of socialist construction, then perhaps its sharpest crystallisation came in the external conflict between the CPSU and the CPC. Many of Mao's own insights of the late 1950s and early 1960s emerge in a specific critique of Stalin, and later, in the heat of the polemic, through a more sweeping indictment of Soviet policy. The experience of the Border Region Years is repeatedly applied to an analysis of Soviet errors.

When the Soviet Union claimed that China had completed the socialist revolution in 1957, Mao replied that only the first victory towards this had been won.[68] His argument remained that the class struggle to prevent the restoration of capitalism would continue for a very long time. Triumph is not achieved, he insisted, merely by changing the legal deeds of ownership.[69]

The Soviet withdrawal of aid in summer 1960 provoked a mounting official antagonism which finally graduated into open polemic in 1963. The CPC published the letters of each side in the exchange, and despatched a long and detailed series of 'comments' arguing precisely the points about socialist construction and class struggle that were in contention internally. The apogee of this was probably Comment IX, *On Khrushchev's Phoney Communism*. This included Mao's fifteen theses on socialist construction, a detailed discussion of Soviet press reports on corruption in collective farms and their underlying social causes, and an onslaught on Khrushchev's concept of a 'state (and Party) of the whole people'. This last was seen as a denial of class struggle and so of the tradition of Stalin and Lenin;[70] its proclamation of security for socialism was seen as itself a move in the direction of capitalist restoration.

We have criticised interpretations of conflicts within the PRC which analysed them as merely power battles at the top. More seriously, where these arguments come from the Left we have averred that they represent a retreat from marxist analysis. If marxism is to fulfil the claims it makes for itself, it must be able to analyse social processes in transitional societies as well as in capitalism. If the analysis is to be marxist it must proceed beyond the phenomenal to reveal the essential processes at work. And for a marxist the main forces at work, in whatever form, must be the struggle between classes in dealing with societies which have overthrown bourgeois control but not all elements of capitalism.

Having insisted on these points we are compelled to follow through their significance for certain aspects of the PRC's own policies. To have attempted this for the USSR and to have elaborated only upon the positive elements of the Chinese experience (i.e. where the proletarian line in the struggle has been made explicit and had gained the upper hand) would be to lay ourselves open to two just charges. The first is that ours would seem a predominantly geopolitical exercise, using the cover of marxist scholarship to vindicate China against the Soviet Union. The second, also a fault of most 'Friends of China', would be to acclaim the theory of the ubiquity of class struggle and in the same breath to praise any policy officially supported by the government of the PRC, thereby denying the possibility of mistakes or a period of ascendancy for the capitalist line. These same 'friends' then launch virulent attacks on the claimed total destruction of socialism in the Soviet Union. They should recall that Mao warned, 'do not negate everything'; but they should also bear in mind the corollary, do not affirm everything either.

We shall therefore proceed to indicate certain of the implications of our analysis for the 'foreign policy' of the PRC (which exhibits what we believe are unproletarian elements closely akin to those of Bolshevism); and for the related question of the current CPC analysis of the USSR. This will also involve some brief consideration of the CPC analysis of their own internal conflicts.

In 1962 and 1963,[71] Mao Tsẹ-tung referred to the danger, if the struggles against the forces of restoration and the ideas of capitalism were not maintained, of a slide into fascism. In May 1964, he made the reference more explicit:

> The present-day Soviet Union is a dictatorship of the bourgeoisie, a dictatorship of the big bourgeoisie, a dictatorship like German fascism, a Hitler type of dictatorship . . .[72]

More recently, the Peking and Tsinhua Universities' Group for mass criticism contended:

> . . . the Soviet Union under the yoke of the Soviet revisionist renegade clique has already become an absolute big jail for its people of all nationalities. When this clique speaks of 'humanism', it means ruthlessly suppressing the working people while vindicating renegades, Trotskyites, counter-revolutionaries and bourgeois elements.[73]

Evidently this analysis is sharply at variance with our own, notwithstanding the fact that we have acknowledged ourselves as indebted to what we have described as the practical critique of Bolshevism offered by PRC experience. Yet it would be self-delusion to attribute such a statement merely to false information or to over-exuberant polemics. It is not just the perversion of facts which is in question, but the whole method and style of analysis. The errors here constitute a subordination of marxism-leninism of a piece with those for which we reprimanded the typical leftist China-critic. For an investigation of the historical experience of the efforts of the Soviet people to build socialism, of the achievements and defeats, and a delineation of the class struggle amongst them, they substitute a neglect close to contempt.

The consequent version offered of how the Soviet Union shifted from October 1917 to a state of modern revisionism exhibits a separation of politics and production which is archetypally Bolshevik. Accounts of how 'Khrushchev and his clique' came to 'capture' state power[74] epitomise the impoverished conception of the political.

To follow the course of degeneration of analysis more comprehensibly, it is helpful and important to consider the development of CPC foreign policy *in toto*. As far back as 1946 Mao himself had offered an analysis of the international situation which implied the severance of foreign policy from proletarian internationalism.[75] This endorsed the possibility of diplomatic and trade relations with capitalist states within which oppressed classes might continue their own struggles against their rulers.

After 1950 US imperialism came to be identified as the 'main enemy':

> . . . the focus of post-war contradictions is the contradiction between . . . the U.S. imperialists and their lackeys on the one hand and the oppressed nations and peoples of Asia, Africa and Latin America on the other, and in the contradiction between the old and the new imperialists in their struggles for these areas.[76]

This specific understanding of capitalism thus generated also a notion of a 'Third World' (neither capitalist nor socialist *per se*) of the oppressed. And it produced a picture of the principal contradiction which, in Mao's philosophical frame of reference,[77] would have to be resolved for any others to be successfully handled.

The 1955 Bandung conference of African and Asian nations appears to have marked the explicit acceptance by the CPC that China was a member of the Third World, despite her pursuit of a revolutionary path unlike fellow-members.[78] Also involved here was the affirmation of the PRC's 'Five Principles of Co-existence', clarified in 1963 as 'mutual respect for territorial integrity and sovereignty, mutual non-aggression, non-interference in each other's internal affairs, equality and mutual benefit, and peaceful co-existence'.[79] It will be noted that these principles come dangerously close to reifying 'nations' and 'states' in a manner reminiscent of Pontius Pilate's infamous style when it comes to considering the effects on class struggle within these states. This in turn seems to have had certain important consequences for the conscious conception of capitalist societies and the meaning of diplomacy in recent years, as we shall see.

In 1958 the theory of the 'intermediate zone' was publicly revived by Mao. In 1946 he had advanced it as the major section of the world over which the USA, unwilling to directly attack the USSR, was bent on gaining control. China remained part of that zone.

In 1958 also, we find the explicit fracturing of diplomacy from both production and proletarian control. A CPC resolution indicated that once the 'legacies of the old society' had vanished, 'the function of the state will be limited to protecting the country from external aggression but it will play no role internally'.[80] The statement is, of course, tendential rather than immediate, but it nevertheless severs 'matters of state' and 'concerns of the people' conceptually in the same manner as we argue that 'foreign policy' and 'socialist construction' are separated in practice. The conception of the Party as the link between 'internal' and 'external' matters, moreover, is distinctively Bolshevik and jarringly out of tune with other aspects of CPC practice we have discussed. The strengthening perspective of 'zones' reflected and perhaps itself engendered a growing sense of common interests with the 'Third world' on China's part. The chief motive forces, however, were clearly those that led to the gradual intensification of the CPC/CPSU polemic following the Soviet withdrawal. In 1963 it was still possible for the CPC to declare, in the early stages of the polemic:

> There now exist two essentially different world economic systems, the socialist system and the capitalist system, and two mutually antagonistic camps, the socialist camp and the imperialist camp. (CPC, 1964: 185)

The USSR was still included in the socialist camp here, but as we know its status in this respect was already being questioned in the CPC. Thus in 1962 Mao had already relegated the contradiction between socialism and imperialism to a secondary list behind the primary one now designated as 'the contradiction between the people of the whole world and imperialism' (1962b: 192).[81] This last seems to hint strangely at something akin to Khrushchev's reviled notion of the 'whole people'. Succeeding policy evolution was to make this seem still more true.

By 1964 the rejection of the USSR was near enough total (remember this was the year of Mao's 'fascist' description) to sanction a hardening of the 'intermediate zones' theory, but with a crucial recasting. The panorama now offered was of a bi-polar world, dominated by the conflict between the two great imperialist 'superpowers'. Between the USA and the Soviet Union there were now identified two intermediate zones. To the Third World was added a Second World, 'developed' nations which were nevertheless increasingly subject to the threat of domination by the superpowers.[82] Significantly, this second group of nations exhibits a 'dual character';

> While their ruling classes are exploiters and oppressors, those countries themselves are subjected to U.S. control, interference and bullying. (*Peking Review*, (4) 1964: 7)

For now we seek only to register the opposition here between ruling classes and 'those countries themselves', a theoretically indicative ambiguity in so far as it prefigures the *class*lessness of such more recent blanket concepts as 'hegemonism'.

The significance of the bi-polar concept becomes apparent when one recalls the 1950 analysis quoted above of the principal contradiction as being between old and new imperialists. This constitutes the core rationale of Chinese foreign policy to the present; the USSR is *the* new imperialist, and all policy is thus seen as necessarily directed at resolving this contradiction by opposing all advances of Soviet influence. Inevitably, this drowns out other contradictions, in particular that between capitalism and socialism, proletariat and bourgeoisie. Hence, to quote an example provoking utmost revulsion, the PRC has consorted, traded and offered aid to the Pinochet regime in Chile,[83] this a state which *is* virulently fascist and the product of raw imperialism.

In 1965 Lin Piao's text on People's War[84] was published, illustrating vividly the conflicting tendencies, the class struggle, between lines in China's perspective on the outside world. On the one hand the principal contradiction is still between the 'revolutionary peoples' of the Third World and imperialism headed by the USA. Yet the main conceptualisation is *in terms* of the 'rural areas of the world' (i.e. 'underdeveloped' nations) rising up against the 'cities of the world' (North America and Western Europe). This is to be a grand mirror of revolution in China. It flows in one sense from Mao's thinking as expressed in his 'Reading Notes':

> Lenin said: 'the more backward the country, the more difficult the transition from capitalism to socialism'. Now it seems that this way of thinking is incorrect . . . the more backward the economy, the easier . . . the transition . . . The important question is the remoulding of human beings.[85]

Yet at the same time, it will be observed that Lin Piao's formulation seems once again to subordinate classes to 'nations'.

The political report of the Ninth Congress of the CPC in 1969 stated the theme (and separations) of official foreign policy plainly:

> The foreign policy of our Party and government is consistent. It is: to develop relations of friendship, mutual assistance and co-operation with socialist countries on the principle of proletarian international-

ism; to support and assist the revolutionary struggles of all the oppressed peoples and nations; and to strive for peaceful co-existence with countries having different social systems on the basis of the Five Principles . . . Our proletarian foreign policy is not based on temporary expediency; it is a policy in which we have long persisted.[86]

We leave the reader to judge the proletarian content and consistency of this policy for him or herself. One thing is irrepressible – a sense of *déjà vu* from reading the foreign policy statements issued at Congresses of the CPSU.

Having finally been admitted to the United Nations, the Chinese government despatched the then chairman of their delegation to the Sixth Special Session of the UN on the problems of raw materials and development. Teng Hsiao-ping's speech of 10 April 1974[87] reiterated and confirmed the world picture we have traced the emergence of. It further advocated trade based on 'equality' (something which an analysis of capitalism could never countenance as a meaningful possibility) and the transfer of technology and experts to developing countries. China's own status is made explicit:

China is a socialist country, and a developing country as well. China belongs to the Third World.

Let us then attend to some of the theoretical and practical consequences of the CPC analysis of 'foreign policy' matters. One has been the almost fanatical expediency-diplomacy (*pace* the Ninth Congress statement) which has characterised the orchestration of tactics against the major enemy, identified as the Soviet Union. A stark example is the apparent collusion with the CIA in seeking to establish rival (anti-socialist) groups as opposition to a Soviet-aided genuine liberation movement, the MPLA, in Angola.

Second, the attitude towards the Second World has seemingly led to a progressive elision of *practical* awareness of the class struggle in such countries. Increasingly as French, German, British and even American (Nixon, Ford, Kissinger) leaders, architects of the continuance of bourgeois domination and exploitation of the working classes in those countries, accept invitations to visit Peking, they are greeted as representatives of their 'people'. They are praised for their resistance, in the name of their 'people', to the Soviet quest for hegemony. They are assured of the friendship of the Chinese 'people'.[88]

Thirdly, expediency has been starkly exposed by the about-turn in official attitudes towards, to give particular examples, the European Economic Community and Yugoslavia. In the course of the polemic the EEC was understood as part of 'an increasingly fierce scramble of the imperialist powers' (CPC, 1963: 196). In 1964 the USSR was accused of being like the EEC:

> . . . you have introduced the law of the capitalist world into relations between socialist countries. You openly follow the example of the Common Market which was organised by monopoly capitalist groups. (Cit. Macciocchi, 1971: 506)

A decade later we find the EEC suddenly emerging as a bulwark against Soviet avarice. A warm welcome is proclaimed for Britain's entry to the Market in 1974, and an ambassador is sent with the establishment of official diplomatic relations between the PRC and the EEC in 1975.

The case of Yugoslavia is similar. In 1963 the CPC issued a detailed and searching appraisal of factual material concerning socialism in Yugoslavia (Comment III, 26 September, in CPC, 1965). We do not agree with the consequent blanket characterisation of Yugoslavia as capitalist (or, as we saw Mao suggesting in 1962, fascist) but the factual material gathered clearly serves as a strong indictment against the course of socialism there. Certainly we are familiar now with the grounds on which 'capitalist' and 'fascist' are applied to countries by the CPC since 1963. On this basis, then, they concluded that Yugoslavia had become an imperialist appendage of the United States. As such they urged the Soviet Union to break off all relations with Yugoslavia, thereby following the PRC's own 'principled stand'. The dangers of not doing so are made clear:

> . . . *revisionism is the product of imperialist policy* . . . Sparing no cost, imperialism has now expanded the scope of its operations and is buying over leading groups in socialist countries and pursues through them its desired policy of 'peaceful evolution'. (CPC, 1965: 182)

How then are we to interpret this somersault in policy which contained fraternal and close relations between the PRC and a Yugoslavia which has hardly effected much change in the direction of socialism in the past decade? How do we explain (and how are the Chinese people *themselves* meant to take) the insistence by Li Ta, Deputy Chief of the General Staff of the Red Army, greeting a Yugoslav People's Army delegation, that 'Our two peoples have always sympathised with, supported and encouraged each other, both in the past struggle against fascism and the present struggle against imperialism and hegemony' (*Peking Review*, (44) 1974). The answer lies, of course, at the end of Li Ta's sentence. The Yugoslavs have consistently supported 'non-alignment' and Li Ta praises this explicitly in his speech. In short, Yugoslavia can now do what she wishes as long as that is not joining the Soviet Bloc. The fatuous notion, considered in class terms, of 'non-alignment' needs no elaboration.

These kinds of opportunist diplomacy have not gone unnoticed amongst either Trotskyist or orthodox communist critics of the PRC. Characteristically, however, their analysis tends to stop with the observation of the phenomenon of unholy alliances. To infer from these alone that China is a 'degenerate workers' state' or 'state capitalist' *simpliciter* is, however, an error as colossal as the CPC's own inferences concerning the USSR in both its procedure and consequences.

What is more profoundly disturbing, and indicative of the essential, class-relational import of CPC strategy, is that which is usually presumed beyond question: the salience, and indeed the very notion, of 'foreign policy' itself. The separation of discrete policy areas so typical of Bolshevism is once again in evidence. President Mobutu of Zaire, for example, can pour libations to his ancestors in the Hall of the People in Peking – and be celebrated in the Chinese press doing so – at the same time as the campaign to criticise Confucius is in full flood. Distinguished foreign dignitaries are, it appears, beyond mass criticism.

The critique of Bolshevism which we have traced in the practical experience of the PRC has patently not been extended to embrace 'foreign policy'. Rather, we find a replication of many of the inglorious features of Bolshevism itself. The line on foreign trade is more equivocal than that on diplomacy. In large part it remains constrained by the General Line which opposes productive dependence,[89] but nevertheless a growing volume of trade, and a large deficit with Japan and the West, has been a feature of the mid-1970s. Ill omens are afforded by the argument that trade is fairly safe so long as it takes place through State handling of all dealing. Again a Bolshevik understanding, in mechanical rather than relational terms, of how capitalist imperialism works, rears its head. Indeed such a stance is inherent in the 'non-interference' notions of the Five Principles of Peaceful Co-existence themselves. All of this betrays, amidst the proclamations of first the precariousness and then the snuffing out of socialism in the USSR, an insidious encroachment of the feeling that socialism is secure against outside influences in the PRC.[90]

This may seem paradoxical given the continued stress on internal class struggle in China. Yet having noted the voluntaristic, cabalistic understanding of how a supposedly bourgeois group came to control the USSR (or, as formerly claimed, Yugoslavia) it is severely unsettling to reflect on at least the official presentation to the people of the nature of attempts (and of their defeat) to gain control in China. Liu, Lin,

Teng and their fellow 'conspirators' are repeatedly referred to as 'bourgeois agents' who 'plotted' to 'capture' power. They are each referred to along with their 'clique' or 'gang'. Once again, notwithstanding the constant underlying theme of class struggle as the need to fight ways of thinking and acting, this reduction of the battle at the top to one between caricatures betrays surviving elements of Bolshevism. Indeed, these are present in the very unpreparedness to recognise such a phenomenon as that we have called 'the Bolshevik problematic', indicating the limits of the application of marxism and the need to ceaselessly pursue, and study the experience of, class struggle.

6 'Never Forget Class Struggle . . .'

We made it clear, at the start of this book, that we were engaged upon a *theoretical* project. Historical experience, we were convinced, and particularly, though by no means exclusively, that of the socialist accomplishments of the workers and peasants of People's China, had made the limitations of Bolshevism as a problematic of transition visible. Our major concern was to articulate this practical critique; and our book, in consequence, would not centrally be 'about' the USSR and China. Rather, it would be a book which sought to bring the historical experience of the Soviet and the Chinese peoples to bear upon certain prematurely closed issues in marxist theory. Hence our title. And hence also various emphases in our text; polemical emphases on the restrictions Bolshevism places on socialist transformation, and parallel, and equally polemical, emphases on the emancipatory qualities inherent in those experiences which had initially allowed us to see those restrictions. Such biases were legitimate and indeed unavoidable given the nature of our project; but they carried with them the serious danger that despite our frequent protestations to the contrary, our book would be read as a simple eulogy of the theories and practices of the CPC, as against those of the CPSU. For this reason if for no other it behoves us to state here, in what we hope are unambiguous terms, the implications of our arguments for analysis of the USSR and PRC as social formations. Another, no less compelling consideration also induces us to begin our concluding thus. The historical experience we have endeavoured to theorise, we believe, equally amounts to a practical critique of both the conclusions, *and* the methodologies, of most of what currently pass for marxist analyses of the Soviet Union, China, and the rest of the countries of the socialist camp. Against these latter analyses we think it necessary to be brutally and insistently empirical.

In Moscow and Leningrad rents amount to less than 5 per cent of take-home pay and have not risen *since 1922*. Soviet tram and bus fares, and gas charges, have been constant *since the 1930s*, while the prices of bread, sugar, flour, meats, potatoes and other staples have been stable *for the last ten years*. In 1976, Britain's year of capitalist crisis, the Soviet working class enjoyed substantial increases in disposable income (in excess of 15 per cent on average), *and* price reductions on a wide range of electrical and mechanical goods.[1] We could readily extend this list of what Marx would call 'great facts' of working-class experience.[2] The point, however, is that they are exactly that.

Both China and the USSR are for us social formations which are in transition, in Charles Bettelheim's phrase, 'between' capitalism and socialism. In neither case do we see capitalism as having been restored (or as never having been overthrown): neither in the PRC, nor in the USSR, is the production of commodities the dominant mode of production or the making of surplus value its motive force; in neither formation is labour-power merely a commodity. These, as Marx several times reminds us,[3] are the defining characteristics of capitalist production, and to the extent that they remain absent socialism remains the dominant mode of production in both the PRC and the Soviet Union. The 'great facts' of the kind we have instanced are the phenomenal forms of that dominance. They are its record and its reality in the lives of working-class people. However fettered, in sum, socialism in the USSR may be (and however beleaguered socialism in China) it remains, over a wide range of experiences, *socialism*; protecting the lives of working-class men and women as no Welfarism and no Social Democracy could ever do in a capitalist social formation. People do not starve, or die for want of warmth or medical facilities, nor do they risk homelessness or unemployment, as is in varying degrees the experience of the working class wherever capital rules. Such gains matter; they are in the end the only valid measure of socialism. For, simply, only the socialisation of production has historically been capable of guaranteeing them.[4]

To take our stand on such 'great facts' (and the conditions that make them possible, which were first secured by the Bolshevik revolution and have since been extended elsewhere) is not merely to declare a substantive commitment. It is equally to adopt a *methodological* stance, and one which must in our view be that of any enterprise which considers itself to be marxist. This stance is that of what Gramsci called an 'organic intellectual': one who seeks to found and validate his or her analysis in the historical experience of the working class. Class, in other words, is not just a category of marxist analysis but a ground of its possibility. Now, the above brute facts were cited against, primarily, those (CPC, and others of 'Maoist' inclination,[5] SWP[6]) who declare that the USSR is 'capitalist'. The experiences they record, and the conditions that make such experiences possible, are not, on any evidence, compatible with the requisites of the capitalist mode of production; and to have adopted the viewpoint of working-class experience would have precluded any possibility of such facts being 'overlooked'.

The same methodology, however, equally draws our attention to other facts of working-class experience and equally militates against another form of marxist interpretation. We refer to the kind of facts which have been central to our critique of Bolshevism, and the style of analysis which views the USSR, or the PRC, as socialist societies *simpliciter*. This point applies particularly to 'Friends of China'.[7] We have argued throughout this book that certain capitalist relations endure in both the USSR and the PRC. In neither case has the division of labour or 'bourgeois right' been overcome; Marx's 'muck of ages' still clings. Consider, for example, how far the emancipation of Soviet and Chinese women has still to go.[8] Such relations, we have urged, are not mere epiphenomena, but constituents of capitalist production. Moreover, they will not wither away 'naturally' in the course of time (nor, as is more commonly assumed, with the development of the productive forces), but can be transformed only through continuing class struggles. We are the first to acknowledge that the CPC and the CPSU have endeavoured to lead these struggles. We do not endorse the rhetoric of 'betrayal', in its Trotskyist or Maoist incarnations. We do however believe that both Communist Parties have made costly errors, from which we can and should learn. Often, capitalist relations have not been recognised for what they are; they have rather been seen as secondary or merely superstructural phenomena, or, most damagingly, as resources which can temporarily be used in the building of socialism. This last error is most evident in Bolshevik perspectives on production; but as Chapter 5 showed, the CPC is no stranger to such thinking either. In foreign and foreign trade[9] policy, in particular, it has embraced an opportunism almost without precedent in the most utilitarian of Bolshevik judgements; an opportunism furthermore which exactly parallels the marxist analyses we are presently criticising, in its failure to grasp just how strong the forces of capitalism *are* during the transitional era.

Analyses which declare the USSR (or PRC) capitalist, then, overlook the socialism which their peoples have built. But conversely, purely apologetic analyses ignore the legacies of capitalism which exist within both countries and have in some particulars been reproduced, however unwittingly, by CPSU and CPC policies. For us, by contrast, the USSR, China, and the rest of the countries of the socialist camp are *contradictory* social formations, in which socialism is dominant but not triumphant, and capitalism is subordinated, but not vanquished. This means that their defining feature, their 'general illumination', to adapt a famous metaphor of Marx's, is continuing *class struggle*; a struggle whose many fronts, both 'internal' and international,[10] whose varied and complex forms, and whose intricate and chequered progression will we hope at the least have been suggested in the preceding chapters. Now, there is not a hint of this contradictoriness, this struggle or its complexities, in either of the preceding analyses; the Soviet Union and China are viewed, with a singular absence of dialectic, as capitalist or socialist monoliths. This lacuna, in our view, rests on a familiar methodological disorder. Such unitary judgements are possible only on condition that one or the other of the two, contradictory, facets of workers' experience we have cited above is forcibly abstracted from. For to attempt, via a marxist critique, to establish the historical conditions under which people can partake of such conflicting experiences must lead inexorably to the acknowledgement of the persistence within both China and the USSR of both capitalist and socialist relations and the struggle between them. Only this recognition can explain the whole gamut of Soviet or Chinese working-class experience, and only by selectively, and thus violently abstracting from this whole can the contradictions it manifests be effaced.

Clearly the two kinds of analyses we have indicted thus far do not exhaust marxist perspectives on the socialist bloc; but similar methodological defects mar other accounts which are in many respects closer to our own. Unfortunately we lack space here to substantiate this assertion. It will none the less be useful briefly to clarify our position in respect of two contemporary interpretations which fall into this latter category: modern Trotskyist theories, as best exemplified in the work of Ernest Mandel; and the in many ways pioneering *œuvre* of Charles Bettelheim. What follows, we stress, is a statement, and not a defence of our position; its justification (where we have not elaborated in other writings[11]) must be sought in the arguments of this book as a whole.

On modern Trotskyism we may be exceedingly brief since most of what was said in Chapter 3 concerning Trotsky applies *a fortiori* to his contemporary followers. In particular, however, we would stress that in contrast to the kinds of analysis we have considered hitherto in this chapter modern Trotskyism demonstrates the continuing marxist strengths of its Bolshevism in its recognition that socialist relations persist in the countries of the socialist camp, and in the sometimes very perceptive insights into the class struggles therein that this sustains.[12] These strengths are well illustrated in Mandel's devastating polemic against the theorists of the SWP (formerly the International Socialist Group) and his *Ten Theses* on the transition to socialism, which convincingly refutes Bettelheim's (and the CPC's) current positions on the USSR.[13] But these same texts equally reveal Bolshevism's inadequacies; a technical-economic concept of production (and a tacit theory of productive forces), together with a voluntarist notion of politics, ultimately ground their analysis. That internal relation of productive and State forms we have argued throughout this book is rarely recognised, and Mandel's empirical comprehension of the modalities of class struggle is attenuated as a result. We have exemplified in Chapter 3.

Bettelheim, of course, follows the CPC in their view that the USSR is now capitalist (cf. his 1974, *Preface*). He is therefore vulnerable both to the objections we have advanced above, and to the more extended criticisms of in particular, Mandel (1974a) and Hindess (1976).[14] And without doubt, this monumental error is anchored in certain theoretical deficiencies in his work. Nevertheless, there are several reasons for extending Bettelheim a more serious and sympathetic consideration than his colleagues amongst the 'left' enemies of the USSR. Above all, he is one of the very few marxists in the West (Althusser must be counted as another[15]) whose work has engaged with, and sought to theorise, the historical experience of the class struggles for socialism in China. In consequence, he has articulated many of precisely the theoretical lessons of this history which we have emphasised, and has helped us immeasurably in our own attempt to do so. We differ from Bettelheim only in what we consider to be a failure on his part to take his critique far enough. This, we believe, accounts for his mistaken view of the USSR.

Central to what Bettelheim criticises as *'marxisme figé'*[16] are two theses: first, a mechanical identification of ownership and class relations; second, the primacy of the productive forces. Against the former, he reiterates Balibar's[17] distinction of the 'property connection' and the 'real connection' between labourer and means of production. Against the latter, he asserts the dominance of production relations over productive forces.[18] From his first argument, he insists that a change in ownership of the means of production, following a proletarian revolution, does not *ipso facto* entail their socialisation at the level of the real connection; concretely, the 'dual separation' of labour from these means and productive enterprises from one another continues within the actual production process.[19] And these separations are relations of capitalist production. The era of transition is therefore characterised by what Bettelheim (somewhat unfortunately) characterises as a 'non-correspondence' of 'political and economic levels'. But from his second argument, it follows that 'development of the productive forces' alone will not resolve this contradiction; rather, how such forces will develop will depend precisely on how this contradiction is handled. Hence, 'politics' rather than 'economics' must be 'in command'; for to ensure a socialist correspondence of economy and polity requires the active transformation of the capitalist relations which survive as 'real connections' and this is supremely a matter of class struggle. This implies amongst other things that it is less the existence of a Plan than the correctness of a Party's General Line which distinguishes the socialist from the capitalist road.

Now, there is clearly much here with which we would concur. But there are also difficulties, which relate directly to Bettelheim's analysis of the USSR. Two points in particular may be mentioned here. The first concerns Bettelheim's understanding of 'politics in command'. It is significant that he characterises *marxisme figé* as an economism, and as a specifically Stalinist deviation from Leninism. We, on the other hand, see the formulae Bettelheim attacks as endemic to Bolshevism as such, but not, crucially, in a merely economistic form; rather, their economism is systematically linked to a definite and voluntaristic conception of politics. Hence to reject Bolshevik economism means equally to reject its voluntarism. Bettelheim, however, is blind to this link; indeed, he is oblivious to the Bolshevik problematic as such.[20] And this myopia, we believe, severely limits his critique, for he in fact substantially reproduces the Bolshevik notion of politics, even while repudiating the theory of productive forces which grounds it. Thus he often tends simply to reverse the equations of the Second International, without querying their terms; 'politics in command' is understood as the domination of politics *over* (as opposed to *in*) production, the two still being construed as independent spheres of activity. This in turn leads him, as Sweezy (1971) and Mandel (1974a) have perceived, into a radical idealism wherein the Line of the ruling Party becomes effectively the sole criterion of the nature of a transitional formation.

This tendency is compounded by the second problem to which we wish to draw attention. This relates to Bettelheim's use of Balibar's distinction. As we have seen, Bettelheim (correctly) refuses to reduce relations of production to property relations, and in this context denies that planning suffices to establish a formation as socialist. From this theoretical foundation he argues that it is possible for what he terms a 'statebourgeoisie' to employ the machinery of planning to exploit labour. Such exploitation will be capitalist in so far as the State, and hence the means of production which it owns, are not subject to genuine proletarian control, and the relation of labour-power with such means continues to be a wage relation.[21] Bettelheim regards this as presently the situation in the USSR. Leaving aside the question of when it was ever *not* the situation, there is a clear inadequacy in these criteria.

Marx identifies 'two characteristic features' of capitalism: first, 'being a commodity is the dominant and determining characteristic of its products', which implies that 'the labourer himself comes forward merely as the seller of commodities . . . the relation between capital and wage-labour determines the entire character of the mode of production'; second, 'the production of surplus-value is the direct aim and determining motive of production' (Marx, 1865a: 878f.). Now, clearly Bettelheim's 'dual separation', at the level of the 'mode of material appropriation', is a necessary condition of this process; it is not, however, of itself a *sufficient* condition. Marx makes it clear elsewhere that 'production founded on capital . . . posits itself in the forms adequate to it only in so far as and to the extent that free competition develops' (Marx, 1858a: 650). For only competition ensures the operation of the law of value and it is this law which grounds both the specifically capitalistic form of exploitation and capital's compulsion to accumulate; with competition, in Marx's words, 'the inner laws of capital . . . are for the first time posited as *laws*' (ibid., emphasis added). The clear implication is that the absence of the capitalist market-form indicates that the capitalist mode of production does not dominate a social formation, even if, as is clearly the case in the USSR, capitalist relations, of the sort noted by Bettelheim, have some presence. Mandel has rightly developed this argument.

Our concern, however, is once again centrally with an issue of methodology. Like his cruder co-believers Bettelheim has a penchant for forced abstraction. From the (correct) proposition that the Plan/market opposition does not suffice to distinguish capitalism from socialism, he contends that the Plan and the market are mere phenomenal forms and hence should be discounted.[22] But the point about such forms is precisely that they need to be accounted *for*, in terms of their conditions. And, simply, the conditions in which capitalist market-forms are not dominant are those in which the tendencies inscribed in a 'mode of material appropriation' which exhibits Bettelheim's 'dual separation' do not have the force of laws. Had Bettelheim recognised this, he would further have had to recognise that the suppression of these forms constitutes a precise measure of the degree to which proletarian politics are 'in command' still in the Soviet Union. This would in turn have led him to consider to what extent the survival of certain capitalist relations there is a consequence of the quality of that politics. But here, Bettelheim's blindness to the singularity of Bolshevism, like Mandel's, is a critical obstacle to his in many ways extremely searching analysis.

We wish finally, if extremely briefly, to state what we see as the key general conclusions of our investigations. We do not intend by this the abstraction of some ideal 'model' of the road to socialism, 'Chinese' or otherwise; indeed, a key lesson of the historical experience on which we have focused is precisely that the relations involved in the imposition of any *a priori* model suppress the initiative and fetter the self-emancipation of the direct producers, who rather than Parties (or machines, or experts) are the true builders of socialism. Our aim is on the contrary one of stating certain principles, whose validation is to be found in that experience, but whose relevance extends to the class struggle everywhere. Our remarks are in other words *theoretical* in Stalin's sense of the term.

Marx rarely used the notion of a 'fundamental law'. But one occasion on which he did so was to link together as basic to capitalism its systematic production of profit *and* poverty. For him '*the absolute general law of capitalist accumulation*' (and the italics are his own) is that which

> establishes an accumulation of misery, corresponding with an accumulation of capital. Accumulation of wealth at one pole is, therefore, at the same time accumulation of misery, agony of toil, slavery, ignorance, brutality, mental degradation, at the opposite pole, i.e. on the side of the class that produces its own product in the form of capital. (Marx, 1867a: 645)

This is neither rhetoric nor exaggeration. In particular, those disposed to overlook the misery *currently* accumulating in imperialism's heartlands might recall that we are talking of a *world*-market system of exploitation. That class which produces its product in the form of, say, 'British' capital, slaves in, amongst other places, the tea-gardens of Sri Lanka, the gold and diamond mines of South Africa and the child labour sweatshops of Hong Kong.[23]

It is in *this* context that socialism must be understood, first and foremost, in terms of having enough to eat, being decently clothed and housed, enjoying adequate medical facilities. To define it thus is to point precisely to that experience which capitalism cannot guarantee for all. This of course means that socialist construction is *centrally* concerned with ensuring the fullest development of the social forces of production; indeed, it *is* that development. And this in turn is exactly why the theory of productive forces which, in its Bolshevik form, has hitherto provided the dominant problematic of transition must emphatically be rejected. There is no paradox in this assertion.

On the contrary: historical experience has amply confirmed (and extended) the central insight we drew from Marx in Chapter 1 – that material production is always and irreducibly a *social* activity. This means that it is impossible to sever development of the forces from transformation of the relations of production and subordinate the second to the prior accomplishment of the first. In Bettelheim's words, 'the relations of production exert a dominating effect on the characteristics of the means of labour' by 'imposing the conditions under which the productive forces are reproduced' (Bettelheim, 1970a: 86, 1973: 91). We would add a forceful reminder that the relations to which Bettelheim refers comprise the entire, extensive repertoire of moral, cultural and political conditions which sustain any given way in which men and women produce their means of subsistence. To develop a particular form of labour process is *ipso facto* to develop the relations necessary to its performance. There can therefore be no socially neutral development, no development which obeys technical imperatives alone. The choice facing socialists lies between socialist and capitalist roads.

Development of the productive forces, and class struggle, are not therefore *separate* practices. It is inaccurate even to conceive them as complementary. Simply, to secure a *socialist* development of the productive forces (one that is capable of giving everyone enough to eat) *is* a class struggle. For to give everyone enough to eat demands that the producers consciously and collectively organise their efforts to that end, and this in turn requires their emancipation from the many shackles capital places on their cooperation. Prominent among the latter is the division of labour. Class struggle is, in other words, the *productive* motor of socialist construction. For only through its unleashing will the conditions be created under which the productive forces embodied in the voluntary cooperation of labour can flourish. This struggle is as extensive as are the relations in which capital presently enslaves the working class. It is in these terms that we must understand the injunction to 'put politics in command'. It does not refer to a relation between distinct 'economic' and 'political' activities, concerns or institutions but to production *itself*. Politics, understood as the self-emancipation of the producers, in and through collective production, is the *means* through which *socialist* development is assured.

The struggle for socialism, then – conceived *as* a struggle for production – does *not* lie between 'backwardness' and 'modernisation'. It lies between what Marx in 1867 described as the *political* economies of capital and labour. This has clear implications for any Communist Party. Estimates of the resources of socialism (and capitalism) must be political judgements. The criterion by which we evaluate techniques, institutions, practices (including our own) must be: do they foster or fetter the emancipation of labour; do they help the people extend their control over their lives, or do they reproduce the shackles of free wage slavery; do they in a word serve socialism or capitalism? To repeat, this injunction applies across the board; we cannot separate 'base' and 'superstructure', 'forces' and 'relations', and postpone the transformation of the latter term of each pair. To do so is to rob the producers of the means of their emancipation and *therefore* in the end to hold back socialist production too. Finally, this injunction equally applies to revolutionary strategies *here and now*. As Marx, Lenin, and Mao have all stressed, the political economy of labour is present in the workers' struggles of the existing world order; it is they which alone allow us to see it. Socialist construction begins long before any moment which can be called 'the' Revolution. It begins with capital's creation of the working class.

A Restatement

MARX AND ENGELS ON PRODUCTION, CAPITALISM AND SOCIALISM

We close this book with a number of passages from Marx and Engels which together provide a restatement of its major arguments. The quotations fall into three groups. The first set indicate why production is central to historical materialism, what it is, and how to study it. The second set relate class, division of labour, and State-form in capitalism. The third set discuss socialist construction.

This may, perhaps, seem an unusual way to end. But as we have stressed throughout, the historical experience discussed in this book is of massive *theoretical* import. Part of what it teaches us is the need constantly to re-examine Marx anew; familiar texts take on new dimensions when seen thus. These quotations are cited with that objective. When read in the light of the historical experience of the Soviet and the Chinese peoples, they present, we believe, a marxism untrammelled by the closures integral to the Bolshevik problematic; one in which the fullness of what is involved in production and thus in the class struggles to transform its capitalist into its socialist mode, can be grasped. It is with this aim in mind that we choose to end where we began, with Karl Marx. Lenin stated the same point introducing his *State and Revolution*:

> in view of the unprecedentedly widespread distortion of Marxism, our prime task is to *re-establish* what Marx really taught . . . (Lenin, 1917b: 391)

PRODUCTION

. . . we must begin by stating the first premise of all human existence and, therefore, of all history, the premise, namely, that men must be in a position to live in order to be able to 'make history'. But life involves before everything else eating and drinking, a habitation, clothing and many other things. The first historical act is thus the production of the means to satisfy these needs, the production of material life itself. And indeed this is an historical act, a fundamental condition of all history, which today, as thousands of years ago, must daily and hourly be fulfilled merely in order to sustain human life.

Marx and Engels, *The German Ideology* (1846a: 39)

The way in which men produce their means of subsistence depends first of all on the nature of the actual means of subsistence they find in existence and have to reproduce. This mode of production must not be considered simply as being the reproduction of the physical existence of the individuals. Rather it is a definite form of activity of these individuals, a definite form of expressing their life, a definite *mode of life* on their part. As individuals express their life, so they are. What they are, therefore, coincides with their production, both with *what* they produce and with *how* they produce. The nature of individuals thus depends on the material conditions determining their production.

Marx and Engels, *The German Ideology* (1846a: 31–2)

In the process of production, human beings do not only enter into a relation with Nature. They produce only by working together in a specific manner and by reciprocally exchanging their activities. In order to produce, they enter into definite connections and relations with one another, and only within these social connections and relations does their connection with Nature, i.e. production, take place.

Marx, *Wage-Labour and Capital* (1847b: Bottomore and Rubel, 155)

The fact is, therefore, that definite individuals who are productively active in a definite way enter into these definite social and political relations. Empirical observation must in each separate instance bring out empirically, and without any mystification and speculation, the connection of the social and political structure with production.

Marx and Engels, *The German Ideology* (1846a: 36)

The production of life, both of one's own in labour and of fresh life in procreation, now appears as a double relationship: on the one hand as a natural, on the other as a social relationship. By social we understand the co-operation of several individuals, no matter under what conditions, in what manner and to what end. It follows from this that a certain mode of production, or industrial stage, is always combined with a certain mode of co-operation, or social stage, and this mode of co-operation is itself a 'productive force'.

Marx and Engels, *The German Ideology* (1846a: 41)

Man himself is the basis of his material production, as of any other production that he carries on. All circumstances, therefore, which affect man, the *subject* of production, more or less modify all his functions and activities, and therefore too his functions and activities as the creator of material wealth . . . In this respect it can in fact be shown that *all* human relations and functions, however and in whatever form they may appear, influence material production and have a more or less decisive influence on it.

Marx, *Capital, IV: Theories of Surplus Value,* I (1863a: 288)

CAPITALISM

The specific economic form, in which unpaid surplus-labour is pumped out of direct producers, determines the relationship of rulers and ruled, as it grows directly out of production itself and, in turn, reacts upon it as a determining element. Upon this, however, is founded the entire formation of the economic community which grows up out of the production relations themselves, thereby simultaneously its specific political form. It is always the direct relationship of the owners of the conditions of production to the direct producers – a relation always naturally corresponding to a definite stage in the development of the methods of labour and thereby its social productivity – which reveals the innermost secret, the hidden basis of the entire social structure, and with it the political form of the relationship of sovereignty and dependence, in short, the corresponding specific form of the state.

Marx, *Capital, III* (1865a: 791)

Division of labour only becomes truly such from the moment when a division of material and mental labour appears.

The greatest division of material and mental labour is the separation of town and country.

. . . it is quite immaterial what consciousness starts to do on its own: out of all such muck we get only the one inference that these three moments, the forces of production, the state of society, and consciousness, can and must come into contradiction with one another, because the *division of labour* implies the possibility, nay the fact that intellectual and material activity – enjoyment and labour, production and consumption – devolve on different individuals, and that the only possibility of their not coming into contradiction lies in the negation in its turn of the division of labour . . .

With the division of labour, in which all these contradictions are implicit, and which in its turn is based on the natural division of labour in the family and the separation of society into individual families opposed to one another, is given simultaneously the *distribution*, and indeed the *unequal* distribution, both quantitative and qualitative, of labour and its products, hence property: the nucleus, the first form, of which lies in the family, where wife and children are the slaves of the husband. This latent slavery in the family, though still very crude, is the first property, but even at this early stage it corresponds perfectly to the definition of modern economists who call it the power of disposing of the labour-power of others. Division of labour and private property are, moreover, identical expressions: in the one the same thing is affirmed with reference to activity as is affirmed in the other with reference to the product of the activity.

Further, the division of labour implies the contradiction between the interest of the separate individual or the individual family and the communal interest of all individuals who have intercourse with one another . . .

And out of this very contradiction between the interest of the individual and that of the community the latter takes an independent form as the *State*, divorced from the real interests of individual and community, and at the same time as an illusory communal life, always based, however, on the real ties existing in every family and tribal conglomeration – such as flesh and blood, language, division of labour on a larger scale, and other interests – and especially . . . on the classes, already determined by the division of labour, which in every such mass of men separate out, and of which one dominates all the others.

Marx and Engels, *The German Ideology* (1846a: 43, 65, 43–4, 45)

. . . capital is not a thing, but rather a definite social production relation, belonging to a definite historical formation of society, which is manifested in a thing and lends this thing a specific social character. Capital is not the sum of the material and produced means of production. Capital is rather the means of production transformed into capital, which in themselves are no more capital than gold or silver in itself is money. It is the means of production monopolized by a certain section of society, confronting living labour-power as products and working conditions rendered independent of this very labour-power, which are personified through this antithesis in capital. It is not merely the products of labourers turned into independent powers, products as rulers and buyers of their producers, but rather also the social forces [of their labour and socialized] form of this labour, which confront the labourers as properties of their products.

Marx, *Capital, III* (1865a: 814–15)

. . . how does this strange phenomenon arise, that we find on the market a set of buyers, possessed of land, machinery, raw material, and the means of subsistence, all of them, save land in its crude state, the *products of labour*, and on the other hand, a set of sellers who have nothing to sell except their labouring power, their working arms and brains? That the one set buys continually in order to make a profit and enrich themselves, while the other set continually sells in order to earn their livelihood? The inquiry into this question would be an inquiry into what the economists call *'Previous, or Original Accumulation'* but which ought to be called *Original Expropriation*. We should find that this so-called *Original Accumulation* means nothing but a series of historical processes, resulting in a *Decomposition of the Original Union* existing between the Labouring Man and his Instruments of Labour . . . The *Separation* between the Man of Labour and the Instruments of Labour once established, such a state of things will maintain itself and reproduce itself upon a constantly increasing scale until a new and fundamental revolution in the mode of production should again overturn it, and restore the original union in a new historical form.

Marx, *Wages Price and Profit* (1865b: 210)

SOCIALISM

It is the working millions of Great Britain who first have laid down – the real basis of a new society – modern industry, which transformed the destructive agencies of nature into the productive power of man. The English working classes, with invincible energies, by the sweat of their brows and brains, have called into life the material means of ennobling labour itself, and of multiplying its fruits to such a degree as to make general abundance possible.

By creating the inexhaustible productive powers of modern industry they have fulfilled the first condition of the emancipation of Labour. They have now to realise its other condition. They have to free those wealth-producing powers from the infamous shackles of monopoly and subject them to the joint control of the producers, who, till now, allowed the very products of their hands to turn against them and be transformed into as many instruments of their own subjugation.

The labouring classes have conquered nature; they have now to conquer man. To succeed in this attempt they do not want strength but the organisation of their common strength . . .

Marx, *Letter to the Labour Parliament* (1854: 417)

After a thirty years' struggle, fought with most admirable perseverance, the English working classes . . . succeeded in carrying the Ten Hours Bill . . . [which] was not only a great practical success; it was the victory of a principle; it was the first time that in broad daylight the political economy of the middle class succumbed to the political economy of the working class.

But there was in store a still greater victory of the political economy of labour over the political economy of capital. We speak of the co-operative movement . . . The value of these great social experiments cannot be over-rated. By deed, instead of by argument, they have shown that production on a large scale, and in accord with the behests of modern science, may be carried on without the existence of a class of masters employing a class of hands; that to bear fruit the means of labour need not be monopolized as a means of dominion over, and extortion against, the labouring man himself; and that, like slave labour, like serf labour, hired labour is but a transitory and inferior form, destined to disappear before associated labour, plying its toil with a willing hand, a ready mind, and a joyous heart.

Marx, *Inaugural Address* of the International Working Men's Association, St Martin's Hall, Long Acre, London, 28 September 1864 (1864: 345–7)

. . . state power forms in fact the creation of the middle class, first a means to break down feudalism, then a means to crush the emancipatory aspirations of the producers, of the working class. All reactions and all revolutions had only served to transfer that organized power – that organized force of the slavery of labour – from one hand to the other, from one fraction of the ruling classes to the other . . . [The Commune] was, therefore, a Revolution not against this or that, legitimate, constitutional, republican or Imperialist form of State Power. It was a Revolution against the *State* itself, of this supernaturalist abortion of society, a resumption by the people for the people of its own social life. It was not a revolution to transfer it from one fraction of the ruling classes to the other, but a Revolution to break down this horrid machinery of Class-domination itself . . .

Such is the *Commune – the political form of the social emancipation* of the liberation of labour from the usurpations (slaveholding) of the monopolists of the means of labour, created by the labourers themselves or forming the gift of nature . . . The Commune does not [do] away with the class struggles, through which the working classes strive to the abolition of all classes, and, therefore, of [class rule] . . . but it affords the rational medium in which that class struggle can run through its different phases in the most rational and humane way. It could start violent reactions and as violent revolutions. It begins the *emancipation of labour* – its great goal – by doing away with the unproductive and mischievous of the state parasites, by cutting away the springs which sacrifice an immense portion of the national produce to the feeding of the statemonster on the one side, by doing, on the other, the real work of administration, local and national, for workingmen's wages. It begins therefore with an immense saving, with economical reform as well as political transformation.

Marx, *Civil War in France*: first draft (1871b: 165–6, 171–2)

. . . from the conception of history we have sketched we obtain these further conclusions: (1) In the development of productive forces there comes a stage when productive forces and means of intercourse are brought into being, which, under the existing relationships, only cause mischief, and are no longer productive but destructive forces (machinery and money); and connected with this a class is called forth, which has to bear all the burdens of society without enjoying its advantages, which, ousted from society, is forced into the most decided antagonism to all other classes; a class which forms the majority of all members of society, and from which emanates the consciousness of the necessity of a fundamental revolution, the communist consciousness, which may, of course, arise in the other classes too through the contemplation of the situation of this class. (2) The conditions under which definite productive forces can be applied, are the conditions of the rule of a definite class of society, whose social power, deriving from its property, has its *practical*-idealistic expression in each case in the form of the State; and, therefore, every revolutionary struggle is directed against a class, which till then has been in power. (3) In all revolutions up till now the mode of activity always remained unscathed and it was only a question of a different distribution of this activity, a new distribution of labour to other persons, whilst the communist revolution is directed against the preceding *mode* of activity, does away with *labour*, and abolishes the rule of all classes with the classes themselves, because it is carried through by the class which no longer counts as a class in society, is not recognised as a class, and is in itself the expression of the dissolution of all classes, nationalities, etc., within present society; and (4) Both for the production on a mass scale of this communist consciousness, and for the success of the cause itself, the alteration of men on a mass scale is necessary, an alteration which can only take place in a practical movement, a *revolution*; this revolution is necessary, therefore, not only because the *ruling* class cannot be overthrown in any other way, but also because the class *overthrowing* it can only in a revolution succeed in ridding itself of all the muck of ages and become fitted to found society anew.

Marx and Engels, *The German Ideology* (1846a: 86–7)

What we have to deal with here is a communist society, not as it has *developed* on its own foundations, but, on the contrary, just as it *emerges* from capitalist society; which is thus in every respect, economically, morally and intellectually, still stamped with the birth marks of the old society from whose womb it emerges . . .

Between capitalist and communist society lies the period of the revolutionary transformation of the one into the other. Corresponding to this is also a political transition period in which the state can be nothing but *the revolutionary dictatorship of the proletariat.*

Marx, *Critique of the Gotha Programme* (1875: *MESW*, 323, 331)

Our doctrine – said Engels, referring to himself and his famous friend – is not a dogma, but a guide to action. This classical statement stresses with remarkable force and expressiveness that aspect of Marxism which is constantly being lost sight of. And by losing sight of it, we turn Marxism into something one-sided, disfigured and lifeless; we deprive it of its living soul; we undermine its basic theoretical foundations – dialectics, the doctrine that historical development is all-embracing and full of contradictions; we sever its connection with the definite practical task of the epoch, which may change with every new turn of history.

Lenin, *Certain features of the historical development of Marxism* (1910: 39)

Notes

INTRODUCTION

1. Our citations refer to the bibliography for fuller details of the sources we have used. The citation will consist of three parts: for example (Marx, 1867a: 715) refers to a book by Marx, written or published in 1867, to the 715th page of that book. If the next reference is to the same book we will use simply (ibid., 716) meaning the same author, the same title, page 716. A full explanation of the bibliographical arrangement is given with the Bibliography.

CHAPTER 1

1. This chapter represents a condensation of arguments we have developed at length elsewhere. See, in particular, Corrigan, 1976, Ch. 2; Corrigan and Sayer, 1975; Ramsay, 1976; and Sayer, 1975a, 1975b, and 1977.
2. In using the plural 'men' here and elsewhere Marx and Engels do not intend denying the productive power of women in making history, as their remarks on the family (1846a: 44, i.e. five pages beyond the passage cited) make clear. The point may seem too obvious to bear mention; but historical experience both negative and positive has shown that without specific organisations 'armed' for struggle against them, socialist construction will be deformed by the reproduction of capitalist definitions of *some* people as less than fully human.
3. Cf. Marx, 1863a: 285, where he relates spiritual production, the structure of society, and human beings' relation to nature to 'the *definite historical* form' of material production.
4. As, e.g., in his 1847b: 28.
5. Cf. Marx, 1858a: 706, where he describes 'forces of production and social relations' as 'two different sides of the development of the social individual' (and goes on to speak of 'general social knowledge' as 'a *direct force of production*').
6. Cf. Anderson, 1974a: 204f.; Balibar, in Althusser and Balibar, 1968: 233f.
7. For a critique of this 'theory of productive forces' see the post-1967 texts of Charles Bettelheim as listed in our Bibliography; and *Three Major Struggles on China's Philosophical Front*, Peking FLP 1973.
8. In, principally, his 1890b,c and 1894f.

9. Sayer, 1975a: 791f.
10. This empirical criterion is likewise insisted upon in Marx and Engels, 1846a: 31, 38, 40. It was no mere 'early' phenomenon; cf. Marx, 1865a: 792 (which calls for 'analysis of the empirically given circumstances') or his 1880 *passim.*
11. Cf. Corrigan, 1976: Ch. 2; Hal Draper's texts; R. N. Hunt, 1974; Chang, 1931.
12. 'In each historical epoch, property has developed differently and under a set of entirely different social relations. Thus to define bourgeois property is nothing else than *to give an exposition of all the social relations of bourgeois production.* To try to give a definition of property as of an independent relation, a category apart, an abstract and eternal idea, can be nothing but an illusion of metaphysics or jurisprudence' (Marx, 1847a: 154, emphasis added). Compare the analysis in his 1858a: 491f.
13. In 1890 Engels wrote: 'Force (that is State power) is also an economic power' (Engels, 1890c). This is elaborated in his 1888, expanding earlier sketches in the first edition of *Anti-Duhring*. Cf. Marx, 1867a: 751, quoted below, p. 11.
14. Cf. Marx, 1868.
15. Cf. Corrigan and Gillespie, 1974.
16. On Marx's ambiguities see Colletti, 1974: 40f.
17. Thus Marx (and Engels) wrote, for example: 'the communist revolution, which removes the division of labour, ultimately abolishes political institutions . . .' (1846a: 427; cf. ibid., 96). Colletti, op. cit., grasps this essential point of continuity between the 1843 *Critique* and *The Civil War in France.*
18. Marx, 1867a: 72–3.
19. See Engels, 1894a: Pt. III, Ch. III, and Marx and Engels, 1846a, Pt. I, *passim.*
20. Cf. Marx and Engels, 1846a: 96, 427.
21. Cf. Marx, 1850a: 330. This is *not* to be confused with Trotsky's concept of permanent revolution, on which we comment at length in Ch. 3 below.
22. Cf. Marx, 1857: 85–8.
23. Our account of Marx's 'appearance/essence' distinction owes much to G. A. Cohen (1972), Geras (1971) and Mepham (1972); see also Godelier, 1964a. For elaboration, see Sayer, 1975b: Ch. 1.
24. Cf., *inter alia*, Marx, 1867a: 77, 236f., 539–40, 568f.; 1865a: 790f.; 1863c: 484; 1865b: sect. IX.
25. Compare, for example, the *apriorism* of Althusser and Balibar, 1968, or Hindess and Hirst, 1975.
26. Discussed in Sayer, 1975b: 147–70.
27. See Sayer, loc. cit.
28. Ch. XXIV of Dent ed.
29. Further criticism of the lunacy may be found in Anderson, 1976.
30. See, conversely, Marx's 'Seventh and Last Observation' on 'The Metaphysics of Political Economy' in his 1847b: 120f.
31. We elaborate this thesis in Corrigan and Sayer, 1975.

32. Cf. Sayer, 1975b: Ch. 1, for fuller discussion.
33. What is too often overlooked here is the way the passage continues: 'The ruling ideas are nothing more than the ideal expression of the dominant material relationships, the dominant material relationships grasped as ideas; hence of the relationships which make the one class the ruling one, therefore, the ideas of its dominance' – a position thoroughly consonant with the analysis we develop below.
34. Sayer, 1975b: Ch. 1, Sects. 2 and 3, discusses in detail Marx's attempts to do this in connection with, respectively, fetishistic theories of value and the trinity formula.
35. Largely because of the seminal articles of Geras and Mepham referred to above, which rightly take this analysis as paradigmatic.
36. And that of his family, since we are talking of the manufacture of a *class*. See Marx, 1867a: 170f.
37. See Marx, 1867a: ch. XIX.
38. Cf. Marx and Engels, 1846a: 83–4; Marx, 1863a: 389, *et seq.*
39. Marx, 1865a: 830.

CHAPTER 2

1. See especially Marx, 1871b: 171–2 (quoted in 'A Restatement', below p. 160); Mao, 1964a, 2nd thesis.
2. We document the Trotsky/Stalin debate in Ch. 3, and the CPC/CPSU polemic in Ch. 5. We comment briefly upon one central debate within the Trotskyist movement, that between Mandel and the theorists of the SWP, and provide relevant references in Ch. 3 nn. 59 and 60 and in Ch. 6.
3. This concept, which was Khrushchev's, was central to the CPC/CPSU polemic of the early 1960s. See CPC, 1965, and 1964, which contain the key CPC documents.
4. It is important here to indicate two significant, though partial, exceptions to the charges which follow. The first is the post-1967 work of Charles Bettelheim, which we discuss briefly in Chapter 6 and in more detail elsewhere (Corrigan, 1976b, Ramsay, 1977). Despite our substantial disagreements with Bettelheim over his claim that capitalism has 'now' been restored in the USSR we owe him much. The second exception is Louis Althusser. Recently, beginning with his 1972 reply to John Lewis in *Marxism Today*, Althusser has shown how he has sought to relate the positive and negative experiences of what he (mis)construes as the 'Stalinian deviation', and the Great Proletarian Cultural Revolution. Unlike Althusser, we see this 'deviation' as rooted in Bolshevism as such. But he must be applauded for seeing in it 'the *posthumous revenge of the Second International*' (1972a: 89), and for recognising that 'the only *historically existing* (left) "critique" of the fundamentals of the "Stalinian deviation" to be found . . . is a concrete critique, one that exists in the facts, in the struggle, in the line, in the practices, their principles and their forms, of the Chinese Revolution' (1972b: 92). This is also the place to mention the impressive CPC critique of what is misunderstood as 'Stalinism'; see Mao,

1956c, and CPC, 1965 and other texts noted in later chapters. We have drawn much from here also, notwithstanding our *total* disagreement with subsequent CPC pronouncements on the USSR (on which we elaborate in Chapters 5 and 6). None the less, *all* these materials are uniformly blind to *Bolshevism*.

5. E.g., at length in his 1920b: II–IV.
6. Thus, for instance, Althusser writes of science that 'it can only pose problems on the terrain and within the horizon of a definite theoretical structure, its problematic, which constitutes its absolute and definite condition of possibility, and hence the absolute determination of *the forms in which all problems must be posed* . . .'. This implies that 'any object or problem situated on the terrain and within the horizon, i.e. in the definite structured field of the theoretical problematic of a given theoretical discipline, is visible', while 'the same connexion that defines the visible also defines the invisible as its shadowy obverse. It is the field of the problematic that defines and structures the invisible as the defined excluded, *excluded* from the field of visibility and *defined* as excluded by the existence and peculiar structure of the field of the problematic' (Althusser and Balibar, 1968: 25–6). Like Althusser we identify a problematic as an implicit framework which renders a particular set of practices possible and in the same operation *excludes* others. We would also, however, stress a point which Althusser concedes only for *ideology*: 'to think the unity of a determinate ideological unity . . . by means of the concept of its *problematic* is to allow the *typical systematic structure* unifying all the elements of the thought to be brought to light, and therefore to discover in this unity a *determinate content* which makes it possible both to conceive the *meaning* of the "elements" of the ideology concerned – *and to relate this ideology to the problems left or posed to every thinker by the historical period in which he lives*' (Althusser, 1961: 67). Despite such good intentions Althusser tends far too often to treat 'scientific' problematics (and revolutions) in particular as merely ideational, rather than social, structures and events.
7. On the marxism of the Second International, Colletti, 1968, is a sustained critique; see also Lukács, 1924, and 1925 (which latter is a critique of Bukharin, 1921, and should be read with Gramsci's criticisms of the same text in his 1934a: 419f.), and Goldmann, 1971. Rubin's polemic against technicist accounts of marxist economics in his 1928 is also directly relevant here and cannot be praised too highly. More general theoretical resources for a critique of this impoverished marxism include Ollman, 1971, with its exposition of the *internal* relatedness of all that the theorists of the Second International separated. On the roots in the later Engels, see G. S. Jones, 1973, and Hodges, 1965. The important difference between Engels's and Marx's criticisms of Hegel, which is pertinent here though not discussed in our text, is clarified in McLellan, 1969. The best critique of the 'theory of productive forces' has been developed within the CPC; see Li Cheng, 1973, *Three Major Struggles on China's Philosophical Front*, Peking 1973, First Essay, and, more broadly, the texts of the CPC/CPSU polemic within which this was a key implicit issue. Relatedly, see the post-1967 work of Charles Bettelheim, *passim*, and note the complementary remarks of

Balibar, in Althusser and Balibar, 1968: 233f., and Anderson, 1974a: 204f. The recent publication of Marx, 1866, abundantly confirms these authors' central contention. Finally, by way of a 'corrective' to the overwhelmingly negative appraisal of Second International marxism presented in both our text and these sources, it is worth stressing, with Anderson, 1974c: Ch. 1, that notwithstanding its undoubted limitations this marxism actually *engaged* politically and theoretically with capitalism to a far greater extent than has most of the 'Western marxism' produced subsequently, which has all too often retreated, both metaphorically and literally, into the ivory towers of academia.

8. Marx's *Critique of Hegel's Philosophy of Right* (1843b) was first published in 1927, his *Paris Manuscripts* (1844c) and his and Engels's *The German Ideology* (1846a) in 1932, and the first draft of *Capital*, the *Grundrisse* (1858a) in a limited edition in 1939–41. The first accurate and complete edition of Volume 4 of *Capital, Theories of Surplus Value* (1863a,b,c), was published in three parts between 1956 and 1966. This is of course to mention only major texts; numerous articles, letters, drafts and preparatory and manuscript materials likewise remained long buried. To take an example very pertinent to the theses argued in this book, the two drafts of Marx's *Civil War in France* (1871b and c), a text on which we have drawn heavily, were not published until 1934. A good deal of Marx's work, for example his extensive notes on mathematics, natural science and technology reported by Professor E. Colman in his 1931, have yet to see the light of day. It is worth pondering the fact that *none* of this material was available to Lenin and the early Bolsheviks.
9. Speaking of this text in the 1920s, Ryazanov said: 'All the young Marxists, who entered the public arena in the early eighties – Bernstein, Kautsky, Plekhanov – were brought up on [*Anti-Duhring*]' (cit. G. S. Jones, 1973: 19). Lenin considered it 'wonderfully rich and instructive' (MESW, 20). In 1936 it was still spoken of thus: 'This book has played an enormous role in the development and propagation of marxism, and is to this day one of the best expositions of its principles' (Lenin, *Selected Works*, 4, Moscow 1936, p. 448, editorial note).
10. The notion was originally Joseph Deitzgen's. See Buick, 1975.
11. See his 1886a: 62f. and *passim* (but note this was *not* published until 1925), and 1894a: 26–31, and *passim.*
12. Principally *The German Ideology*. See Sayer, 1975b: Ch. 1, sect. 1.
13. Plekhanov's *Notes* to Engels's *Ludwig Feuerbach* (with Peking ed. of the latter) are revealing on these issues. See also his 1895.
14. Both Althusser and Balibar, 1968: Part 1, and Colletti (1968) make pertinent criticisms here, though their remedies differ radically.
15. This unfortunate analogy was also prefigured in Engels. See his 1883a.
16. Lenin quotes this proposition in *What is to be Done?*, and it is central to the distinction between 'Trade Union' and 'political' consciousness, and the consequent view of the form and role of the revolutionary Party, which that work develops. When the latter was republished, Lenin made no changes, but – importantly – stated that the text 'controversially corrects Economism, but it would be wrong to study its contents outside this task'

(LSW (1936), 2: 501). This is consonant with what we identify later in this chapter as a progressive break on Lenin's part with Kautsky's epistemological legacy. In view of this it is disturbing to realise the extent to which *What is to be Done?* continues to provide marxists with a paradigm for what is equally disturbingly construed as *merely* a theory of organisation; see, for example, Mandel, 1971. Here, in our view, lies one of Mao's greatest advances: the epistemology elaborated in his *On Practice* (1937b) and the 'mass-line' conception of Party work it sustains. We amplify this in Chapter 4 below.

17. This theory has been superbly criticised in the PRC. See, in particular, Li Cheng, 1973, and *Three Major Struggles on China's Philosophical Front*, Peking, FLP, 1973. See also the work of Charles Bettelheim since 1967.
18. In particular, the divisions between town and country, agriculture and industry, and mental and manual labour – the 'Three Great Differences', as they are referred to in China.
19. On Tsarist Russia see, apart from the relevant works of Lenin and Trotsky as cited in this and the next chapter, Carr, 1950: Part 1, and Anderson, 1974b: Part II ch. 6, for a short account. More extended or specific discussions include the following: on Tsarist 'development', Brutzkus, 1934, Falkus, 1972, Grossman, 1971, Kemp, 1969, Shanin, 1972: 17f., Sontag, 1968, *Tsarist Takeoff*; on the relatedness of 'agrarian' and 'industrial sectors', Rimlinger, 1960, 1961, Von Laue, 1961, Walkin, 1954, Yaney, 1971, Zelnick, 1968; on Stolypin's reforms, Gerschenkron, 1964, Haimson, 1964, Shanin, 1972: 37, Wolf, 1969, Yaney, 1971; on the peasantry and peasant movements more generally, Owen, 1937, Perrie, 1972, G. T. Robinson, 1932, Shanin, 1971c, 1972, Watters, 1968, Wolf, 1969. One should also, as it were, read Male or Lewin retrospectively. On the Tsarist State and its policies, see Alston, 1969, Pipes, 1974b, Sinel, 1968, 1973, Starr, 1972, Yaney, 1974; on the Russian revolutionary movement, marxist and otherwise, Baron, 1953, Cliff, 1975, Haimson, 1974, Lane, 1968, Lichteim, 1970, Liebman, 1973, Perrie, 1976, Walicki, 1969.
20. Shanin (1972: 17) argues that the Tsarist economy was on the edge of an 'extended downward turn' in 1913/14; Grossman (1971: 487) amongst many others argues that 'real development' was taking place. In an important sense both are correct; *capitalist* development is always uneven, moving forward in fits and starts. Further, such development always involves active underdevelopment.
21. See e.g., Mao, 1926, 1927, 1928, 1939c.
22. The concept 'pre-capitalist' (and *a fortiori* the peasant/wage labourer and enclave/hinterland notions employed in the next few pages) are liable to be *extremely* misleading unless taken in the context of our insistence that Tsarist development *itself* reproduced social relations of the sort conventionally seen as merely 'backward'. That this is the *normal* path of capitalist development is a point we have argued in detail elsewhere (Corrigan, 1977).
23. See Anderson, 1974b: 347f.
24. See amongst others Falkus, 1972: ch. 9; Grossman, 1971: 492f.; Shanin, 1972: 17f.; *Tsarist Takeoff*.

25. And often, though by no means always, technically sophisticated.
26. See Kemp, 1969; Anderson, 1974b: 352–3; and, for an exemplary early Bolshevik analysis, Trotsky, 1909b: chs 1–4.
27. Anderson's account of the tensions between the Tsarist Ministries of the Interior and Finance (1974b: 357) is revealing on this contradiction. On the political structures of Tsarist rule more generally, see ibid., 353f. (and the related comments in his 1976); Pipes, 1974b; Yaney, 1974.
28. 'Some ten or so revolutionaries shared in the founding of the old *Iskra* in 1900, and only about forty attended the birth of Bolshevism at the illegal congresses in Brussels and London in 1903. In 1912–13, when the legal Bolshevik *Pravda* came into being it had the support of hundreds of thousands of workers . . . In November 1917, nine million electors out of a total of thirty-six million voted for the Bolsheviks in the elections to the Constituent Assembly' (Lenin, 1922e: 350–1. Cf. his 1920b).
29. Carr, 1950: 19f. provides a useful summary. For fuller reference see n. 19 above.
30. More precisely, sections of them; *narodnism* was a heterogeneous movement, not a unitary Party.
31. The central works here are, of course, those of Lenin (e.g. 1922e) and Trotsky (e.g. 1930b), plus many of those cited in n. 19 above and throughout the next chapter. Again, Carr (1950: Part 1) provides a useful sketch.
32. Trotsky did not of course join the Bolshevik Party until 1917; but, as we argue in Chapter 3, his thought lies very much within the Bolshevik problematic none the less. It is in this sense that we take various of his pronouncements as being representatively Bolshevik here and elsewhere in this chapter.
33. *Above all* in his *What is to be Done?* (1902: Pt. 4). The historical rootedness of the 'model' of Party organisation in this text cannot be overemphasised. On Lenin's (and our own) further reservations, see n. 16 above.
34. For documentation see n. 1 above.
35. Compare Marx and Engels, 1846a: 86–7, quoted in 'A Restatement', below p. 161.
36. Carr is very perceptive here, and points to an enduring tendency in the whole Trotskyist tradition. We argue in Chapter 3 that it is in emphases of this kind that Trotsky, to a greater extent than *any other* prominent Bolshevik, reveals his roots in the Second International's 'theory of productive forces'. The tenacity of this theory in modern Trotskyism is perhaps expressed best in the SWP analysis of China, which denies that a proletarian revolution ever took place in that country (it being *a priori* too 'backward')! See *International Socialism*, 92. In view of this Trotskyist claims to present *the* socialist alternative to the practices which fettered socialism in the USSR must be seen as more than a little ironic.
37. In important ways for socialism, given the crude technicism on which Trotsky's internationalism in the end rested. We exemplify this distinction between Stalin and Trotsky in Chapter 3.
38. Lenin, 1918b: 259. Compare Trotsky, 1920a: 121.
39. We lack space here to substantiate this assertion. But the rootedness of both

Bukharin's 'Enrich yourselves!' and Preobazhensky's 'primitive socialist accumulation' within the Bolshevik problematic as outlined here should be sufficiently evident. Both see 'development' in capitalist terms and both suppose the capacity of the socialist State to hold its capitalist consequences in check. We record various other congruences in the notes to Chapter 3. It follows that the challenge we believe historical experience poses to Bolshevism as such applies *a fortiori* to these as much as to its other variants.

40. And also – demonstrating how long the struggle to transcend the limitations in Bolshevism will be – it is present in the CPC notion of the 'relative autonomy' of the State as regards foreign policy and foreign trade, in the PRC, with very similar consequences. See Chapter 5 below.

41. As one of us has argued at length (Ramsay, 1973b, 1974, 1976) the concept of rationality, as related by bourgeois intellectuals to production, is of no little significance when it recurs in Soviet and other Bolshevik writing. It comes here under the general heading of 'economic rationality', and is an integral part of 'socialist economics'. In common with their bourgeois counterparts, and in a manner which reproduces in its most categorical form the separation of 'base' and 'superstructure' (the 'economics' and 'politics' of their bourgeois acclaimants), these writers wrench production as an activity into a realm populated only by objects, objects which can then be optimally organised in the name of a purportedly politically neutral deity named efficiency. Its close affinity to belief in Taylorism as a mechanism transferrable to socialist organisation of human resources, where political impact is seen as zero since political power has already been captured, has been noted. This conception of economic rationality can be found to pervade not only the work of Soviet and East European (or Tengist in the PRC) 'economists' but also the official pronouncements of political leaders on production in countless cases (see e.g. Brezhnev addressing the 24th or 25th Congresses of the CPSU for countless examples). It informs the whole logic of the 1965 Soviet reforms and their counterparts in the other CMEA countries. Therein the problem becomes one of methods of administrative regulation rather than of social relations; and this too, of course, slavishly echoes the judgements of Western analysts, who represent a particularly effective imperialist force in this respect.

   The existence of such an absolute (hence politically neutral) concept of rationality has been undermined by the work of marxist anthropologists (e.g. Godelier, 1972, 1973; Sahlins, 1972). It is shattered, in our view, by any consideration of the lessons of socialist construction unhampered by the blinkers of bourgeois ideology (masquerading as 'pragmatism'). Thus relations of production come to be seen as a material force, as argued in Chapter 1; whilst capitalist rationality and efficiency are found to be internally related to a division of labour and to repressive controls which can only constrain and debilitate the realisation of that force. In short, the rationality of which the proponents of capitalism are so proud (in the face of all the absurd consequences which are the everyday result of real-world capitalism) is an ideology of that system and so carries its contradictions and its brutalities with it; it cannot be turned to the service of socialism, for it is a relation of socialism's antithesis. Nor can its 'development' be a formula for producing enough for all the people to eat.

42. On the significance of these, which provide the context in which our criticisms are made, see Chapter 6.
43. We deal briefly with this extremely un-marxist style of analysis, and provide relevant documentation, in Chapter 6.
44. This is merely a suspicion; but certain of the so-called 'crimes' with which Lin Piao, and subsequently the Gang of Four have been charged appear to exhibit a certain *dogmatic* notion of putting politics in command which effectively does counterpose the political to the productive. At the same time it is *crucial* that we ask ourselves who is making such charges, and what alternatives are proposed. 'Ultraleftism' is a capacious and a dangerous concept. We recall Charles Bettelheim, in the *Postscript* to his 1973, warning against the ultraleftism of those who were attacking eight-grade wage-scales in the PRC. Three years later Mao was to issue instructions urging the people of China to do just that. This once again illustrates the complexities of class struggle under the dictatorship of the proletariat, and the foolhardiness of relinquishing marxism for blind faith in a ruling Party's policies whatever their shifts of line. We need analysis, not apologetics.

CHAPTER 3

1. Welcome – if still far from satisfactory – moves in the right direction are to be found in recent work by Liebman, 1973 (cf. Mandel, 1975) and Cliff, 1975. Cf. Bettelheim, 1974; Harding, 1976.
2. Lenin, 1917c; first published in *Pravda* (18) 22 January 1925. Cf. the more famous formulations in Lenin, 1923 texts.
3. Lenin, 1899 – cf. Harding, 1975; A. Hunt, 1976. Lenin's agrarian theses 1907b and 1908b were not published until 1917 and 1918, but they and the notebooks of 1900–16 (1916a) warrant much study.
4. Lenin, 1918b; we now have the draft version, 1918ba, and his important Six Theses from it, 1918bb; Lenin defended it against *Kommunist* critics in his 1918c.
5. On the use of experts cf. Lenin 1917f; 1919c; 1921b.
6. Note to the crucial set of texts *Lenin on the Soviet State Apparatus* (Moscow 1969) p. 442; see also note 26 in Lenin's *What is Soviet Power?* (Moscow 1973: 101) and note 302 to the one volume *Selected Works*.
7. On these conferences compare Day, 1973, pp. 51–65; Carr, 1953, ch. 29; Deutscher, 1959, ch. 1. The recent biography of Hammer (Considine, 1975) provides a mass of empirical data on this, as does Vol. 45 of Lenin's *Collected Works*. For example, on 22 May 1922 Lenin, with Stalin's approval, issued extra concessions to Hammer, because the latter's Allied American Co. was 'to be distinguished from the usual capitalist companies in that it is well disposed towards the Soviet Union' (*CW*, 37: 365). Trotsky not only agreed to supply Soviet troops to guard Hammer's property, he also urged Hammer to tell other capitalists to invest in Russia because

'capital was safer there than anywhere else because Russia, no longer in ferment, would adhere to any agreements it might make' (cf. Considine, pp. 36f.). Brezhnev, 1972, 1974, and Chossudovsky, 1973, make use of these and similar formulations from Lenin, for Détente (cf. *Observer Business News*, 30 June 1974).

8. Cf. Carr, 1964: ch. 44; Jackson, 1966; 1974. On Comintern peasant politics see Ho, 1928; Mao, 1964b: 218.
9. Marx, 1877; 1881a, b; cf. Engels, 1875; 1894b; Weintraub, 1949; Duggett, 1972, 1975; E. H. Carr, 1952: 381f.; Walicki, 1969; and issues of *Journal of Peasant Studies*, 1973 onwards.
10. Owen, 1937; Perrie, 1972; Gerschenkron, 1964; Haimson, 1964; Shanin, 1972; Yaney, 1971; Wolf, 1969.
11. The seven theses of Lenin here are a classical statement of capitalist modernisation, based on increasing The Three Great Differences which manifest the division of labour.
12. Lenin, 1920a. Cf. his 1907b, 1908b, 1916a; 1917e, g, h; 1919d; 1921b.
13. Akhapkin, 1970: 24. The distance of Bolshevism from the reality and experience of agrarian production can be seen from Lane, 1968, and the minutes of the CC itself 1917–18, Institute, 1958; the confusion and chaos of the latter should always be remembered, cf. *Lenin on the Soviet State Apparatus*. For a very good set of documents, McCauley, 1975.
14. Cf. Stalin, 1925; 1928b.
15. On Bukharin, see Dallemagne, 1975, and the contrasting reviews of S. F. Cohen, 1974, by Carr, 1974, and Liebman, 1975. On Bukharin's Marxism cf. Lenin, 1920d; 1921a; Lukács, 1925; Gramsci, 1934a: 419f., and S. F. Cohen, 1970.
16. Cf. Stuart, 1971; 1972; Matthews, 1972: 154; Salisbury, 1973: 89 and *Inside a People's Commune* (Peking, FLP, 1974).
17. Goodey, 1974; Brinton, 1975; Goodey, 1975; Solomos, 1976.
18. Gershberg, 1973.
19. Lenin, 1920d; 1921a; Carr, 1952: 224f.; Deutscher, 1954; 502f.; Bettelheim, 1974; Solomos, 1976.
20. The letter was published in 1924; there are many similar texts in *Lenin on the Soviet State Apparatus*.
21. Similar clashes may be detected in the useful collection of Lenin: *What is Soviet Power?*
22. For complementary and contrasting analysis cf. Bettelheim, 1974 – and reviews by Miliband, 1975; Sweezy, 1974; Lockett, 1975; Ticktin, 1976, and Liebman, 1973.
23. See Trotsky, 1927a: chs. 11 and 12; 1927b; 1929a; 1929b: chs. 12, 14, 28, 31, 36–42 and *passim*; 1930a; 1930c; 1940a.
24. Writings on 1905 considered here: Trotsky, 1906; 1907; 1908; 1909a, b; 1915; 1922a. This material is reviewed extensively, and its conclusions defended in 1930a. 1940a is a summary of the differences between the positions of Lenin (pre-1917), Trotsky and the Mensheviks on 1905. Trotsky's analysis of the pecularities of Russian capitalism is best expounded in his 1909b: chs 1–4; see also 1906: chs 1–4; 1919c; 1922a; 1930b: ch. 1. 1908, 1909a, 1919c and 1922a contain strident critiques of

'that spurious Marxism which nourishes itself on historical clichés and formal analogies' together with a plea for detailed materialist analysis. The theory of permanent revolution is most fully presented in 1930a, with its main propositions summarised as ch. 10; see also 1906, 1909a, 1940a.

25. The need for moving over to socialist tasks and the ensuing contradictions are detailed by Trotsky in his 1906; especially ch. 6, but also chs 8 and 9; and in the critique of Lenin's formula of the 'democratic dictatorship of the proletariat and peasantry' contained in his 1909: sections VI and VII. Trotsky is absolutely emphatic, in his early work, on the dependence of the Russian on the international revolution: see his 1906: 237, 247; 1909a: 325 (quoting from his own 1905 Preface to Lassalle's *Speech before a Jury*), 332–3. In his 1906 Trotsky stresses that socialist policies will come up against 'political obstacles' before 'the technical backwardness of the country' (1906: 237); in his 1909a he defines the principal contradiction as between 'the low level of productive forces and the hegemony of the working classes' (1909a: 329); 'the country's economic backwardness' will prevent solution of 'the objective problems of socialism' (ibid., 332). Trotsky maintained this view when in power: see, e.g. 1921b: 306.
26. See also Trotsky, 1908: 307, where Tscherewanin is accused of substituting 'formalist deduction' for 'materialist analysis of social relations', which takes up 'the most important question; the question of the actual inner social forces and class mechanisms of a bourgeois revolution.'
27. This is evident from *all* Trotsky's writings on 1905; but see especially 1907 and the fuller 1909a, in which Trotsky's differences with Lenin are clearly spelt out. See also 1930a: Introduction to Russian edition and ch. 3; 1930e: 354f.
28. See Trotsky, TP, 2, document 510. Trotsky's proposals to the Central Committee are appended to 1923b: ch. 6. The incident is described in 1929: 463f.
29. See, for example, 1920c: 138–9; 1921h: 157; 1921c: 214, 223.
30. See, for example, Trotsky, 1906: 202–3; 1919b: 40–1; 1920a.
31. It is worth listing some of Trotsky's descriptions of peasants: 'political barbarism, social formlessness, primitiveness and lack of character' (1906: 208); 'primitiveness and petty-bourgeois character, . . . limited rural outlook, . . . isolation from world-political ties and allegiances' (ibid., 209); 'local cretinism is history's curse on all peasant riots' (1909b: 65); 'Dispersed, cut off from the cities which were the nerve-centres of politics and culture, dull-minded, its intellectual horizons hemmed in like its meadows and fields, indifferent towards everything that the cities had created by invention and thought . . .' (ibid., 70); 'the dull-wittedness of the muzhik' (ibid., 73); 'grey illiterates of the infantry' (ibid., 222); 'backwardness and distrustful passivity of the muzhik-soldier' (ibid., 224); 'the peasant . . . who still cannot see beyond the spires of his village church . . . social layers thrust back by capitalism away from the mainstream of development' (1919a: 26).
32. See, particularly, Trotsky, 1906: ch. 6; 1930e: 354.
33. Note that in his 1909b Trotsky saw 'American-type farming', i.e. 'a free farming economy at a high technological level', as 'the only way' of solving

the 'agrarian problem' (1909b: 52); note also his view that even if there *had* been a revolution in the West, 'a retreat along the lines of the New Economic Policy would have been inevitable just the same' (1930e: 371).

34. Stated in many places, notably Trotsky (*et al.*), 1927a: 35; 1936: 38. See also the discussion in 1932: ch. 11.
35. The premises of Trotsky's internationalism and critique of socialism in one country are most explicitly set out in his 1928, Introduction to the German edition of 1930a, and 1930e; though they clearly permeate all his work. There can be little doubt of the *genuineness* of Trotsky's internationalism: *vide* his willingness to help Soviet Hungary by military means (TP, 1: documents 182, 188) or his stance on Brest-Litovsk (1929: ch. 31), and generally, his commitment to Comintern (CI, 1, 2: *passim*).
36. In 1939, in an essay called 'Presenting Karl Marx', Trotsky wrote: 'The programme of technocracy which flourished in the period of the Great Crisis of 1929–32 was founded on the correct premise that economy can be rationalised only through the union of technique at the service of science and government at the service of society. Such a union is possible, provided technique and government are liberated from the slavery of private ownership. That is where the great revolutionary task begins. In order to liberate technique from the cabal of private interests and place the government at the service of society, it is necessary to "expropriate the expropriators". Only a powerful class, interested in its own liberation and opposed to the monopolistic expropriators, is capable of consummating this task. Only in unison with a proletarian government can the qualified stratum of technicians build a truly scientific and a truly national, i.e. a socialist economy' (1939f.: 41–2). This should be read in the context of (*a*) Trotsky's reply to Kollontai's criticisms of technocracy in his 1921f.; and (*b*) his *own* awareness of the contribution of this modernisation strategy to 'degeneration', discussed below.
37. . . . 'if we analyse capitalism in the spirit of Marx's genuine teachings, . . . then the development of Russian capitalism *with all its peculiarities* will appear wholly "natural", as an *indispensable, component part of the world capitalist process*' (Trotsky, 1919c: 55–6, our emphasis).
38. Compare the incredibly abstract, hazy and banal formulation of 1930a: 24 with, for example, the very much more precise (because historically grounded) formulation of 1919c: 55–6, partly quoted in previous note.
39. For a typical formulation of Trotsky's 'relative autonomy' variant of the distinction, see 1919c: 53; 1921a: 293–5; 1940d: 148–9. Note that he instructively defines *revolution* as 'part of the superstructure', which *ipso facto* does not do away with the hegemony of 'the laws of world economy' (1930a: 30).
40. See Trotsky, 1922c: 13–14, in which Trotsky (following Lenin) distinguishes state capitalism (a bad thing) from state 'capitalism' (a good thing) solely on the grounds of *control*; providing that it is the proletarian state which controls enterprises which are 'capitalist' (in the sense that they 'operate along commercial lines based on the market') 'the more our "state capitalism" develops . . . the firmer will become the foundation of socialism'. See also his 1933: 16–18.

41. Principally, Trotsky, 1923b, 1925, 1927a, b, 1928.
42. The decimation of the proletariat during the Civil War is particularly stressed, especially in the *Revolution Betrayed* account. See 1923b: 12–15 on immediate pressures for the 'internal dictatorship of the Old Guard'; 1936: ch. 5 for the fuller account of Trotsky's hindsight, where 'backwardness' plays a much heavier role. It is disturbing to realise the extent to which this crude proportionalist methodology is accepted by marxists: cf. Deutscher, 1959: ch. 1; Harman, 1969, 1971; Sweezy, 1971: 51 and fn.
43. See Trotsky, 1923b: 22: 'In the last analysis, the question will be resolved by two great factors of international importance: the course of the revolution in Europe and the rapidity of our economic development.' See also ibid.: ch. 4, 40, 46 and *passim.*
44. This assertion totally dominates the perspectives set out in *Whither Russia?* (Trotsky, 1925, *passim*).
45. See also 1923b: 40–2, 85–6; and 1927a, chs 1, 4 and *passim.*
46. See especially Trotsky, 1923b: 42, and Appendix 3; 1927a: 3, 27, 37, 42–3, 100–1.
47. Trotsky, 1932: 156–9; 1936: 40–1.
48. This text is saturated with Trotsky's statist brand of voluntaristic optimism. See also pp. 29–30 (the State and 'peasant' economy) and 43–5 (the State and the world market); on the latter, see also 1921f. In both cases Trotsky assumes that Bolshevik control of the State will damp down the contradictions attendant upon utilising capitalism for socialist construction.
49. See, especially, the proposals on 'the situation of the working class and the trade unions' (Trotsky, 1927a: 19–24) and 'the agrarian question and socialist construction' (ibid., 30–4). In both cases, fiscal redistribution plays a key role. On this, see also 1925: 44; 1936: 75. The main point about fiscalism is its locus in *distribution* rather than *production.* For to attempt 'socialist' distribution of wealth without transforming its mode of *production* is likely to lead to the worst of all possible worlds, in both political and productive terms. But again Trotsky envisages State activity as a substitute for or more accurately the main form of class struggle. These proposals contain *nothing* about workers' control; indeed, particularly in regard to trade unions, they largely presuppose the persistence of wage relations, of managerial structures, etc., characteristic of capitalism.

    We have shown above how Lenin endorsed this State machinery of judicial and fiscal coercion and manipulation: of course Stalin politicised it, thoroughly, in 1929 and after. It was perhaps Stalin's greatest contribution to marxism to have made the Bolshevik apparatus so visible, thereby showing the problems to be *political* and not technical.
50. Trotsky's admiration for bourgeois 'technique' – regarded as utterly distinct from bourgeois social relations – and his corresponding stress on political control – as opposed to political forms – are perhaps most evident in his military policies and writings. Ironically, it is in this sphere, as 'maker of the Red Army', that he is most often celebrated. See, *inter alia,* his 1921j: 21; 1922b: 111. Compare Bettelheim, 1971: 45, and our ch. 4 below, on the PLA in China.
51. See, particularly, Trotsky 1925 *passim*; 1927a: ch. IV.

52. Trotsky, 1925: 40–1. See also Trotsky's technocratic dismissal of Kollontai's doubts about 'utilising' capitalist forces in his 1921f.
53. The analysis of 'degeneration' is most fully presented in Trotsky, 1936. See also, in particular, 1933: and, for defence and elaboration of the analysis against Laurat, Rizzi, Urbahns, Schachtman *et al.*, DM, *passim*.
54. The two are frequently coupled: 'In the last analysis the problem reduced itself to the isolation of the Soviet Republic and its backwardness' (Trotsky, 1930a: 366).
55. E.g. on peasantry, Trotsky, 1936: 39f., 74; proletariat, ibid., 89; politburo, ibid., 23–4; and Stalin, ibid., ch. 5, and above all the opening pages of Trotsky's *Stalin* (1940b). The tradition of summating the historical experience of the dictatorship of the proletariat by Stalin's 'Asiatic' qualities continues – see, e.g. Deutscher, 1949: 25f.; Colletti, 1970. A curious reiteration of Kautsky's notion of 'Tartar Communism': Kautsky, 1918, 1922.
56. See Trotsky, 1936: ch. 9; 1939a, b; and above all 1939e, and 1940d: 152–3.
57. On Urbahns and Laurat, see Trotsky, 1933; on Burnham and Rizzi, his 1939e.
58. What Trotsky means by this is clarified in his 1939b: 19f.; 1939c: 35f.; 1939d; 1940d: 158f.; 1940e: 219f.
59. Similarly with the work of his followers. See, for example, Mandel's excellent analysis of why, in the USSR and the People's Democracies of Eastern Europe, (*a*) there should be pressure towards 'market socialism'; and (*b*) this should meet with resistance from *both* the State machine *and* the working class (Mandel, 1969).
60. Kidron (1969) and Harman (1970) accuse Mandel of 'reifying' the Plan. Mandel, having defined production relations (correctly) as '*all* relations between producers which are indispensable for the "production of their material life" at a given level of development of productivity of human labour' (1970: 34), replies with the point that ' "Planning" . . . is a specific set of relations of production resulting from the suppression of private property in the means of production and the beginning of the withering away of commodity production, through which labour performed in collectively owned factories is recognised as immediately social labour' (ibid., 34). Mandel is of course right to define 'planning' as a set of social relations of production: but his formula remains 'algebraic'. The social relations are defined *negatively*: *not* private property, *not* commodity production. Were Mandel to attempt to provide a *positive* account of these production relations, he would be forced to specify the *kind* of planning involved, its institutional mechanisms, etc., in short the *content* of 'collective ownership'. And here, the nature of the State machine and Bolshevik productive strategy would be central. He would then be compelled, on his own definition of planning as a set of production relations, to recognise the persistence of class and two-line struggle *within* 'planning', rather than, as he tends to, simply *between* 'the Plan' and 'the Market'.
61. The CPC analysis of Stalin is a partial exception here. See many of Mao's texts in the *Wansui* collection, especially his 'Speech on the ten great relationships', his published *On the correct handling of contradictions* . . . and

his notes on Stalin's *Economic Problems*. Several texts in the *Unrehearsed* selection show a critique of Stalin (and the Comintern) which dates from the 1930s. For those materials see Chapter 4 below. Two texts of the polemic are also particularly crucial here: *On the question of Stalin* (1963) and *On Khrushchev's phoney communism* . . . (1964; the famous 'Ninth Reply' whose fifteen theses on socialist construction are by Mao Tse-tung). As the 1963 text states (p. 2): the question is really 'how to sum up the historical experience of the proletariat and of the International Communist Movement since Lenin's death.' Both texts are in CPC, 1965. Althusser has clarified the significance of wrong criticism of Stalin in his recent texts (collected in his 1976 book; of which see especially his 1972b: 92). On Mao and Stalin see Fernbach, 1974 and Gray, 1976a.

62. Likewise, for Pipes (1974a) Stalin is the 'pock-marked god', for Ignotus (1974) 'the Bolshevik Tsar', for Nove (1974a) 'Uncle Joe in command'. These, like Ratcliffe (1974), are all reviews of the almost simultaneously published commentaries of Hingley (1974), Tucker (1974) (the first of three volumes) and Ulam (1974). The Trotskyist combination of these two approaches is recognised and criticised in Miliband, 1973a: 378. Cf. M. Johnstone, 1968a: 123, and the texts by Krasso. Gramsci's refutation of the theory of permanent revolution is a masterful example of how to expose the essential fatalism of Trotsky's theories (Gramsci, 1934a: 241, and Carr, 1959: 56f.). Trotsky's defenders (e.g. Mandel, 1968b; Woods, 1969) perform a useful service in showing the adherence to a theory of productive forces of modern Trotskyism. In places, even Miliband seems to see nothing but 'inevitability' (1973a: 383).
63. Lenin, 1921c: 277.
64. But see Trotsky's own strictures on the limitations of this analogy in his 1933 (and the accompanying 'The Question of Thermidor . . .').
65. Cf. Marx, 1852b: 170 and 1871b: 228 (Draper ed., pp. 196f.). Generally see: 1871a: 165; 1871b: 230; and 1871c: 69f.
66. Cf. Stalin, 1924a, b; 1926; 1927c; 1937b.
67. Stalin (1924b: 91) quotes Lenin saying that Bolshevism is 'a model of tactics for all' (cf. Stalin, 1926: Part 2). On the Bolshevisation of the Comintern see Carr (1964: chs 27, 30) and Poulantzas's important analysis of Bolshevism's General Line (1970: 223f.). Mao and CPC resistance to Bolshevism as the theory of socialist revolution and construction is discussed in Chapter 4 below.
68. Carr, 1958: 205; 303f.; 1969: Ch. 1, Ch. 2, Ch. 3. Cf. Nove, 1962, 1969; Lewin, 1965, 1966; Shanin, 1971c, 1972; Male, 1971; Karcz, 1971. Carr, 1967, and Carr, 1969: Ch. 11 are both high-water marks in empirical history. We stress here the many warning signs given about agrarian production-politics: Kalinin in 1925 (cit. Male, 1971: 122; Lewin, 1966: 82); Kritsman in 1926 (cit. Carr, 1958: 255; 1969: 283–4, this analysis being vastly superior to that of Trotsky, cit. Carr, 1958: 380fn. 1); Molotov in 1927 (cit. Carr, 1959: 389; 1969: 36f.; Male, 1971: 123; Lewin, 1966: 184f.). The formation of the historic blocs referred to is best illustrated by Carr's volumes, but for a good local study on Kazakhstan see Lane, 1975.
69. Nove's point concerning the additional strains following the mid-twenties

shift from post-war 'reconstruction' to industrial *con*struction is relevant here. See his 1969: 138.

70. Cf. here, Mao, 1955, and Chapter 4 below.
71. In February 1925 a conference more or less abandoned the *kolkhozi*; certainly for the Ukraine (Carr, 1958: 238f.; the related Milyutin-Varga debates are entirely constrained within Bolshevism. Cf. ibid., 259f.). Lewin, Male and Carr also show a wealth of possible initiatives from below – including appeals for help from socialist collectives of peasants in *Pravda* (10 March 1928, cit. Lewin, 1966: 272) – and in the same year (*Bolshevik*, 6, 1928) it was possible for Zdanovich to advance the thesis of class struggle from within, by poor and middle peasants, to win over the communes to socialism (cf. Narkiewicz, 1970: 132). But 75 per cent of the communes and rural Soviets had no poor peasant (*bednyaki*) group at all and, most significantly of all, as Male reports: 'the Commune tractor was never tried . . .' (1971: 200).
72. Stalin's 1929b concludes: 'when we have put the USSR on an automobile, and the *muzhik* on a tractor, let the esteemed capitalists, who boast so loudly of their "civilisation", try to overtake us! We shall see which countries may then be "classified" as backward and which as advanced' (p. 305, published in *Pravda*, 7 November 1929). This, like much of what we document below, betrays those very Bolshevik notions of 'catching up by copying' and 'American, not Prussian, forms of capitalism' which, as we have seen, are firmly grounded in Lenin.
73. Both options, of course, lie squarely within the Bolshevik problematic: as is revealed, *inter alia*, by the fact that Stalin four years previously had chaired a Central Committee meeting which had agreed in supporting 'the efficient and well-to-do farmer' (Carr, 1958: 303f.); while Bukharin was also thoroughly Bolshevik in declaring of the countryside: 'We shall conquer thanks to scientific management, or we shall not conquer at all' (*Pravda*, 20 January 1929, cit. Carr, 1969: 264).
74. Stalin concludes his seminal 1924 study of Leninism with this declaration (our interpolations): 'The combination of the Russian revolutionary sweep [which we have indicated as Bolshevik voluntarism] with American efficiency [which we call capitalist techniques considered as necessary] is the essence of Leninism in Party and state work' (Stalin, 1924a: 85).
75. For a summary of these points, see Nove (1969: chs 7–9).
76. Even Trotsky's biographer, Deutscher (cit. Miliband, 1973a: 385) uses the term 'decimated' to describe their fate. There is evidence to suggest that workers and peasants frequently saw the Purges as representing their revenge on their erstwhile oppressors. See the peasants in *Bednota*, 1925 (cit. Carr, 1958: 199) and material used by Miliband (1973a: 387f.). Nove's analysis of who *was* purged or terrorised (1975: Ch. 2) is partial confirmation. *These* aspects of 'Stalinism' are usually conveniently forgotten in Trotskyist accounts. The real nature of the problem is well established in the Draft Programme of the 'Revolutionary C.P.S.U. (Bolshevik)', 1966, which argues: 'Stalin's fight against the bureaucratic strata which developed in the building of an industrialised socialist state was just and necessary. But he tried to fight these bureaucratic strata from within the

bureaucratic apparatus itself. For this reason he was not able to defeat them decisively' (*Hammer and Anvil*, Supplement No. 6). This is very much the major thesis in the critique of Stalin within the CPC; Stalin mishandled contradictions among the people, he failed faithfully to rely on the masses to defeat petty-bourgeois elements within the Party and State by subjecting the latter to all-round criticism from below, and so on. But, despite its insistence on treating Stalin as a phenomenon of the International Communist Movement, the CPC fails to ground Stalin's errors in the legacy from Bolshevism, *including* Lenin's.

77. See, *inter alia*, the 'High Tide' collection (Mao, 1956a) together with Jack Gray's article (1970) on its significance.
78. Cf. *Bolshevik*, No. 18, 1950 (cit. Mehnert, 1952: 66f.).
79. We might note, in this connection (1) Trotsky's assertion, in 1924, that 'The Party is in the last result always right, because the Party is the unique historical instrument given to the proletariat for the fulfilment of its fundamental tasks' (13th CPSU Congress, cit. Carr, 1954: 370, and Deutscher, 1959: 139, whose translations differ); (2) Bukharin's endorsement of this, which he in 1926 raised to an epistemological premise: 'If we are to reject the decision of the majority [of the Party] and say that truth consists in conformity with reality – which is in itself true – the question at once arises: Who decides what *is* or is *not in conformity* with reality?' (cit. Carr, 1959: 151 fn.); and (3) the extent to which Lenin – as Stalin is frequently able to show by quotation (see Stalin's 1924a: 32f.; 1926: 131f.; 1934: Part 3, and the volume *Lenin on the Soviet State Apparatus*, *passim*) – led a violent fight against the bureaucratic and intellectual windbags in State and Party.
80. In Great Britain 60,595 civilians died in the Second World War (about a third in London alone) and 265,000 members of the British Armed Forces died (Longmate, 1973: 133 and 84). Kochan (1962: 312f.) reports casualties of 'perhaps ten million' in the USSR in the Great Patriotic War; Spencer reports: 'Nearly 4,000,000 Red Army prisoners died in German hands. At least 750,000 Russian Jews were "exterminated". Between 3,000,000 and 5,000,000 other Soviet citizens died in one way or another because of the occupation' (1967: 391). Brown states: 'Subsequent Soviet statistics have implied that twenty million people died of injury or privation during, or immediately after, the Great Patriotic War. In the summer of 1945, one person in every eight was homeless' (Brown, 1970: 19). 'It has been calculated', writes Kochan, 'that one quarter of all Soviet property was destroyed – 17,000 towns, 70,000 villages and hamlets, 31,000 factories, 84,000 schools, 40,000 miles of railway track, not to speak of almost forty-five million horses, head of cattle and pigs' (Kochan, 1962: 312f.).

    In the siege of Leningrad over 600,000 people died, and whilst many people see Stalingrad as a definitive turning point in the war (Anderson, 1974c: 24), few comprehend the enormity of the general suffering and destruction, crystallised in Leningrad's refusal to surrender. Those 600,000 who died are symbolised in the Piskarevsky Memorial cemetery and in the war rooms of the Museum of Leningrad's history. Their theoretical/political significance has been one of the guiding themes of our attempt to comprehend the historical experience of Bolshevism.

81. See Nove, 1969: 190–1.

CHAPTER 4

1. For sources cf. the bibliographical appendix to this chapter.
2. Mao, 1936: 186f.; cf. Mao, 1958b: 99; 1963, 1964b and *Philosophy is no mystery* (Peking, FLP, 1972).
3. His emphasis removed.
4. Almost identical formulations – of the simultaneous changing of circumstances and people – are to be found in many places in Marx's work: cf. Part One of the *German Ideology*; Marx's 1851 polemic with the Communist League; the opening page of his *Eighteenth Brumaire* and, above all, the drafts and text of his *Civil War in France*, together with the amending preface to the *Manifesto* which it occasioned.
5. Marx, in the *Critique of the Gotha Programme*, and Lenin, in *Leftwing Communism*, agree, in the latter's words, that 'no other approach to this task [building socialism] is serious enough to warrant discussion' (Lenin, 1920b: 50).
6. Mao, 1943c.
7. We mean here Mao, 1927; 1941a, b; 1942d; 1956a and his frequent microstudies of exemplary transformations 1955, 1957a, 1958a, later encapsulated in GPCR *Instructions*.
8. We take this opportunity to record our special indebtedness to Gray's excellent studies of China, which repay the closest study.
9. Snow, 1941: 191f.; cf. also R. O. Hall's *China's fight for freedom* (London, Odhams Press, n.d.).
10. Cf. Mao, 1936; 1938a, b; 1942d; 1943a, b; 1945a, b, e, f, g; Belden, 1949, and Epstein quoted by Chesneaux, 1973: 135.
11. Cf. Mao, 1949c: 415.
12. The resolution is Mao, 1945c. See also Mao, 1958b: 97f.; 1962a. Vladimirov, 1973, reports that on 29 July 1942 Mao said 'Stalin does not and cannot know China. And yet he presumes to judge everything. All his so-called theories on the revolution are the blabberings of a fool.' We also know Mao's and Lin Piao's low opinion of the military manuals which Stalin 'suggested' they use, cf. Bianco, 1971: 174 fn. 5 and Mao, 1958c: 127f. In 1958 Mao argued: 'If we had followed Wang Ming's, or in other words Stalin's, methods the Chinese revolution couldn't have succeeded' (Mao, 1958b: 102). Speaking of the 28 Bolsheviks sent by Stalin to stiffen up the CPC and the other advisers Mao argued in 1962 that they 'did not understand, or we could say they utterly failed to understand, Chinese society, the Chinese nation, or the Chinese Revolution' (Mao, 1962a: 172). In 1964 Mao added 'Stalin felt that he had made mistakes in dealing with Chinese problems, and they were no small mistakes' (Mao, 1964b: 217). Fernbach (1974) provides an outline of CPC views on Stalin – these texts are simply ignored by many marxists; see especially Mao's long analyses

of Stalin explicitly (1956c) and implicitly (1957a), together with his notes on Stalin's *Economic Problems of Socialism in the U.S.S.R.* (Mao, 1958f.; 1959b), and a key text of the polemic documents *On the question of Stalin* (Peking, FLP, 1963, in CPC, 1965). There is also much of value to be found in many texts in the *Unrehearsed* volume.

13. Cf. Mao, 1958b: 99f., and several other texts in the important collection *Mao Tsetung Unrehearsed.*
14. On these two months cf. the Memoirs of Khrushchev, 1974.
15. It is instructive to take these canons to both Mao's own historical texts (e.g. his 1945c); and the polemic texts after 1964 (which by and large generally *do* 'negate everything').
16. This policy was congruent with material reality: the massive concentration of capitalist production in China. In 1947 Mao estimated 'during their twenty-year rule the four big families . . . have piled up enormous fortunes valued at ten to twenty thousand million US dollars' (Mao, 1947: 167). Cf. the rest of this text, and the article 'Public ownership of the means of production in China' (*Peking Review*, (51) 1972), which reveals that the four families owned 80 per cent of the fixed assets of China's industry in 1949. Belden, 1949: 217f., carries an illuminating interview with one of the big four, T. V. Soong; which should be contrasted with Belden, 1949: 643f. A commentary by bourgeois experts which recognises that the major obstacles to 'Development' in pre-1949 China were not 'material factors', nor yet the supposed inadequacies of the people (which together define the prevailing notions of China's *poverty*) but 'the nation's governmental and social structure', is Perkins (1974).
17. Central here are the texts in: *The struggle between the two roads in China's countryside* (Peking, FLP, 1968) and Chou En-lai's analysis of Liu Shao-ch'i of 15 April 1967 (Collier, 1973: 148f.) which reveals that Mao's key speech of 1955 was specifically a commentary upon and criticism of Liu.

CHAPTER 5

1. See also the letter of the CC/CPSU to the CC/CPC, 30 March 1963, reprinted in CPC, 1963: 77–8.
2. Contrast Lenin, 1920c, and the Chinese view of doing a good job of production (see below, this chapter).
3. Katz, 1972: 127.
4. Decree of 10 April, quoted by Katz, 1972: 3.
5. Kosygin, quoted Katz, 1972: 132.
6. See e.g. Lenin, 1921h.
7. See e.g. Lenin, 1921i: 57f.; 1921j.
8. CPSU, 1971: 69.
9. CPSU, 1976: 19.
10. See also Berliner, 1952, on enterprise directors' methods of 'making out' by illicit means to perform well on official plan indicators.
11. F. Chapple, quoted in the *Observer*, 25 January 1975.

12. Bukharin and Preobazhensky, 1920: 343.
13. Bukharin and Preobazhensky, 1920: 346.
14. Andrle, 1976, provides a large fund of information on the powers and activities of the enterprise director.
15. Again, bear in mind Lenin's predilection for Taylorism.
16. Nove, 1969: 334.
17. Nove, 1969: 362.
18. Jacobs (Wiles, 1971) provides figures that suggest that in 1967 2·9 per cent of arable land consisted of private plots. These produced 26 per cent of agricultural output, however; this testifies to the impact of local knowledge and initiative, and (*pace* bourgeois commentators) promises vast untapped potential if the fetters on true collective cooperation were unleashed.
19. Gross profits rose from 100 million rubles in 1965 to 617 million rubles in 1970 (Wilczynski, 1973: 113).
20. See the *Observer*, 4 February 1973, *Guardian*, 9 August 1973, 17 October 1974, and 24 June 1976.
21. See *Guardian*, 24 June 1976, *Sunday Times*, 12 October 1975, 7 March 1976.
22. P. Neuberg, *Times*, 16 June 1976.
23. R. Davy, *Times*, 28 August 1975, on Soviet press reports.
24. See e.g. Karcz, 1971; Stuart, 1971, 1972.
25. Matthews, 1972: 154.
26. These two model charters are reproduced in Stuart, 1972: 191 and 211.
27. Borisova, 1973: 321–2.
28. CPSU, 1961.
29. *Financial Times*, 29 July 1976.
30. See e.g. Wilczynski, 1973: 150 on the growing role of capitalist motor manufacturers in this respect.
31. C. Foley, 1974. Today, of course, oil is more than ever the focus of eager efforts by the Soviet Union to make agreements on exports and technological/finance cooperation with Japan and Western capitalism. Incredibly, too, Brezhnev's trading linkman, an oil magnate by the name of Dr Armand Hammer, turns out to be the same 'Comrade Hammer' used by Lenin to sell Soviet sugar to the West (Foley, 1974; Chossudovsky, 1973).
32. See e.g. Nove, 1973a, b.
33. Cf. Ticktin, 1973.
34. For reviews of the evidence see Burt (1972); Benson (1974); Hunnius (1973); and also Obradovic (1975).
35. Bilandzic, 1967; Rus, 1970.
36. Tito, 1948, in his 1970: 58–9.
37. In the Twenty-Three article document of January 1965.
38. Mao, 1956a (Introductory Note to 'This township went co-operative in two years', December 1955, quoted in MTSR: 341; slightly different translation in *Socialist Upsurge*: 44).
39. Lenin, 1921a: 83, 84 (see discussion in Ch. 3 above).
40. See e.g. Myrdal, 1963, 1970; Chen, 1973; Chu Li, 1974.
41. This is one of a whole series of statements quoted by the authors from their visits to Chinese factories. See Macciocchi, 1971, for an example of the radical change of motivation since the GPCR.

42. Quoted by Levy, 1975: 116 from the collection of Mao's speeches and articles known as *Wansui* 1967 and *Wansui* 1969. Schram II and *Miscellany* are selections from these sources. The particular passage quoted in the text here is from Mao's 'Reading Notes on the Soviet Union's *Political Economy*' and is variously dated some time between 1960 and 1962.
43. See e.g. Howe, 1973a, b; 1974 for an economist's account.
44. Big character posters, a form of public criticism, self-criticism, and public debate made popular in the GPCR.
45. Mao, 17 May 1958, quoted from the set of documents known as *Wansui* (1969 ed.), by Gittings (*Guardian*, 1 October 1974).
46. This theme is also explored in the better-known essay Mao, 1957a: 478.
47. First advanced at the Tenth Plenum in 1962.
48. See Corrigan, 1974; and the work of Jack Gray *passim*.
49. Levy, 1975: 102 refers to another use of this metaphor by Mao in criticising Stalin, at the Second Chengchow Conference, 27 February 1959 (from *Wansui*, 1967 ed.).
50. Mao's argument is quoted by Levy, 1975: 115.
51. For an account of this period see especially Gray, 1974: 37–40.
52. Quoted by Gray, 1974: 38.
53. Compare Myrdal, 1963, with his 1970 for a vivid concretisation of the change.
54. See Mao, 1964b: 216, where he adamantly declares that 'To consolidate New Democracy . . . is to engage in capitalism.'
55. In a talk reported in Collier, 1973: 148–50. Liu's other four mistakes are described as: calling for 'peace and democracy' in 1945; proclaiming a need for more, not less capitalists in 1949; opposing the move to increase agricultural cooperation (in fact calling for its reduction) as mechanisation was at too low a level in 1955; and misdirection of the methods and style of the 'Four Clean-ups' movement of 1963–5.
56. This forms the basis of Mao's 1957 formulation, which survives intact in the 1975 constitution:

    The state shall ensure the masses the right to use [debates and tatsebao] to create a political situation in which there is both centralism and democracy, both discipline and freedom.
57. Cf. Rossanda, 1970: 17.
58. See Daubier, 1974: 180–3; Collier, 1973: 140; Karol, 1975: 117–19 for discussions of Liu's text. A more literal translation of the title is *On the Self-Cultivation of Communists* and amongst the major criticisms now levelled at it is the (near-Confucian) stress on the cultivation of personal moral values. Others include the de-emphasis on class struggle; the advocation of obedience without question to orders; the portrayal of the Party as the fount of all wisdom; and the encouragement amongst Party members of the idea that appropriate faithfulness would bring individual advancement as its end.
59. See J. Robinson, 1973; Bettelheim, 1973.
60. Report on the Work of the Government to the Fourth National People's Congress of the PRC, in CPC, 1975: 56 (13 January 1975).

61. See e.g. Maccio, 1970.
62. From various figures on individual factories given to visitors, differentials of up to 7:1 appear to persist.
63. 1971: 126.
64. Articles which Western academics prefer to scoff at for being primitive, quaint or merely ideological echoes of the CPC official line, since they are not the product of persons designated a specific task of 'analyst' or 'intellectual', in fact offer a rich harvest of practical insights. 'Study Political Economy and Run the Docks well' (*Peking Review*, (24) 1974) reported a discussion session amongst workers in Shanghai harbour, for instance. Equally indicative are collections such as: *Philosophy Is No Mystery: Peasants Put Their Study To Work* (Peking, FLP, 1972), a compilation from Chinchien Production Brigade, Kiangshan County, Chekiang Province; and *Serving the People with Dialectics: Essays on The Study of Philosophy by Workers and Peasants* (Peking, 1972).
65. See *Peking Review*, (40) 1975: 6, for a report of Teng's speech. After Teng's fall, and the riot in Tien An Men square organised by his supporters on the right, it became clear that most of his backing was centred (as our own analysis would have predicted) in the economic and technical ministries (Gittings, *Guardian*, 22 April 1976).
66. See the account of the Mass Criticism Group of Peking and Tsinghua Universities, *Peking Review*, (28) 1976: 9–12.
67. Chih Heng, 1976; Cheng Yueh, 1976.
68. See Levy, 1975: 109. (The reference is to the 'Reading Notes'.)
69. Levy, 1975: 109 n. 59 (from *Wansui*, 1969, Talk at the Peitaho Central Committee Work Conference, 9 August 1962).
70. Though it was in fact Stalin who had argued in 1950 that socialism could change gradually, without ruptures. He reasoned that this was possible because of the revolution being 'from above' (a classic consummation of the 'capture' thesis). Cf. Schram I: 120.
71. Mao, 1964b.
72. 11 May 1964, quoted by Gittings, 1974: 764 from *Wansui*, 1969.
73. 'Dead soul of Confucius, Fond Dreams of New Tsars', reprinted from *People's Daily* in *Peking Review*, (6) 1974: 6.
74. At the 10th CPC Congress in 1973, Chou En-lai stated:

    > Over the last two decades the Soviet ruling revisionist clique, from Khrushchev to Brezhnev, has made a socialist country degenerate into a social-imperialist country. Internally, it has restored capitalism, enforced a fascist dictatorship, and enslaved the people of all nationalities . . . (*Peking Review*, (35–6) 1973: 25)

75. Mao, 1946b.
76. *Red Flag* (theoretical journal of the CC/CPC), (3–4) 1963. Translated in CPC, 1964: 200.
77. See in particular 1937c.
78. Macciocchi, 1971: ch. 15. Cf. also Gittings, 1974; Yahuda, 1974.
79. *Peaceful co-existence – two diametrically opposed policies*, Peking, FLP, 1963. Reprinted in CPC, 1965.

80. From 'Resolution on the establishment of People's Communes on the Rural Areas', CC/CPC, 29 August 1958.
81. In his 'Democratic Centralism' talk (1962a: 182) Mao also reaffirmed the desire to seek alliances with anti-communist forces on the basis of the 'Five Principles'. He did add (though rather ambiguously) that 'these matters are in a different category from the matter of uniting with the people of all countries' (p. 182).
82. See e.g. Chen, 1975: 449–52; Gittings, 1974: 757. A few days after the announcement Mao is alleged to have made the following celebrated observation to visiting French diplomats:

    France herself, Germany, England, on the condition that she ceases to be the courier of America, Japan and we ourselves – there is your Third World. (*New York Times*, 24 February 1964; cf. Yahuda, 1974)

    It is probably best to treat this as a statement for dramatic effect on the occasion rather thân a refutation of the otherwise accepted analysis of Second and Third World.
83. E.g. $100 million aid from PRC of Chile, reported by the General Secretary of the Socialist Party of Chile in his speech to the 25th Congress of the CPSU, quoted in Supplement IV to *Socialism: Theory and Practice* (Moscow), July 1976: 12. Proletarian Internationalism is not simply separate from other PRC diplomacy, as this makes clear. The two are utterly opposed.
84. Lin Piao, 1965.
85. Quoted by Levy, 1975: 108.
86. Quoted by Chen, 1975: 321.
87. Reproduced in *Peking Review*, (16) 1974 – see also the *Renmin Ribao* editorial of 9 April 1974, reprinted in *Peking Review*, (15) 1974.
88. In one absurd, almost satirical instance, at a banquet given for the visit of Edward Heath (one-time Prime Minister of capitalist Britain as the leader of the ruling class party) Teng Hsiao-ping proclaimed: 'The Chinese and British peoples have always been friendly to each other' (*Peking Review*, (22) 1974: 8). The amnesia about the history of the brutality of British colonialism (Opium Wars and all that), of tacit support for the US forces aiding the KMT, and of the periodic demonstrations in Peking against the colonial authorities' actions in Hong Kong since 1949 (see Chen, 1975: 291–2) is enough cause for concern. Worse is the anaesthetic it implies has been administered concerning the awareness of potential effects of modern neo-colonialism through trade, aid and diplomacy.
89. See for instance the closing section of Chou En-lai's Report to the 10th National Congress of the CPC, *Peking Review*, (35–6) 1973, reprinted in CPC, 1973.
90. Thus one 'Friend of China' may be found arguing that:

    . . . peaceful co-existence includes trade and diplomacy with imperialism. The power of socialism is such that it will continue to grow and will benefit more out of such an exchange than a capitalist power. (S. Mauger, 1973: 14)

This constitutes a serious misjudgement of the strengths and nature of both socialism and imperialism, the latter afforded neither the necessary strategic contempt nor the requisite tactical seriousness.

CHAPTER 6

1. For background statistics of this kind see *USSR* (Novosti Press Agency Yearbook); Parker, 1973; and occasional, revealing coverage in the press as in *The Times*, 24 December 1976, or *Guardian*, 16 September 1974. The relevant article in the latter begins: 'Imagine a country without unemployment and without inflation, where prices have remained stable for 20 years or more, where the gross national product has grown during the same period at a rate from 5 to 6 per cent a year; . . . where there is no balance of payments problem, and where there are no capitalists and no beggars.' The country in question is the GDR.
2. The absence of such great facts in most accounts is notable. Consider, e.g. David Lane's recent work (1976), which mentions rent only in terms of differentiation, ignoring the basic extent of housing distribution. Even in those accounts which focus on 'facts' (e.g. Matthews, 1972) bourgeois writers do not comprehend what they are listing; exemplary here is the frequent, almost throwaway illustration of the pervasive *ordinariness* of book buying and reading in the USSR, even in what these writers think of as the 'backward rural sector'. None of them consider what (in their terms) the cultural level is amongst unskilled workers in capitalist countries. This, of course, is only a part of comparing bourgeois life-style in the capitalist West with proletarian living in the USSR or China; taking the books for granted is only the other side of their complaints about queues and lack of choice. Much class struggle in the Soviet Union and China turns on safeguarding and extending these great facts. Such a reality informs the writings and debates within *Voprosy Filosofii* and *Istoriya SSSR*, as well as around the tables of many a *stalovaya* or *buffyet*.
3. See Marx, 1865a: 878f. (quoted below, p. 150–1); and compare 1863a: 45; 1863c: 471–2, 490–1; 1865b: Pt. VII; 1867a: Ch. 6, and p. 430; 1878: 119–20, 357, 389.
4. This is why Marx and Engels write at the end of the second section of their *Manifesto* that socialist construction involves an 'association, in which the free development of each is the condition for the free development of all'. They time and again stress that such development depends upon material necessities, upon transformed circumstances, which accompany and as Mao puts it, 'make solid', self-changing. This is also to emphasise that the working class is *international* and no one of its national fractions can be free to develop when, as is the case under capitalism, the 'development' in question rests upon the wholesale exploitation and oppression of workers beyond the prism of the 'nation'. If the latter alone forms the boundary of study then capitalism can momentarily *appear* (*but* recall the rediscovery of poverty in all Western countries at roughly ten-year intervals throughout the twentieth century) capable of overcoming want, suffering and

degradation. The condition which sustains the illusion is the impoverishment of whole peoples 'elsewhere' which fuels such 'prosperity'. On the world-market features of capitalism see Nicolaus, 1970, Corrigan, 1977.

5. Two such CPC converts, depressingly, are Charles Bettelheim, whom we discuss below, and Martin Nicolaus.
6. Formerly the International Socialism Group. The SWP position is classically stated in Cliff, 1970 – an appallingly phenomenal analysis. See also Harman, 1969, 1970, and Kidron, 1969. The two latter are ably demolished by Mandel, 1969 and 1970.
7. We have in mind here those who have faithfully followed changes in the CPC analysis of the USSR (or, as we discussed in Chapter 5, the EEC or Yugoslavia) and those who find they can justify *all* of China's policies including such as its $100m. credit to Pinochet's Chile (reported at the 25th CPSU Congress, cit. *Socialism, Theory and Practice*, Supplement IV, July 1976) or its support of reactionary forces in, e.g., Pakistan, Zaire, Sri Lanka or Angola. These, as we have suggested in Chapter 5, need to be understood in terms of continuing class struggle in the PRC. 'Friend of China' articles pervade such journals as *China Now*, CPSG *Bulletin*, *Politics and Money*, and most stridently of all, the proliferating 'Maoist' press; though it is fair to note some partial exceptions here, like Reg Birch's dissent from Third Worldism and related critique of the CPC analysis of the EEC, though he and the CPB (ML) none the less accept that the Soviet Union is unproblematically capitalist. Such texts are distinguished by a reliance on merely phenomenal evidence, and so are unable to penetrate the historical movement within the USSR. Importantly (and here their apologetic character is at its most evident), were they to acknowledge the *extent* to which similar phenomenal evidence of 'capitalism' is present in the PRC, they would be obliged, in terms of their own methods, to conclude that China is a capitalist country too. In sum, the *struggle* we have emphasised throughout this book (whose depth, ironically, Mao and the CPC have done much to reveal) finds no place in 'Friend of China' writings on either China or the USSR.
8. See here Scott, 1974, Davin, 1976. It should be stressed, however, as these women do, just how far *by comparison with capitalism* the emancipation of women in socialist countries *has* proceeded.
9. Central to China's foreign trade policy has been the homogenisation of the world into *countries* of particular types ('within the Third World', 'developing', etc.) noted in Chapter 5. This is clear from, e.g., a special issue of *Chinese Economic Studies* (winter 1974–5, vol. 8, no. 2) which translates the 1973 'Primer on International Trade' of the Liaoning Fiscal Institute's Foreign Trade Department's Writers Group. This links 'international trade' *within capitalism* very clearly to foreign policy, imperialism, trade wars and plunder. But it then declares that the trade 'among all fervently Marxist-Leninist socialist states and between them and the developing nations of Asia, Africa, and Latin America is a new form of international trade, entirely different from that of the past. Here, reciprocity based on equality has replaced plunder and exploitation' (p. 4). Given this it is not surprising to find that the dominant notions (ably criticised, somewhat

ironically, by Bettelheim in his remarks on Emmanuel) used to comprehend international trade are 'balance of trade' and 'exchange of equivalents'. This is territory we should be familiar with by now, of obeisance before certain technical-administrative 'laws of world economy'. But, as we have emphasised before, texts like this are texts of struggle. In this case, the USSR is included within the list of socialist social formations, which are correctly seen as being under attack from capitalism, while the United States is identified as the 'main enemy'. Further, certain social organisations like UNCTAD and the EEC, which are seen later simply as 'progressive', are identified as capitalist organisations first and foremost.

10. When Lenin died, *The Times* (23 January 1924) acknowledged Bolshevism's 'wide impact' and argued that Lenin ('short, bald-headed, snub-nosed' – they did not yet refer to the colour of the eyes as with Stalin) 'set himself the task of making the restless masses of the Russian people the centre and starting-point of a great world upheaval'. This is quite correct, and the bourgeoisie has never lost sight of it. The Soviet Union stands as a beacon, as an alternative image of a different and new social form. Hence the international vilification, sabotage, and intervention by the forces of the imperialist countries in the 'civil' war, hence the delay in supporting the Soviet armies against Hitler (in the hope that the Nazis might extinguish the beacon first), hence the so-called 'Cold' War which followed. The war against Bolshevism, against socialist alternatives to capitalism, never stops; it has raged since over Korea, Malaya, Egypt, Vietnam, Cuba, Laos, Cambodia, Angola, Dhofar, to name only the most prominent of its theatres. Détente is another kind of invasion, a continuation of the same war to convert the labour and other resources of socialism to the service of capital. A central dimension of this is the notion of the 'free movement of labour' embodied in the Jackson amendment, which seeks to capitalise on the superb medical, social and educational facilities of the USSR by urging that once educated (at the expense of the Soviet State) people should be 'free to move' to where their 'talents' will be best rewarded. Bourgeois (and often, socialist) newspapers keep largely silent about the many among such *émigrés* who have sought to return, finding their 'true homeland' strangely inhospitable or the 'great' city of New York too expensive. Neither have the dissidents proved an unmixed blessing for the propagandists and intelligence services which worked for their emigration; in their way, Bukhovsky and Solzhenitsyn have proved quite good workers for socialism. It is important to record, finally, that neither Détente, nor the 'peaceful road', are universally admired in the USSR; see, e.g., Ponomarev, 1974, Zarodov, 1975, Cherepin, 1975. On the other hand nothing is more comprehensible than the Soviet people's desire for *peace* given the immense sufferings (see Ch. 3, n. 80) capitalist interventions have imposed on them.
11. See Corrigan, 1976b, Ramsay, 1977.
12. See above, Ch. 3, nn. 59 and 60.
13. Mandel, 1969, 1970, 1974a. His comments on Ticktin (Mandel, 1974b) are also relevant here, as are the pertinent chapters in his 1968a.
14. Other reviews of Bettelheim's *Luttes* are Miliband, 1975, Sweezy, 1975,

Lockett, 1975, China Policy Study Group *Broadsheet* 12, 1975, and Ticktin, 1976.

15. See above, Ch. 2, n. 4.
16. In the Preface to his 1974.
17. See Althusser and Balibar, 1968, Pt. III, Ch. 1.
18. As does Anderson, 1974a: 204f.
19. This forms the theoretical basis of Bettelheim's crucial recognition of the need to attack the division of labour. See his 1973, Ch. 3 and *passim*, and his (important) 1972.
20. A *partial* exception here lies in his doubts about the programme enshrined in Lenin's *Immediate Tasks* as expressed in his 1973: 73f. But Bettelheim has hardly built on the insights of these scant paragraphs.
21. See Bettelheim, 1971: 59.
22. Read, carefully, Bettelheim, 1971: 34f.
23. See n. 4 above.

Bibliography

This bibliography is arranged as follows:

PART ONE A Marx/Marx and Engels
B Engels
C Lenin
D Trotsky
E Stalin
F Mao

PART TWO All other sources.

In Part One, for each author we first list collections, then individual texts. Collections are identified by letter-codes, texts by year of composition, plus, where required, a suffix (e.g. 1843a). It is the latter which are cited in our text and notes. Our listing of texts within any given year does not necessarily follow the order of their composition. For each text we give, where possible, a variety of sources. Our own citations in text and notes refer always to the first source listed unless we specifically state otherwise.

In Part Two we list works alphabetically by author (or in the case of anonymous authorship, title) with subdivision by date and/or suffix. Here dates are those of publication unless a separate publication date is given at the end of the entry. Throughout we abbreviate London as L, Moscow as M, New York as NY, and Peking as P. All other abbreviations, as in journal titles, should be self-explanatory.

Our intention has not been to produce an 'exhaustive' bibliography in any sense, though *de facto* Part One represents a reasonably full list of the major writings of the authors it treats. We have, in general, listed only sources explicitly referred to in this book. Details are kept brief, but we have always sought to provide sufficient information to enable texts to be located in bibliographies and library catalogues. Fuller details may be found through: *British Books in Print* (UK annual); *Books in Print* (US annual); *Paperback Books in Print* (UK annual); *British National Bibliography* (weekly, cumulative).

The following addresses may be useful to readers who wish to keep up with literature on socialist construction and marxist theory as this bibliography becomes outdated:

Central Books Ltd, 37 Grays Inn Road, London WC1X 8PS. For M, Progress, eds of Marx, Engels and Lenin, current Soviet material and Left literature more generally.

New Park Publications Ltd, 186a Clapham High Street, London SW4 7UG; Pathfinder Press, 47 The Cut, London SE1 8LL; IMG Publications, 182 Pentonville Road, London N1; Pluto Press Ltd, Unit 10 Spencer Court, 7 Chalcott Road, London NW1 8LH; for works by Trotsky, and of the Trotskyist movement's various tendencies.

Red Star Press, PO Box 71, London SW2, for reprints of works by Stalin.

Guozi Shudian, PO Box 390, Peking, China, for P, FLP eds of Marx, Engels, Lenin, Stalin and Mao and current Chinese material.

PART ONE

A *MARX/MARX AND ENGELS*

Note. For more bibliographic information on Marx, see Rubel, 1956, 1960, McLellan, 1973.

COLLECTIONS

I Karl Marx (KM) and Frederick Engels (FE) *Collected Works*. M, Progress, NY, International, L, Lawrence and Wishart, 1975 onwards. To comprise 50 volumes. Cited as: MECW, 1, 2, etc.

II **General Collections**
KM/FE *Selected Works in Three Volumes*. M, Progress, 1969–70. Cited as: MESW I, II, III.
KM/FE *Selected Works in One Volume*. M, Progress, 1968. Cited as: MESW.
KM/FE *Selected Correspondence*. M, FLPH, 1956; reprinted with additions, M, Progress, 1965; revised ed., M, Progress, 1975. Cited as: MESC 1956, 1965, 1975 respectively.
KM/FE and V. I. Lenin *The Essential Left*. L, Allen & Unwin, 1960. Cited as: EL.

III **Anthologies**
KM *Early Writings*. Ed. T. B. Bottomore, C. A. Watts, 1963. Cited as: BEW.
KM *Early Writings*. Ed. L. Colletti, L, Penguin, 1975. Cited as: CEW.
KM *Writings of the Young Marx on Philosophy and Society*. Ed. L. Easton/K. Guddat, NY, Anchor, 1967. Cited as: YM.
KM *Early Texts*. Ed. D. McLellan, Oxford, Blackwell, 1971. Cited as: ET.
KM *The Revolutions of 1848*; *Surveys from Exile*; *The First International and*

After. Pelican Marx Library, Political Writings Vols 1–3. Ed. D. Fernbach, L, Penguin, 1973, 1973, 1974 respectively. Cited as: MPW, 1, 2, 3.
KM/FE *Articles on Britain*. M, Progress, 1971. Cited as: AB.
KM/FE *On Britain*. 2nd ed., M, FLPH, 1962. Cited as: OB.
KM/FE *On Colonialism*. M, Progress, 1968. Cited as: OC.
KM *On Colonialism and Modernisation*. Ed. S. Avineri, NY, Anchor, 1969. Cited as: OCM.
KM/FE *On the Paris Commune*. M, Progress, 1971. Cited as: PC.
KM/FE *Writings on the Paris Commune*. Ed. H. Draper, NY, Monthly Review Press, 1971. Cited as: WPC.
KM/FE *On Religion*. M, FLPH, 1957. Cited as: OR.
KM/FE *The Russian Menace to Europe*. Ed. P. Blackstock/B. Hoselitz, L, Allen & Unwin, 1955. Cited as: RM.
KM *Texts on Method*. Ed. T. Carver, Oxford, Blackwell 1975. Cited as: TM.
KM *Value: Studies by Karl Marx*. Ed. A. Dragstedt, L, New Park, 1976. Cited as: V.

IV **Selections**

KM *Selected Writings in Sociology and Social Philosophy*. Ed. T. B. Bottomore/M. Rubel, L, Penguin, 1963. Cited as: BR.
KM *Essential Writings*. Ed. D. Caute, L, Panther, 1964. Cited as: EW.
KM/FE *Basic Writings on Politics and Philosophy*. Ed. L. Feuer, L, Fontana, 1969. Cited as: BW.
KM *On Economics*. Ed. R. Freeman, L, Penguin, 1962. Cited as: OE.
KM, FE and V. I. Lenin *On the Dictatorship of the Proletariat*. P, FLP, 1975. Cited as: DP.

TEXTS

1842 'Proceedings of the Sixth Rhine Province Assembly. Third Article. Debate on the Law on Thefts of Wood.' MECW, 1, 224–63. Excerpted, ET.

1843a 'Justification of the Correspondent from the Mosel.' MECW, 1, 332–58. Excerpted, YM.

1843b *Contribution to the Critique of Hegel's Philosophy of Law*. MECW, 3, 3–129. Alt. trans.: *Critique of Hegel's Philosophy of Right*, ed. J. O'Malley, Cambridge University Pr., 1970; *Critique of Hegel's Doctrine of the State*, CEW, 57–198. Excerpted, YM, ET.

1843c 'On the Jewish Question.' MECW, 3, 146–74, BEW, 3–40, CEW, 211–42, YM, ET.

1844a 'Contribution to the Critique of Hegel's Philosophy of Law: Introduction.' MECW, 3, 175–87, BEW, 41–58, CEW, 243–58, YM. 249–64, ET, 115–29, OR, 41–58, and appended to O'Malley ed. of 1843b. Excerpted, BW.

1844b 'Comments on James Mill, *Elémens d'économie politique*.' MECW, 3, 211–28, CEW, 259–78. Excerpted, YM, ET.

1844c *Economic and Philosophic Manuscripts of 1844* [the 'Paris Manuscripts']. MECW, 3, 229–348, BEW, 66–219, CEW, 279–400. Separate edition, ed. D. J. Struick, L, Lawrence & Wishart, 1970. Excerpted, YM, ET.

1844d 'Critical Marginal Notes on the Article "The King of Prussia and Social Reform". By a Prussian.' MECW, 4, 189–206, CEW, 401–20, ET, 204–22, YM.

1844e *The Holy Family* (with FE). MECW, 4, 5–211. Sep. ed., M, Progress, 1975. Excerpted, YM.

1845 'Theses on Feuerbach.' Two variants exist, Marx's own, and that edited by Engels. Both are given in MECW, 5, and appended to Ryazanskaya ed. of 1846a; Marx's in BR, 82–4, CEW, 421–3, YM, 400–3; Engels's in MESW, I, 13–15, MESW, 28–30, OR, 69–73, BW, 283–6.

1846a *The German Ideology* (with FE). Ed. S. Ryazanskaya, M, Progress, 1968. MECW, 5. Pt. I and selections from the rest published separately, ed. C. J. Arthur, L, Lawrence & Wishart, 1970. Pt. I also in MESW, I, 16–80, and YM.

1846b Letter to P. V. Annenkov, Dec. 28. MESC, all eds. MESW, I, 517–28, MESW, 669–79, and appx. to NY ed. of 1847a.

1847a *The Poverty of Philosophy*. NY, International, 1963; M, Progress, 1973. MECW, 6.

1847b *Wage Labour and Capital*. M, Progress, 1970. MESW, I, 142–74, MESW, 64–94.

1848a *Manifesto of the Communist Party* (with FE). M, Progress, 1973; P, FLP; Penguin (under title *The Communist Manifesto*) L, 1967. MESW, I, 98–137, MESW, 31–63, EL, 7–48, MPW, I, 62–98, BW, 43–82.

1848b 'On the Question of Free Trade.' With NY ed. of 1847a.

1850a 'Address to the CC of the Communist League (March 1850).' MPW, 1, 319–30.

1850b *The Class Struggles in France: 1848–1850*. MESW, I, 205–99, MPW, 2, 35–142; and as sep. pamphlet from M, Progress. Excerpted, BW, 322–57.

1852a Letter to J. Weydermeyer, March 5th. MESC, all eds. Excerpted, MESW, I, 528, MESW, 669, DP.

1852b *The Eighteenth Brumaire of Louis Bonaparte*. MESW, I, 394–487, MESW, 97–180, MPW, 2, 143–249; and as sep. pamphlet from M, Progress. Excerpted, BW, 358–88.

1853a 'The British Rule in India.' MESW, I, 488–93, AB, 166–72, OB, 391–8, OC, 35–41, OCM, 88–95, MPW, 2, 301–7, BW, 511–17.

1853b 'Future Results of the British Rule in India.' MESW, I, 494–9, AB, 197–203, OB, 399–406, OC, 81–7, OCM, 132–9, MPW, 2, 319–24.

1854 Letter to the Labour Parliament. OB, 416–17, AB, 216–17, MPW, 2, 277–9.

1856 'Speech at the Anniversary of *The People's Paper*.' MESW, I, 500–1, AB, 262–4, OB, 466–8, MPW, 2, 299–300.

1857 'General Introduction [to 1858a].' With full ed. of 1858a. Alt. trans.: with 1859b, and Arthur ed. of 1846a; in TM; in McLellan selections from 1858a; and in sep. pamphlet, with 1859a, from P, FLP, 1976.

1858a *Grundrisse*. Full edition, ed. M. Nicolaus, L, Penguin, 1973. Selections: *Marx's Grundrisse*, ed. D. McLellan, L, Macmillan, 1971; *Precapitalist Economic Formations*, ed. E. Hobsbawm, L, Lawrence & Wishart, 1964.

1858b Letter to F. Lassalle, 22 Feb. MESC, all eds.

1859a Preface to 1859b. With 1859b. MESW, I, 502–6, MESW, 181–5, CEW, 424–8, and with P ed. of 1857. Excerpted BR, 67–9, BW, 83–7.

1859b *A Contribution to the Critique of Political Economy*. L, Lawrence & Wishart, 1971.

1863a, b, c *Theories of Surplus Value* [*Capital*, Vol. IV]. Parts I–III. M, Progress, 1963, 1968, 1971. Selections, ed. E. Burns, L, Lawrence & Wishart, 1951.

1864 'Inaugural Address of the Working Men's International Association.' AB, 340–9, MESW, II, 11–18, OB, 483–92, MPW, 3, 73–81, and in *Documents of the First International*, 5 vols, M, 1962 onwards, Vol. 1.

1865a *Capital*, Vol. III. Ed. F. Engels, M, Progress, 1971.

1865b *Wages, Price and Profit*. P, FLP, 1973. MESW, II, 31–76, MESW, 186–229, and as sep. pamphlet from M, Progress. In EL under title *Value, Price and Profit*.

1865c 'On Proudhon' [Letter to J. B. Schweitzer, 24 Jan.]. MESC all eds, MESW, II, 24–30, and with NY ed. of 1847a.

1866 'Results of the Immediate Process of Production' [Ms. of a planned further part of *Capital* I]. With Penguin ed. of 1867a. Alt. trans., V.

1867a *Capital*, Vol. I. Ed. F. Engels, tr. S. Moore/E. Aveling from 3rd German ed., incorporating changes made by Engels in 4th German ed., L, Lawrence & Wishart, 1967. Pt. VIII of this ed. is separately available in MESW, II, 100–45, and from M, Progress, as a pamphlet entitled 'Genesis of Capital'. Other English full eds include: Chicago, Kerr, 1905; L, Allen & Unwin, 1970 (a facsimile of the first English ed. of 1887); L, Dent, 1974 (a trans. of the 4th German ed.); L, Penguin, 1976 (a trans. of KM/FE *Werke* Vol. 23, which incorporates changes in both German eds and the French ed. of 1872–5). To note the different German eds here is not scholastic; Marx, and Engels as his literary executor, altered both the text and its arrangement through successive impressions. Material from the first German ed., deleted by Marx from subsequent eds or substantially rewritten, can be found in V.

1867b Preface to 1st German ed. of 1867a. With all full eds of 1867a.

1868 Letter to L. Kugelmann, 11 July. MESC, all eds, MESW, II, 418–20.

1871a *The Civil War in France*. P, FLP, 1970. MESW, II, 202–44, MESW, 273–313, PC, 48–102, WPC, 35–101, MPW, 3, 187–235, and as sep. pamphlet from M, Progress. Excerpted BW, 389–430.

1871b First draft of 1871a. With P ed. of 1871a. PC, 102–81, WPC, 103–78. Excerpted, MPW, 3, 236–68.

1871c Second draft of 1871a. With P ed. of 1871a. PC, 182–224, WPC, 179–213.

1871d Notebook on the Paris Commune [press excerpts and notes for 1871a]. Ed. H. Draper, Berkely, Independent Socialist Pr., 1971.

1872a Preface to 2nd German ed. of 1848a. (With FE.) With M, P, and Penguin eds of 1848a. MESW, I, 98–9, MESW, 31–2.
1872b Speech at Amsterdam. MPW, 3, 323–6. MESW, II, 292–5.
1873 Afterword to the 2nd German ed. of *Capital*. With all full eds of 1867a.
1874 Conspectus of Bakunin, *Statism & Anarchy*. MPW, 3, 333–8. Excerpted, MESW, II, 411–12.
1875 *Critique of the Gotha Programme*. P, FLP, 1972 (with relevant letters by KM and FE). MESW, III, 13–30, MESW, 315–35, MPW, 3, 339–59, BW, 153–73, and as sep. pamphlet from M, Progress.
1877 Letter to the Editorial Board of *Otechestvenniye Zapiski*. MESC, all eds. OCM, 467–70, BW, 476–9.
1878 *Capital*, Vol. II. Ed. F. Engels, M, Progress, 1967. [The bulk of this was in fact drafted 1865–70; 1878 is the date of the last section of the mss used.]
1879 Circular Letter to Bebel, Leibknecht, Bracke *et al.*, Sept. 17–18 (with FE). MESC, all eds. MESW, III, 88–94, MPW, 3, 360–75.
1880 Marginal Notes on Adolf Wagner, *Lehrbuch der Politischen Oekonomie. Theoretical Practice*, 5, 1972. Alt. trans.: TM, V.
1881a Letter to V. Zasulich, 8 Mar. *Text:* MESC, all eds; RM, 278–9. *Drafts:* 1st draft, in full, MESW, III, 152–61; extracts from various drafts, appx. to Hobsbawm ed. of 1858a; RM, 218–26, gives a 'composite' of all four drafts.
1881b Preface to Russian ed. of 1848a (with FE). With M, P, and Penguin eds of 1848a. MESW, I, 100–1.

B *ENGELS*

COLLECTIONS

All KM/FE collections listed above.
Engels: Selected Writings. Ed. W. O. Henderson, L, Penguin, 1967. Cited as: ESW.
On Marx's Capital. M, Progress, 1972. Cited as: EMC.

TEXTS

1843 'Outlines of a critique of political economy.' MECW, 3, 418–43, ESW, and with Struik ed. of KM, 1844c.
1845 *The Condition of the Working Class in England in 1844*. MECW, 4, 295–596; OB, 1–338. Numerous sep. eds, inc. Oxford, Blackwell, 1968, L, Allen & Unwin, 1968. Extracts, ESW.
1847a Draft of a Communist Confession of Faith [1st draft of the *Manifesto*]. MECW, 6, 96–104.
1847b 'Principles of Communism' [2nd draft of the *Manifesto*]. MECW, 6, 341–57, and as sep. pamphlet from L, Pluto Pr., 1971.

1850 *The Peasant War in Germany*. L, Lawrence & Wishart, 1969. Excerpted, BW, 452–75, ESW.

1852 *Germany: Revolution & Counter-revolution* (with KM). L, Lawrence & Wishart, 1969. MESW, I, 300–87. Extracts, ESW.

1867a 'Karl Marx, *Das Kapital*' [Review]. EMC.

1867b Synopsis of *Capital* [Vol. I, opening chs only]. EMC.

1868a 'Marx's *Capital*' [Review]. EMC, ESW.

1868b 'Karl Marx on Capital' [Review]. EMC.

1873 *The Housing Question*. M, Progress, 1970. MESW, II, 295–375.

1875 'On Social Relations in Russia.' MESW, II, 386–98. Excerpted, BW, 507–10.

1876 'The Part Played by Labour in the Transition from Ape to Man.' With his 1891a, 251–64. Sep. pamphlet, M, Progress. MESW, III, 66–77, MESW, 358–68.

1880 *Socialism, Utopian and Scientific* [3 chs of his 1894a, slightly amended, published independently]. M, Progress. MESW, III, 95–151, MESW, 379–434, EL, 103–46, BW, 109–52, ESW.

1883a Speech at Marx's Graveside. MESW, III.

1883b Preface to 3rd German ed. of *Capital*, I. With all full eds of KM, 1867a.

1884 Preface to 1st German ed. of *The Poverty of Philosophy*. With NY and M eds of KM, 1847a.

1885 Preface to *Capital*, II. With KM, 1878.

1886a *Dialectics of Nature*. M, Progress, 1966. Excerpted, OR, 152–93.

1886b *Ludwig Feuerbach and the End of Classical German Philosophy*. P, FLP, 1976 (with Prefaces and Notes by G. Plekhanov). M, Progress, 1969. MESW, III, 335–76, MESW, 594–632, BW, 236–82, OR, 213–68. Extract, ESW.

1886c Preface to English ed. of *Capital*, I. With all full eds of KM, 1867a.

1888 *The Role of Force in History*. L, Lawrence & Wishart, 1968.

1890a Preface to 4th German ed. of *Capital*, I. With all full eds of KM, 1867a.

1890b Letter to J. Bloch, 21–2 Sep. MESC, all eds, ESW.

1890c Letter to C. Schmidt, 27 Oct. MESC, all eds.

1891a *The Origin of the Family, Private Property, and the State*. L, Lawrence & Wishart, 1972. MESW, III, 204–334, MESW, 455–593. Extract, ESW.

1891b Introduction to *Wage Labour and Capital*. With M ed. of KM, 1847b. MESW, I, 142–9, MESW, 64–71.

1891c Introduction to *The Civil War in France*. With KM, 1871a, P, M, PC and WPC eds. ESW.

1894a *Anti-Duhring: Herr Eugen Duhring's Revolution in Science*. NY, International, 1972; M, Progress. Excerpted, BW, 311–21.

1894b Afterword to 'On Social Relations in Russia'. MESW, II, 398–410.

1894c 'The Peasant Question in France & Germany.' MESW, III, 452–76, MESW, 633–50.

1894d Preface to *Capital*, III. With KM, 1865a.

1894e Afterword to *Capital*, III. With KM, 1865a.

1894f Letter to H. Starkenburg, 25 Jan. MESC, 1956.

1895 Introduction to *The Class Struggles in France*. With M ed. of KM, 1850b. MESW, I, 186–204, MESW, 651–68, ESW.

C *LENIN*

COLLECTIONS

I *Collected Works*, M, Progress, 1960 onwards. 45 vols. Cited as LCW, 1, 2, etc.

II **General Collections**
Selected Works in Twelve Volumes. L, Lawrence & Wishart, 1936 onwards. Cited as LSW (1936) 1, 2, etc.
Selected Works in Three Volumes. M, Progress, 1970–71. Cited as LSW (1970) 1, 2, 3.
Essentials of Lenin in Two Volumes. L, Lawrence & Wishart, 1947. Cited as EL, I, and EL, II.
Selected Works in One Volume. M, Progress, 1968. Cited as LSW.

III **Anthologies and Selections**
Amongst those currently in print are: *Against Dogmatism*; *Against Imperialist War*; *On the Foreign Policy of the Soviet State*; *On the Great October Socialist Revolution*; *On the Paris Commune*; *On Trade Unions*; *Speeches at Party Congresses*; *Marx-Engels Marxism*; and (with KM and FE) *On Anarchism*. All M, Progress.
The only such anthologies extensively referenced in this book are *What is Soviet Power?*, M, Progress, 1973, cited as SP, and *Lenin on the Soviet State Apparatus*, M, Progress, 1969, cited as LOSS.

TEXTS

Note: texts marked thus * are available in individual eds from M, Progress.

*1894a *What the 'Friends of the People' are*. LCW, 1. Different versions: LSW (1936), 1, 389–455, EL, I, 77–130.
1894b 'The Economic Content of Narodnism and a Critique of it in Mr. Struve's Book.' LCW, 1. Extracts, LSW (1936), I, 456–66.
1899 *The Development of Capitalism in Russia*. LCW, 3.
1901 'Notes on Anarchism and Socialism.' LCW, 1.
*1902 *What is to be Done?* LCW, 5. LSW (1936), 2, 27–192, LSW (1970), 1, 119–272, EL, I, 149–274.
*1904 *One Step Forward, Two Steps Back*. LCW, 7. LSW (1970), 1, 273–454.
1905a 'Party Organisation and Party Literature.' LCW, 10. LSW, 148–52.
*1905b *Two Tactics of Social Democracy in the Democratic Revolution*. LCW, 9. LSW (1936), 3, 39–133, LSW (1970), 1, 459–563, EL, I, 351–455, LSW, 50–147.
1907a 'Against the Boycott.' LCW, 13. LSW (1936), 3, 414–27.
1907b *The Agrarian Programme of Social Democracy in the 1st Russian Revolution, 1905–7*. LCW, 13. Extracts, LSW (1936), 3, 157–286.

1908a Notes on Rey, 1908. In his *Philosophical Notebooks*. LCW, 38.

1908b *The Agrarian Question in Russia towards the Close of the 19th Century*. LCW, 15. LSW (1936), 1, 139–217.

*1908c *Materialism and Empiriocriticism*. CW, 14. Also from P, FLP.

*1910 'Certain Features of the Historical Development of Marxism.' LCW, 17. EL, I, 481–5.

1913a 'The historical destiny of the doctrine of Karl Marx.' LCW, 18. LSW, 17–19.

1913b 'The three sources and the three component parts of Marxism.' LCW, 19. LSW (1970), 66–70, LSW, 20–24; and pp. 7–12 of the LSW (1936) ed. of his 1914.

1914 *The Teachings of Karl Marx*. NY, International, 1930; 2nd ed., with his 1913b, LSW (1936), 11. (Little Lenin Library, I.)

*1915 'The Collapse of the 2nd International.' LCW, 21. LSW (1936), 5, 167–221.

1916a Notebooks on the Agrarian Question. LCW, 40.

1916b Philosophical Notebooks. LCW, 38.

*1916c 'Opportunism and the Collapse of the 2nd International.' LCW, 21. EL, I, 633–42.

*1916d *Imperialism: the Highest Stage of Capitalism*. LCW, 22. LSW (1936), 5, 3–119, LSW (1970), 1, 667–768, EL, I, 643–740, LSW, 169–263.

*1917a *Marxism on the State* [Preparatory material for his 1917b]. M, Progress, 1972.

*1917b *The State and Revolution*. LCW, 25. LSW (1970), 2, 283–376, LSW, 264–351. In EL (q.v. KM/FE Collections) and from P, FLP.

1917c Lecture on the 1905 Revolution. LCW, 23. LSW (1970), 1, 779–94, and in his *On Bourgeois-Democratic Revolution*, M, Novosti, 1975.

1917d 'To the Population.' LCW, 26. LSW (1970), 2, 488–9. LOSS, 95–7.

1917e 'Peasants and Workers.' LCW, 25. LSW (1936), 6, 380–8.

1917f 'Salaries of high ranking office employees and officials.' LCW, 42. LOSS, 100.

1917g Postscript to his 1907b. LCW, 13. LSW (1936), 6, 389–90.

1917h Speeches on the Agrarian Question. LCW, 26. LSW (1936), 6, 352–71, and 421–2.

*1917i Letters from Afar. LCW, 21. LSW (1970), 2, 31–41 [first letter only].

*1917j Letters on Tactics. LCW, 24.

*1917k 'Can the Bolsheviks retain State power?' LCW, 26. LSW (1936), 6, 250–96, LSW (1970), 2, 393–434, LSW, 362–400.

*1917l 'The Tasks of the Proletariat in the present Revolution' [The 'April Theses']. LCW, 24. LSW (1970), 2, 41–7.

*1918a 'How to organise competition?' LCW, 26. LSW (1970), 2, 517–24, LOSS, 111–20.

*1918b 'The Immediate Tasks of the Soviet Government.' LCW, 27. LSW (1970), 2, 643–77, LSW, 401–31.

1918ba Original Draft of 1918b. LCW, 27. LOSS, 135–9.

1918bb Six Theses on the Immediate Tasks of the Soviet Government. LCW, 27. LSW (1970), 2, 678–80, LOSS, 149–52.

*1918c '"Left-Wing" Childishness and the Petty-Bourgeois Mentality.' LCW, 27. LSW (1970), 682–705, LSW, 432–55.

*1918d *The Proletarian Revolution and the Renegade Kautsky*. LCW, 28. LSW (1970), 3, 65–149, LSW, 468–75.

*1919a 'What is Soviet Power?' LCW, 29. LSW, 476–7, SP.

1919b Greetings to the Hungarian Workers. LCW, 29. LSW (1970), 3, 215–18.

1919c 'Salaries for Specialists.' LCW, 42. LOSS, 208.

1919d 'Economics and Politics in the Era of the Dictatorship of the Proletariat.' LCW, 30. LSW (1970), 3, 289–97, LSW, 497–505.

1919e Draft Programme of the RCP (B). LCW, 29. SP, 18–27. Extracts, LOSS, 194–8.

*1919f 'A Great Beginning.' LCW, 29. LSW (1970), 3, 219–42, LSW, 478–96.

*1919g *The State*. LCW, 29. LSW (1970), 3, 259–74, and from P, FLP, 1965.

1920a Preliminary Draft Theses on the Agrarian Question. LCW, 31. LSW (1970), 3, 438–48, LSW, 592–601.

*1920b *'Left Wing' Communism – An Infantile Disorder*. LCW, 31. LSW (1970), 3, 345–430, LSW, 516–91.

1920c 'Tasks of the Youth Leagues.' LCW, 31. LSW (1970), 3, 470–83, LSW, 607–20.

1920d 'The Trade Unions, the Present Situation, and the Mistakes of Comrade Trotsky.' LCW, 32. LSW (1936), 9, 3–27.

1921a 'Once again on the Trade Unions, the Current Situation, and the Mistakes of Trotsky and Bukharin.' LCW, 32. LSW (1970), 3, 523–54.

1921b 'Integrated Economic Plan.' LCW, 32. LSW (1970), 3, 555–62, LOSS, 259–67.

1921c Letter to M. F. Sokolov. LCW, 35. LOSS, 276–8.

1921d 'The Tax in Kind.' LCW, 32. LSW (1970), 3, 589–619. Extracts, LOSS, 268–74.

1921e Instruction of the Council of Labour and Defence to local Soviet bodies. LCW, 32. LOSS, 279–301.

1921f Preliminary Draft Resolution [on Party Unity]. LCW, 32. LSW, 631–4.

1921g Letter on 'the personal touch'. LOSS, 318–19.

1921h Speech closing All-Russia Conference of the RCP (B), 28 May. LCW, 32. LSW (1970), 3, 620–1, LSW, 635–6.

1921i 'The 4th Anniversary of the October Revolution.' LCW, 33. LSW (1970), 3, 641–8, LSW, 645–52.

1921j 'The Importance of Gold Now and After the Complete Victory of Socialism.' LCW, 33. LSW (1970), 3, 649–55, LSW, 653–9.

1922a Draft Theses on the Role and Functions of the Trade Unions under the New Economic Policy. LCW, 42. LOSS, 325–8.

1922b 'Tasks of the People's Commisariat of Justice.' LOSS, 340–5.

1922c Letter to Sokolnikov. LCW, 35. LOSS, 346–7.

1922d Speech at a Plenary Session of the Moscow Soviet. LCW, 33. LSW (1970), 3, 729–38, LSW, 674–80.

1922e 'On the 10th Anniversary of *Pravda*.' LCW, 33. LSW, 668–71.

1923a 'Pages from a Diary.' LCW, 33. LSW (1970), 3, 755–9, LSW, 685–9.

1923b 'On Co-operation.' LCW, 33. LSW (1970), 3, 760–6, LSW, 690–5.
1923c 'Our Revolution.' LCW, 33. LSW (1970), 3, 767–70, LSW, 696–9.
1923d 'Better Fewer but Better.' LCW, 33. LSW (1970), 3, 776–88, LSW, 700–12, LOSS, 410–24.

D *TROTSKY*

COLLECTIONS

I There exists no Collected Works. Pathfinder Press (NY and L) are, however, currently issuing a series of volumes (entitled *Writings of Leon Trotsky*) in which it is intended that all texts of 1929–40 unavailable in English elsewhere be published. We do *not* reference these below.

II **Collections/Anthologies**

The Essential Trotsky. L, Allen & Unwin, 1963. Cited as: ETr.
The Trotsky Papers. 2 vols, ed. J. I. Meijer, The Hague, Mouton/Nijhoff, 1964 and 1971. Cited as: TP1, TP2.
Marxism & Military Affairs. Sri Lanka, Colombo, Young Socialist Pubs, 1969. Cited as: MMA.
The First Five Years of the Communist International. 2 vols, Vol. 1, NY, Monad Pr., 1972, Vol. 2, L, New Park, 1974. Cited as: CI1, CI2.
The Challenge of the Left Opposition, 1923–1925. NY, Pathfinder, 1975. Cited as: LO.
The 3rd International After Lenin. NY, Pioneer, 1957. Cited as: Int.
The Stalin School of Falsification. NY, Pioneer, 1962 (2nd ed.). Cited as: SF.
Germany, 1931–1932. L, New Park, 1970. Cited as: G.
In Defence of Marxism (Against the Petty-Bourgeois Opposition). L, New Park, 1966. Cited as: DM.

III **Selections**

The Age of Permanent Revolution: A Trotsky Anthology. Ed. I. Deutscher, NY, Dell, 1964. Cited as: PR.
The Basic Writings of Trotsky. Ed. I. Howe, L, Heinemann, 1964. Cited as: TBW.

TEXTS

1906 *Results and Prospects*. With his 1930a, L, New Park, 1962.
1907 Speech at London Congress of the RSDLP. With his 1909b.
1908 'The Proletariat and the Russian Revolution.' With his 1909b.
1909a 'Our Differences.' With his 1909b.
1909b *1905*. L, Penguin, 1973. Extract, TBW.
1915 'The Struggle for Power.' With his 1909b.
1917 'After the July Days: What Next?' Colombo, Young Socialist Pubs, 1967.

1919a 'Manifesto of the Communist International to the Workers of the World.' CI, 1.

1919b 'To Comrades of the Spartacus League.' CI, 1.

1919c 'En Route: Thoughts on the Progress of the Proletarian Revolution.' CI, 1.

1919d Preface to his 1906, reissued as 'A Review and Some Perspectives'. M, Comintern, 1921. With his 1906.

1920a 'Manifesto of the 2nd World Congress [of Comintern].' CI, 1.

1920b 'Speech on Comrade Zinoviev's Report on the Role of the Party.' CI, 1.

1920c 'On the Policy of the KAPD.' CI, 1. *Communist International*, 17, 1921.

1921a 'The Main Lesson of the 3rd Congress.' CI, 1.

1921b Report on 'the balance sheet' of the 3rd Congress of the Communist International. CI, 1.

1921c Report on the World Economic Crisis and the New Tasks of the Communist International. CI, 1.

1921d Summary Speech at 3rd Comintern World Congress. CI, 1.

1921e 'Theses of the 3rd World Congress on the international situation and the tasks of the Comintern.' CI, 1.

1921f Speech on Comrade Lenin's Report: 'Tactics of the RCP'. CI, 1.

1921g Letter to Comrades Cachin and Frossard, 14 July. CI, 1.

1921h Speech delivered at the 2nd World Conference of Communist Women. CI, 1.

1921i 'Unified Military Doctrine' [two speeches before the Military Scientific Society attached to the Military Academy of the Red Army]. MMA. *Fourth International*, Jan 1944.

1921j 'Military Doctrine or Pseudo-Military Doctrinairism?' MMA. *Fourth International*, Feb, Mar, Apr 1944.

1922a 'On the special features of Russia's historical development.' With his 1909b.

1922b 'Marxism & Military Knowledge' [Speech before Military Scientific Society attached to the Military Academy of the Red Army]. MMA. *Fourth International*, Dec 1943.

1922c 'The Position of the Republic and the Tasks of Young Workers.' L, Plough Pr. (Young Socialists), 1972.

1923a 'Lenin Ill' [Speech at 7th Conference of Ukrainian CP]. With his 1924b.

1923b *The New Course*. Michigan, Ann Arbor, 1965. LO. Extract, TBW.

1924a Young People Study Politics! [and other speeches]. *Fourth International*, Jan 1966.

1924b *On Lenin: Notes towards a Biography*. Harrap, 1971.

1924c *The Lessons of October*. LO, and as pamphlet from Pathfinder.

1925 *Whither Russia: towards Capitalism or Socialism? International*, Vol. 2, No. 2, 1973. LO, and as pamphlet from Pathfinder.

1926 'Radio, science, technique and society.' *Labour Review*, Nov/Dec 1957. Sep. pamphlet, L, New Park; and in his *Marxism and Science*, Pathfinder.

1927a (*et al.*) *Platform of the Left Opposition*. L, New Park, 1963.

1927b 'Letter to the Bureau of Party History.' SF, and (as 'Stalin Falsifies History') ETr.

1928 *The Draft Programme of the Communist International: a criticism of fundamentals*. Int.

1929 *My Life*. NY, Grosset & Dunlap, 1960. L, Penguin, 1975. Extracts, TBW.

1930a *The Permanent Revolution*. With his 1906.

1930b, c, d *History of the Russian Revolution*. 3 vols, L, Sphere, 1967. Abridged ed., NY, Anchor, 1959. Extracts, PR, TBW.

1930e 'Socialism in a Separate Country.' Appx to his 1930d.

1932 *Germany: What Next?* G. Extract, TBW.

1933 *The Class Nature of the Soviet State*. With *The Question of Thermidor and Bonapartism*. L, New Park, 1968.

1934 *The Young Lenin*. L, Penguin, 1974.

1936 *The Revolution Betrayed*. L, New Park, 1967. Extracts, TBW.

1937 'Stalinism and Bolshevism.' TBW. Sep. pamphlet, L, New Park.

1939a A letter to James P. Cannon, 12 Sep. DM.

1939b 'The USSR in War.' DM. TBW.

1939c 'Again and once more again on the nature of the USSR.' DM.

1939d A letter to Max Shachtman, 6 Nov. DM.

1939e 'A Petty-Bourgeois Opposition in the SWP.' DM.

1939f *The Living Thoughts of Karl Marx*. Greenwich, Conn., Fawcett, 1963.

1940a 'Three Concepts of the Russian Revolution.' Appx to his 1940b. TBW.

1940b *Stalin*. [Only chs 1–7 – that is *until* 1917 – are as Trotsky wrote them. Thereafter the material is edited from notes and mss left behind after Trotsky's assassination, by C. Malamuth.] L, Hollis & Carter, 1947. L, Panther (in 2 vols), 1969.

1940c 'The Class, the Party, and the Leadership.' In T. Cliff *et al.*, *Party & Class*, L, Pluto Pr., n.d.

1940d 'From a scratch – to the danger of gangrene.' DM.

1940e 'Balance sheet of the Finnish events.' DM.

E *STALIN*

COLLECTIONS

I *Collected Works*, M, FLPH, 1952 onwards, reprinted L, Red Star Pr. 1975 onwards. 15 vols. Cited as SCW, 1, 2, etc.

II **Other Collections**

Leninism. L, Lawrence & Wishart, 1942. Cited as: L.

The Essential Stalin. Ed. B. Franklin, L, Croom Helm, 1973. Cited as: ES.

On the Opposition. P, FLP, 1974. Cited as: SO.

TEXTS

1905 'The Proletarian Class and the Proletarian Party.' ES, 39–47. SCW, 1.

1913 'Marxism & the National Question.' ES, 54–84 (abridged). SCW, 2.

1924a *The Foundations of Leninism*. L, 1–85. ES, 89–186, SCW, 6. Sep. ed., P, FLP, 1965.
1924b 'The October Revolution and the Tactics of the Russian Communists.' L, 86–117. SO, 139–82, SCW, 6.
1925 'Concerning the Question of the Proletariat and the Peasantry.' ES, 187–93. SCW, 7.
1926 'On the Problems of Leninism.' L, 118–74. SO, 268–346, SCW, 8 [under title 'Concerning Questions of Leninism' in latter two sources].
1927a 'The Party's Three Fundamental Slogans on the Peasant Problems.' L, 175–86. SCW, 9.
1927b 'The Slogan of the Dictatorship of the Proletariat and the Poor Peasantry in the Period of Preparation for October.' L, 187–96. SCW, 9.
1927c 'The International Character of the October Revolution.' L, 197–204. SCW, 10.
1928a 'Organise Mass Criticism from Below' [from a speech to the 8th Komsomol Congress, 16 May]. ES, 220–3. SCW, 11.
1928b 'On the Grain Front.' L, 205–16 (extracts). SCW, 11.
1928c 'Lenin and the Question of Alliance with the Middle Peasant.' L, 217–27. SCW, 11.
1928d 'The Right Danger in the CPSU (B).' L, 228–39. SCW, 11.
1929a 'The Right Deviation in the CPSU (B).' L, 240–93. SCW, 12.
1929b 'A Year of Great Change.' L, 294–305. SCW, 12.
1929c 'Problems of Agrarian Policy in the USSR.' L, 306–27. SCW, 12 [under title 'Concerning Questions of Agrarian Policy in the USSR'].
1930a 'The Policy of Eliminating the Kulaks as a Class.' L, 328–32. SCW, 12.
1930b 'Dizzy with success.' L, 333–8. SCW, 12.
1930c 'Reply to Collective Farm Comrades.' L, 339–58. SCW, 12.
1931a 'The Task of Business Executives.' L, 359–67. SCW, 13.
1931b 'Some Questions Concerning the History of Bolshevism.' L, 388–400. SCW, 13.
1933 'The Results of the 1st Five Year Plan.' L, 401–40. SCW, 13.
1934 Report on the Work of the CC to the 17th Congress of the CPSU (B). L, 470–539. ES, 224–99, SCW, 13.
1935 'Speech at the 1st All-Union Conference of Stakhanovites.' L, 546–60. SCW.
1936 'On the Draft Constitution of the USSR.' L, 561–90. SCW.
1938 'Dialectical and Historical Materialism.' [From: *History of the Communist Party of the Soviet Union (Bolsheviks): Short Course*, M, FLPH, 1939, reprinted L, Red Star Pr., 1972.] L, 591–618. ES, 300–33, SCW.
1939 Report on the Work of the CC to the 18th Congress of the CPSU (B). L, 619–67, ES, 334–92, SCW.
1950 'Marxism and the Problems of Linguistics.' ES, 407–44. Sep. ed., P, FLP, 1972. SCW.
1952a *Economic Problems of Socialism in the USSR*. P, FLP, 1972. Extracts, ES, 445–507. SCW.
1952b Speech to the 19th Congress of the CPSU. ES, 508–11. SCW.

F *MAO TSE-TUNG*

Note. For a chronological bibliography of Mao's writings (1917–68) see Ch'en II, 163f.

COLLECTIONS

I General Collections

(*a*) Authorised by CC/CPC

Selected Works. 4 vols, P, FLP, 1965 (Vol. 4, 1961) [Note: there are pagination changes between different printings.] Cited as: MTSW, 1, 2, etc.

Selected Readings. P, FLP, 1971. Cited as: MTSR.

Quotations from Chairman Mao Tsetung. P, FLP, 1967. Cited as: MTQ.

(*b*) Unauthorised

The Political Thought of Mao Tsetung. Ed. S. R. Schram, L, Penguin, 1969. Cited as: Schram I.

Mao Tsetung Unrehearsed: Talks and Letters, 1956–71. Ed. S. R. Schram, L, Penguin, 1974. Cited as: Schram II.

Mao. Ed. J. Ch'en, Prentice Hall, 1969. Cited as: Ch'en I.

Mao Papers. Ed. J. Ch'en, Oxford Univ Pr., 1970. Cited as: Ch'en II.

Miscellany of Mao Tsetung Thought. 2 vols, Virginia, Joint Publications Research Service, Nos 61269–1 & 61269–2. Cited as: *Miscellany*.

II Anthologies/Selections

(*a*) Authorised by CC/CPC

Four Essays on Philosophy. P, FLP, 1966. Cited as: MTFE.

Selected Military Writings of Mao Tsetung. P, FLP, 1968. Cited as: MTMR.

Poems. P, FLP, 1976.

(*b*) Unauthorised

Mao Tsé-toung et la construction du socialisme. Ed. Hu Chi-hsi, Paris, Seuil, 1975. Cited as: Hu Chi-hsi.

TEXTS

Note. Texts marked thus * are available in separate eds from P, FLP.

*1926 'Analysis of Classes in Chinese Society.' MTSW, 1, 13–21. MTSR, 11–22.

*1927 Report on an Investigation of the Peasant Movement in Hunan. MTSW, 1, 23–57. MTSR, 23–39 (abridged).

*1928 'Why is it that Red Political Power can exist in China?' MTSW, 1, 63–72.

*1929 'On Correcting Mistaken Ideas in the Party.' MTSW, 1, 108–15.

*1930 'Oppose Book Worship.' MTSR, 40–50.

1933a 'Pay Attention to Economic Work.' MTSW, 1, 129–36.

*1933b 'How to Differentiate the Classes in the Rural Areas.' MTSW, 1, 137–9.

1934a 'Our Economic Policy.' MTSW, 1, 141–5.

*1934b 'Be Concerned with the Well-being of the Masses, Pay Attention to Methods of Work.' MTSW, 1, 147–52. MTSR, 51–7.

*1935 'On Tactics Against Japanese Imperialism.' MTSW, 1, 153–78.

*1936 'Problems of Strategy in China's Revolutionary War.' MTSW, 1, 179–254.

*1937a 'Win the Masses in their Millions.' MTSW, 1, 285–94.

*1937b 'On Practice.' MTSW, 1, 295–309. MTSR, 65–84, MTFE, 1–22.

*1937c 'On Contradiction.' MTSW, 1, 311–41. MTSR, 85–133, MTFE, 23–78.

*1937d 'Combat Liberalism.' MTSW, 2, 31–3. MTSR, 134–7, *Five Articles by Chairman Mao Tsetung*, P, FLP, 1968.

*1938a 'On Protracted War.' MTSW, 2, 113–94.

*1938b 'Problems of War and Strategy.' MTSW, 2, 219–35.

*1939a 'To be Attacked by the Enemy is not a Bad Thing, but a Good Thing.' MTSR, 160–2.

*1939b 'Introducing "The Communist".' MTSW, 2, 285–96. MTSR, 163–78.

*1939c 'The Chinese Revolution and the Chinese Communist Party.' MTSW, 2, 305–34.

*1940a 'On New Democracy.' MTSW, 2, 339–84.

*1940b 'On New Democratic Constitutional Government.' MTSW, 2, 407–15.

*1941a Preface to *Rural Surveys*. MTSW, 3, 11–13. MTSR, 194–7.

*1941b Postscript to *Rural Surveys*. MTSW, 3, 14–16.

*1941c 'Reform our Study.' MTSW, 3, 17–25. MTSR, 198–208.

*1942a 'Rectify the Party's Style of Work.' MTSW, 3, 35–51. MTSR, 209–29.

*1942b 'Oppose Stereotyped Party Writing.' MTSW, 3, 53–68. MTSR, 230–49.

*1942c Talks at the Yenan Forum on Literature and Art. MTSW, 3, 69–98, MTSR, 250–86, *Mao Tsetung on Literature and Art*, P, FLP, 1967, 1–43.

*1942d 'Economic and Financial Problems in the Anti-Japanese War' [Ch. 1]. MTSW, 3, 111–16.

*1943a 'Some Questions Concerning Methods of Leadership.' MTSW, 3, 117–22. MTSR, 287–94.

*1943b 'Spread the Campaigns to Reduce Rent, Increase Production, and "Support the Government and Cherish the People" in the Base Areas.' MTSW, 3, 131–5.

*1943c 'Get Organised!' MTSW, 3, 153–61. MTSR, 295–305.

*1944 'Our Study and the Current Situation.' MTSW, 3, 163–76.

*1945a 'We must Learn to do Economic Work!' MTSW, 3, 239–45.

1945b 'Production is also possible in the Guerrilla Zones.' MTSW, 3, 247–50.

1945c Resolution on Certain Questions in the History of Our Party [Appx. to 1944]. MTSW, 3, 177–225.

*1945d 'On Coalition Government.' MTSW, 3, 255–320.

*1945e 'On Production by the Army for its own Support, and on the Importance of the Great Movements for Rectification and Production.' MTSW, 3, 325–9.

1945f 'Rent Reduction and Production are Two Important Matters for the Defence of the Liberated Areas.' MTSW, 3, 71–3.

1945g 'Policy for Work in the Liberated Areas for 1946.' MTSW, 4, 75–9.

*1946a Talk with Anna Louise Strong. MTSW, 4, 97–101. MTSR, 345–50.

1946b 'Some Points in Appraisal of the Present International Situation.' MTSW, 4, 87–8.

*1947 'The Present Situation and Our Tasks.' MTSW, 4, 157–76.

*1948a 'On Some Important Problems of the Party's Present Policy.' MTSW, 4, 181–9.

1948b 'Different Tactics for Carrying Out the Land Law in Different Areas.' MTSW, 4, 193–5.

1948c 'Correct the "Left" Errors in Land Reform Propaganda.' MTSW, 4, 197–9.

1948d 'Essential Points in Land Reform in the New Liberated Areas.' MTSW, 4, 201–2.

1948e 'Tactical Problems of Rural Work in the New Liberated Areas.' MTSW, 4, 251–2.

1949a 'Turn the Army into a Working Force.' MTSW, 4, 337–9.

*1949b Report to the 2nd Plenary Session of the 7th CC/CPC. MTSW, 4, 361–75.

*1949c 'On the People's Democratic Dictatorship.' MTSW, 4, 411–24. MTSR, 371–88.

1950 Speech at the 3rd Session of the 7th CC/CPC. Extract: 'We must preserve a non-peasant economy.' Schram I, 342–3.

*1955 'On the Question of Agricultural Co-operation.' MTSR, 389–420.

1956a (Ed.) *Socialist Upsurge in China's Countryside*. P, FLP, 1957. [Abridged from *The High Tide of Socialism in the Chinese Countryside*, 3 vols, P, 1955–6. q.v. Gray, 1970.] Extracts, MTSR, 421–31, excerpts, MTQ.

1956b 'On the Ten Great Relationships.' Schram II, 61–83. Ch'en I, 65–85.

1956c *On the Historical Experience of the Dictatorship of the Proletariat*. P, FLP, 1957.

1956d Talk to Music Workers (24 Aug). Schram II, text 2.

*1957a 'On the Correct Handling of Contradictions Among the People.' MTSR, 432–79. MTFE, 79–133.

*1957b Speech at the CPC National Conference on Propaganda Work. MTSR, 480–98. *Mao Tsetung on Literature and Art*, P, FLP, 1967, 142–62.

1957c 'Outline of Views on the Question of Peaceful Transition.' Appx. to *The Origin and Development of the Differences between the Leadership of the CPSU and Ourselves*, P, FLP, 1963, and in CPC, 1965.

1958a 'Introducing a Co-operative.' MTSR, 499–501.

1958b Chengtu Speeches. Schram II, text 4.

1958c Speech [to the Military Affairs Committee] 28 June. Schram II, text 5.

1958d Resolution on the Establishment of People's Communes. Appx. to Ascher, 1972: 45–9.

1958e 'Sixty Points on Working Methods – a Draft Resolution.' Ch'en II, 57–76. Abbreviated as Instruction, 31 Jan 1958, Ch'en II, 82–3.

1958f 'A propos des *Problèmes Economiques du Socialisme en URSS* de Staline.' Hu Chi-hsi, text 1. (Eng. tr. *Miscellany*.)
1959a Speech at Lushan Conference. Schram II, text 6.
1959b 'Annotations des *Problèmes Economiques du Socialisme en URSS*.' Hu Chi-hsi, text 2. (Eng. tr. *Miscellany*.)
1962a 'On Democratic Centralism.' Schram II, text 8.
1962b Speech at the 10th Plenum of the 8th CC/CPC. Schram II, text 9.
*1963a 'Where do Correct Ideas Come From?' [Draft Decision of the CC/CPC on Certain Problems in our Present Rural Work]. MTSR, 502–4, MTFE, 134–6.
1963b 'The Seven Well-written Documents of the Chekiang Province concerning Cadres' Participation in Physical Labour.' Qu. in *On Khrushchev's Phoney Communism*, P, FLP, 1964, 71–2 (this is also in CPC, 1965). Schram I, 367.
1964a Fifteen Theses on Socialist Construction. In *On Khrushchev's Phoney Communism*, P, FLP, 1964, and reprinted in CPC, 1965.
1964b Talk on Questions of Philosophy. Schram II, text 11.
1964c Remarks at the Spring Festival [on Education]. Schram II, text 10. Extracts, Ch'en II, 93–7.
1965 Speech at Hangchow. Schram II, text 14.
1966a 3rd Talk with his Nephew. Schram II, 251–2.
1966b Talk to Leaders of the Centre. Schram II, text 16.
1966c Speech at a Meeting with Regional Secretaries and Members of the Cultural Revolutionary Group of the CC. Schram II, text 17. Another version, Ch'en II, 26–30.
1966d A Letter to the Red Guards of Tsinghua University Middle School. Schram II, text 18.
1966e Speech at the Closing Ceremony of the 11th Plenum of the 8th CC/CPC. Schram II, text 19.
1966eb Sixteen Point Directive, 11th Plenum, 8th CC. In J. Robinson, 1968, 85–96.
1966f Talk at the Report Meeting. Schram II, text 20.
1966g Talk at the Central Work Conference. Schram II, text 21.
1966h Instructions, qu. Machetzkai, 1974: 63. [*Note*. Instructions issued by Mao during the GPCR are collected in Ch'en, II, 77–159, Wheelright & McFarlane, 1970, and Schram I, 368–71.]
1967 Talk at a Meeting of the Central Cultural Revolution Group, 9 Jan. Schram II, text 22. Ch'en II, 45–7.
1969 Talk at 1st Plenum of 9th CC/CPC. Schram II, text 25.
1971 Talks on the Lin Piao Affair. Schram II, text 26.

PART TWO

Adizes, I., 1971. *Industrial Democracy: Yugoslav Style*. Glencoe, Free Pr.
Akhapkin, Y., 1970 (ed.). *First Decrees of Soviet Power*. L, Lawrence & Wishart.
Alston, P. L., 1969. *Education and the State in Tsarist Russia*. [1700–1914]. Stanford Univ. Pr.

Althusser, L., 1961. 'On the Young Marx.' In his *For Marx*. L, Penguin, 1969.
——1972a. 'Reply to John Lewis.' In his 1976.
——1972b. 'Note on "The Critique of the Personality Cult".' In his 1976.
——1973. 'Remark on the category "Process without a Subject or Goals".' In his 1976.
——1974. 'Elements of Self-Criticism.' In his 1976.
——1975. 'Is it simple to be a Marxist in Philosophy?' In his 1976.
——1976. *Essays in Self-Criticism*. L, New Left Books.
Althusser, L., and Balibar, E., 1968. *Reading Capital*. L, New Left Books.
Anderson, P., 1974a. *Passages from Antiquity to Feudalism*. L, New Left Books.
——1974b. *Lineages of the Absolutist State*. L, New Left Books.
——1974c. *Considerations on Western Marxism*. L, New Left Books, 1976.
——1976. Afterword to his 1974c.
Andrle, V., 1973. 'The Factory Director in the "Command Economy": the case of contemporary USSR.' CRRES Science and Industry Seminar, 7/8 Dec.
——1976. *Managerial Power in the Soviet Union*. Saxon House, forthcoming.
Ascher, I., 1972. *China's Social Policy*. L, Anglo-Chinese Educational Institute.
Baron, S. H., 1953. 'Plekhanov on Russian capitalism and the peasant commune.' *Am. Slavic and East European Rev.*, 12:1.
Belden, J., 1949. *China Shakes the World*. L, Penguin, 1973.
Benson, L., 1974. 'Market-Socialism and Class Structure: Manual Workers and Managerial Power in Yugoslav Enterprise.' Paper to BSA Annual Conference 1973, reprinted Parkin 1974.
Berliner, J., 1952. 'The Informal Organisation of the Soviet Union.' *Qu. J. of Economics*, reprinted F. Holzman (ed.), *Readings in the Soviet Economy*, 1962.
——1957. *Factory and Manager in the USSR*. Harvard Univ. Pr.
Bettelheim, C., 1950. 'Discussion on the problem of choice between alternative investment projects.' *Soviet Studies*.
——1966. 'La construction du socialisme.' *La Pensée*, 125 and 126.
——1967. *The transition to Socialist Economy*. Hassocks, Harvester, 1975.
——1969. Preface to Fr. ed. of, and Theoretical Comments on, A. Emmanuel, *Unequal Exchange*, L, New Left Books, 1972.
——1970a. *Economic Calculation & Forms of Property*. L, Routledge, 1976.
——1970b. 'Sur la persistance des rapports marchands dans les "pays socialistes".' *Temps Modernes*, 27.
——1971. His contributions to *On the Transition to Socialism*. With P. Sweezy, NY and L, Monthly Review Pr.
——1972. 'Note de lecture sur l'article: "De la Chine et des racines de la Sinophile occidentale".' *Tel Quel*, 48/49.
——1973. *Cultural Revolution & Industrial Organisation in China*. NY and L, Monthly Review Pr., 1974.
——1974. *Class Struggles in the USSR. 1st period: 1917–1923*. Hassocks, Harvester, 1976.
Bianco, L., 1971. *Origins of the Chinese Revolution, 1915–1949*. Rev. ed., Oxford.
Bilandzic, D., 1967. 'Odnosi, izmedju samoupravljanja i rukovodjenja u poduzecu.' In Dmitrejevic/Kovacevic (ed.) *Savremeno Rukovodjenje i Samoupravljanje*. Beograd, Pravni Facultet.

Blackburn, R. (ed.), 1972. *Ideology in Social Science*. L, Fontana.
Borisova, Y. S., 1973. *Outline History of the Russian Working Class*. M, Progress.
Brandt, C., 1958. *Stalin's Failure in China*. Harvard Univ. Pr.
Brezhnev, L., 1972. *The 50th Anniversary of the USSR*. M, Novosti.
——1974. Speech to the 17th Komsomol Congress, 23 Apr. *Moscow News*, 17 (1216).
——1975. *Following Lenin's Course: Speeches and Articles 1972–1975*. M, Progress.
Brinton, M., 1975. 'Factory Committees and the Dictatorship of the Proletariat.' *Critique*, 4.
Brown, N., 1970. *1945–1968*. L, Pan.
Brus, W., 1964. *The Market in Socialist Economy*. L, Routledge, 1972.
——1971. 'Contradictions and Ways to Resolve them.' *Renascità*, June. Reprinted as ch. 7 of his 1973.
——1973. *The Economics and Politics of Socialism*. L, Routledge.
Brutzkus, B., 1934. 'Historical Peculiarities of the Social and Economic Development of Russia.' In R. Bendix/S. Lipset (ed.), *Class, Status and Power*, 2nd ed., L, Routledge, 1964.
Buchanan, K., 1967. *The South East Asian World*. Bell.
——1970. *The Transformation of the Chinese Earth*. Bell.
Buick, A., 1975. 'Joseph Deitzgen.' *Radical Philosophy*, 10.
Bukharin, N., 1921. *Historical Materialism: A Systematic Sociology*. Michigan, Ann Arbor, 1969.
Bukharin, N., and Preobazhensky, E., 1920. *The ABC of Communism*. L, Penguin, 1969.
Burt, W., 1972. 'Workers' Participation in Management in Yugoslavia.' *Bull. of the Int. Institute for Labour Studies*, No. 9.
Carr, E. H., 1950. *The Bolshevik Revolution, 1917–1923*. Vol. 1. L, Penguin, 1966.
——1952. Id., Vol. 2. L, Penguin, 1966.
——1953. Id., Vol. 3. L, Penguin, 1966.
——1954. *The Interregnum, 1923–4*. L, Penguin, 1969.
——1958. *Socialism in One Country, 1924–1926*. Vol. 1. L, Penguin, 1970.
——1959. Id., Vol. 2. L, Penguin, 1970.
——1964. Id., Vol. 3. L, Penguin, 1972.
——1967. 'Revolution from Above.' *New Left Rev.*, 46.
——1969. *Foundations of a Planned Economy*, 1926–9. Vol. 1 (with R. W. Davies). L, Penguin, 1974.
——1971. Id., Vol. 2. L, Penguin, 1976.
——1974. Review of S. F. Cohen, 1974. *Times Lit. Supp.*, 20 Sept.
Chang, S., 1931. *The Marxian Theory of the State*. NY, Russell, 1965.
Chen, J., 1973. *A Year in Upper Felicity*. Harrap.
——1975. *Inside the Cultural Revolution*. L, Sheldon Pr.
Cheng Yueh, 1976. 'Adhere to the Party's Basic Line: Studying "On the Correct Handling of Contradictions Among the People".' *Peking Rev.*, 5.
Cherepin, N., 1975. 'An unfading example of proletarian heroism.' *Pravda*, 19 Oct.
Chernilovsky, Z., 1970. 'Contemporary views in the USSR on the origin and role of the State.' *Int. Soc. Sci. J.*, 12:3.
Chesneaux, J., 1973. *Peasant Revolts in China, 1840–1949*. L, Thames & Hudson.

Chih Heng, 1976. 'Firmly Grasp Class Struggle as the Key Link.' *Peking Rev.*, 6.

Chossudovsky, E., 1973. 'Why Armand Hammer goes back along the road he first trod with Lenin.' *Times*, 24 Feb.

Chou En-lai, 1973. Report to the 10th Congress of the CPC. *Hsinhua News Agency*, 1 Sep.

Chu Li and Tien Chieh-yun, 1974. *Inside a People's Commune*. P, FLP.

Cliff, T., 1970. *Russia: a Marxist Analysis*. L, IS Books (Pluto Pr.).

——1975. *Lenin*. Vol. 1, L, Pluto Pr.

Cohen, G. A., 1972. 'Karl Marx and the Withering Away of Social Science.' *Philosophy and Public Affairs*, 1.

Cohen, S. F., 1969. 'Bukharin, Lenin and the theoretical foundations of Bolshevism.' *Soviet Studies*, 21.

——1970. 'Marxist Theory and Bolshevik Policy: the core of Bukharin's "Historical Materialism".' *Pol. Sci. Qu.*

——1974. *Bukharin and the Bolshevik Revolution: a Political Biography*. Wildwood House.

Colletti, L., 1968. 'Bernstein and the Marxism of the 2nd International.' In his *From Rousseau to Lenin*, L, New Left Books, 1972.

——1969. 'The concept of the "social relations of production".' Ch. 9 of his *Marxism and Hegel*, L, New Left Books, 1973.

——1970. 'The Question of Stalin.' *New Left Rev.*, 61.

——1974. Introduction to Marx, CEW.

Collier, J. and E., 1973. *China's Socialist Revolution*. L, Stage One.

Colman, E., 1931. 'Short Communication on the unpublished manuscripts of Karl Marx . . .' In *Science at the Crossroads*, L, Kniga.

Communist Party of China (CPC), 1963. *A Proposal Concerning the General Line of the International Communist Movement*. P, FLP.

——1964. *Whence the Differences?* Bath, New Era, n.d.

——1965. *The Polemic on the General Line of the International Communist Movement*. P, FLP. Reprinted, L, Red Star Press, n.d.

——1973. *The 10th National Congress of the CPC: Documents*. P, FLP.

——1975. *Documents of the 1st Session of the 4th National People's Congress of the PRC*. P, FLP.

Communist Party of the Soviet Union (CPSU), 1971. *Report of 24th Congress*. M, Novosti.

——1976. *Documents and Resolutions, 25th Congress of the CPSU*. Supp. to *Socialism: Theory and Practice*, June. M, Novosti.

Considine, B., 1975. *Larger than Life: a biography of the remarkable Dr. Armand Hammer*. NY, Harper & Row, L, W. H. Allen.

Corrigan, P. R. D., 1974. 'On the historical experience of the People's Republic of China.' *J. Contemporary Asia*, Vol. 4.

——1975a. 'On the politics of production.' *J. Peasant Studies*, Vol. 3.

——1975b. 'Dichotomy is contradiction.' *Sociological Rev.*, Vol. 24.

——1976. *State Formation and Moral Regulation in 19th Century Britain: Sociological Investigations*. PhD, Durham, 1977.

——1976b. 'On Socialist Construction.' *J. Contemporary Asia*, Vol. 6.

——1977. 'Feudal Relics or Capitalist Monuments: Notes on the sociology of Unfree Labour.' *Sociology*, Vol. 11.

Corrigan, P. R. D., and Gillespie, V., 1974. 'Class Struggle, Social Literacy, and Idle Time: the provision of Public Libraries in Britain.' Brighton, Labour History Monographs, 1977.

Corrigan, P. R. D., Ramsay, H., and Sayer, D., 1978. *For Mao: Essays in Historical Materialism.* L, Macmillan, forthcoming.

Corrigan, P. R. D., and Sayer, D., 1975. 'Moral Relations, Political Economy and Class Struggle.' *Radical Philosophy*, 12.

Daily Herald, 1917. *What Happened in Leeds: Report published by the Council of Workers' and Soldiers' Delegates.* Reprinted, Nottingham, Spokesman, 1975.

Dallemagne, J.-L., 1975. 'Justice for Bukharin.' *Critique*, 4.

Daubier, J., 1974. *A History of the Chinese Cultural Revolution.* NY, Vintage.

Davin, D., 1976. 'Women in Revolutionary China.' In J. Mitchell/A. Oakley (ed.) *The Rights and Wrongs of Women*, L, Penguin.

Day, R., 1973. *Leon Trotsky and the politics of economic isolation.* Cambridge Univ. Pr.

Deutscher, I., 1949. *Stalin.* Oxford Univ. Pr.

——1954. *The Prophet Armed: Trotsky, 1879–1921.* Oxford Univ. Pr.

——1959. *The Prophet Unarmed: Trotsky, 1921–1929.* Oxford Univ. Pr.

——1963. *The Prophet Outcast: Trotsky, 1929–1940.* Oxford Univ. Pr.

——1967. 'The Unfinished Revolution, 1917–1967.' *New Left Rev.*, 43.

Draper, H., 1962. 'Marx and the Dictatorship of the Proletariat.' *Etudes de Marxologie*, 6 (*Cahiers de l'ISEA* Serie S). [Condensed version, *New Politics* 1:4.]

——1970. 'The death of the State in Marx and Engels.' *Socialist Register.* (L, Merlin Pr.)

Duggett, M., 1972. *The Marxist conception of the Peasant: category and power in the theories of Marx and Lenin.* Oxford, BPhil thesis.

——1975. 'Marx on Peasants.' *J. Peasant Studies.*

Elegant, R., 1951. *China's Red Masters.* L, Westport, 1973.

Ellman, M., 1968. 'Lessons of the Soviet Economic Reform.' *Socialist Register.* (L, Merlin Pr.)

——1971. *Soviet Planning Today: Proposals for an optimally functioning economic system.* Cambridge Univ. Pr. (DAE Paper 25).

——1973. *Planning Problems in the USSR: the contribution of mathematical economists to the solution, 1960–71.* Cambridge Univ. Pr.

Falkus, M., 1972. *The Industrialisation of Russia, 1700–1914.* L, Macmillan.

Fernbach, D., 1974. 'The Chinese view of Stalin.' *China Now*, 14.

Feyerabend, P., 1969. 'Consolations for the Specialist.' In I. Lakatos/A. Musgrave (ed.), *Criticism and the Growth of Knowledge*, Cambridge Univ. Pr., 1970.

Foley, C., 1974. 'The amazing Hammer and sickle show.' *Observer*, 30 June.

Gelder, S. (ed.), 1946. *The Chinese Communists.* L, Gollancz (Left Book Club).

Geras, N., 1971. 'Marx and the Critique of Political Economy.' In R. Blackburn, 1972.

Gerschenkron, A., 1964. 'Reflections on the economic aspects of revolutions.' In H. Eckstein (ed.), *Internal War*, Glencoe, Free Pr.

Gershberg, S., 1973. *The Socialist Emulation Movement.* M, Novosti.

Gide, A., 1937. *Afterthoughts: a sequel to 'Back from the USSR'.* 2nd ed., L, Secker.

Gittings, J., 1973 (ed.). *A Chinese View of China*. L, BBC.

——1974. 'New Light on Mao: 1. His View of the World.' *China Qu.*, 60.

Godelier, M., 1964a. 'Structure and Contradiction in *Capital*.' In R. Blackburn, 1972.

——1964b. 'The measurement of value: a problem of optimum management in a socialist economy.' In his 1972.

——1972. *Rationality and Irrationality in Economics*. L, New Left Books.

——1973. *Horizon, trajets marxistes en anthropologie*. Paris, Maspero.

Goldmann, L., 1971. 'Reflections on "History and Class Consciousness".' In I. Meszaros (ed.), *Aspects of History and Class Consciousness*, L, Routledge.

Goodey, C., 1974. 'Factory Committees and the Dictatorship of the Proletariat.' *Critique*, 3.

——1975. 'Factory Committees . . .; Additional Notes.' *Critique*, 5.

Gramsci, A., 1934a. *Prison Notebooks*. Selections, L, Lawrence & Wishart, 1971.

——1934b. *The Modern Prince*. L, Lawrence & Wishart, 1957.

Gray, J., 1965. 'Political aspects of the Land Reform campaigns in China 1947–72.' *Soviet Studies*, 16.

——1966. 'Some aspects of the development of Chinese agrarian policies.' In R. Adams (ed.), *Contemporary China*, L, Owen, 1969.

——1969a. 'The economics of Maoism.' In H. Bernstein (ed.), *Development and Underdevelopment*, L, Penguin, 1972.

——1969b. 'Recapitulation of factors in the Cultural Revolution.' Hong Kong, Centre for Asian Studies.

——1970. 'The High Tide of Socialism in the Chinese Countryside.' In J. Ch'en (ed.), *Studies in the Social History of China*. Cambridge Univ. Pr.

——1971. 'The Chinese Model.' *L'Est*, 2. In A. Nove/D. Nuti (ed.), *Socialist Economics*, L, Penguin, 1972.

——1972a. 'Mao Tsetung's strategy for the collectivisation of Chinese agriculture.' In E. de Kadt/G. Williams (ed.), *Sociology and Development*, L, Tavistock, 1974.

——1972b. 'Theory of the Great Leap Forward.' Unpublished paper.

——1973a. Contribution to discussion. *Listener*, 5 July.

——1973b. 'The Two Roads: alternative strategies of social change and economic growth in China.' In Schram, 1973c.

——1973c. *Mao Tsetung*. Guildford, Lutterworth Pr.

——1974. 'Politics in Command.' *Pol. Qu.*, 45:1.

——1976a. 'Stalin, Mao, and the future of China.' *New Society*, 1 Apr.

——1976b. 'What is the crime of China's "Gang of Four"?' *New Society*, 4 Nov.

Gray, J., and Cavendish, P., 1968. *Chinese Communism in Crisis: Maoism and the Cultural Revolution*. L, Pall Mall.

Grossman, G., 1971. 'Russia and the Soviet Union.' Ch. 8 of C. Cipolla (ed.), *The Emergence of Industrial Society*, L, Fontana, 1973.

Gurley, J., 1975a. 'The foundation of Mao's economic strategy, 1927–1949.' *Monthly Rev.*, 27:3.

——1975b. 'Rural development in China 1969–72.' *World Development*, 3: 7 and 8.

Haimson, L., 1964. 'The problem of social stability in urban Russia, 1905–1917.' *Slavic Rev.*, 23:4.

——1974 (ed.). *The Mensheviks from the Revolution of 1917 to the Second World War*. Chicago, Univ. Pr.

Hall, R. O. *China's Fight for Freedom*. L, Odhams Pr., n.d.

Han Suyin, 1972. *The Morning Deluge: Mao Tsetung and the Chinese Revolution*. L, Cape.

——1975. *Wind in the Tower: Mao Tsetung and the Chinese Revolution 1949–1975*. L, Cape.

Harding, N., 1975. 'Lenin's Early Writings: the problem of context.' *Pol. Studs.*, 23.

——1976. 'Lenin and his critics: some problems of interpretation.' *European J. of Sociology*, 17:2.

Harman, C., 1969. 'How the revolution was lost.' *International Socialism*, 30.

——1970. 'The inconsistencies of Ernest Mandel.' In Mandel, 1973.

——1971. 'Party and Class.' In T. Cliff *et al.*, *Party and Class*, L, Pluto Pr.

Harrison, J., 1972. *The Long March to Power: a history of the Communist Party of China, 1921–72*. L, Macmillan.

Heren, L. *et al.*, 1973. *China's Three Thousand Years*. L, Times Pubs.

Hindess, B., 1976. Introduction to Bettelheim, 1970a.

Hindess, B., and Hirst, P., 1975. *Precapitalist Modes of Production*. L, Routledge.

Hingley, R., 1974. *Joseph Stalin: Man and Legend*. L, Hutchinson.

Hinton, W., 1966. *Fanshen: a documentary of revolution in a Chinese Village*. NY, Monthly Rev. Pr., 1966; L, Penguin, 1972.

——1969. *China's Continuing Revolution*. L, China Policy Study Group.

——1972a. 'Hundred Day War: the Cultural Revolution at Tsinghua University.' *Monthly Rev.*, 24:3.

——1972b. *Turning Point in China: an essay on the Cultural Revolution*. NY, Monthly Rev. Pr.

——1973. 'Reflections on China.' *Monthly Rev.*, June.

Ho Chi Minh, 1928. 'The Party's Military Work among the Peasants.' In 'A. Neuberg' [i.e. the Comintern Secretariat], *Armed Insurrection*, L, New Left Books, 1970.

Hodges, D., 1965. 'Engels's Contribution to Marxism.' *Socialist Register* (L, Merlin Pr.).

Hofheinz, R., 1969. 'Ecology of Chinese Communist success: rural influence patterns, 1923–45.' In A. D. Barnett (ed.), *Chinese Communist Politics in Action*, Washington, Univ. Pr.

Houn, F., 1973. *A Short History of Chinese Communism*. New Jersey, Prentice-Hall.

Howe, C., 1973a. 'Labour organisation and incentives in industry before and after the Cultural Revolution.' Ch. 4 of Schram 1973c.

——1973b. *Wage Patterns and Wage Policy in Modern China, 1919–1972*. Cambridge, Univ. Pr.

——1974. 'Economic trends and policies.' *Pol. Qu.*, 45:1.

Hunnius, G., *et al.* (ed.), 1973. *Workers' Control*. NY, Vintage.

Hunt, A., 1976. 'Lenin and Sociology.' *Sociological Rev.*, 24.

Hunt, R. N., 1974. *The Political Ideas of Marx and Engels*. Vol. 1. L, Macmillan.

Ignotus, P., 1974. 'The Bolshevik Tsar.' *Sunday Times Review*, 19 May.

Inside a People's Commune. See Chu Li.

Institute for Marxism-Leninism of the CPSU, 1958. [*The Bolsheviks and the October Revolution*] Minutes of the CC/RSDLP (B), Aug 1917–Feb 1918. With extra notes by T. Cliff. L, Pluto Pr., 1974.

International Socialism, 92, Oct 1976 [Obituary issue on Mao].

Isaacs, H., 1951. *Tragedy of the Chinese Revolution*. Stanford Univ. Pr.

Jackson, G., 1966. *Comintern and Peasants in East Europe, 1919–1936*. Columbia Univ. Pr.

——1974. 'Peasant political movements in Eastern Europe.' In H. Landsberger (ed.), *Rural Protest*, L, Macmillan.

Johnstone, M., 1968a. 'Trotsky and the debate on socialism in one country.' *New Left Rev.*, 50.

——1968b. 'Trotsky: Part I – His Ideas.' *Cogito* (YCL).

Jones, G. S., 1973. 'Engels and the end of classical German philosophy.' *New Left Rev.*, 79.

Kant, I., 1781. *Critique of Pure Reason*. L, Dent, 1969.

Karcz, J., 1971. 'From Stalin to Brezhnev: Soviet agricultural policy in historical perspective.' Ch. 2 of J. Millar, 1971.

Karol, K., 1975. *The Second Chinese Revolution*. L, Cape.

Katz, A., 1972. *The Politics of Economic Reform in the Soviet Union*. Praeger.

Kautsky, K., 1899. *The Agrarian Problem*. Cass, 1974.

——1902. *The Social Revolution*. Chicago, Kerr.

——1918. *The Dictatorship of the Proletariat*. Michigan, Ann Arbor, 1974.

——1922. *The Proletarian Revolution and its Programme*. Chicago, Kerr.

Kemp, T., 1969. *Industrialisation in 19th Century Europe*. L, Longman.

Khrushchev, N., 1974. *Khrushchev Remembers*. 2 vols, L, Deutsch, 1971, 1974.

Kidron, M., 1969. 'Maginot Marxism: Mandel's Economics.' In Mandel 1973.

Kochan, L., 1962. *The making of modern Russia*. L, Penguin, 1968.

Konstantinov, F., 1976. 'Historical Materialism.' *Voprosy Filosofii*, 3.

Korbash, E., 1974. *The Economic 'Theories' of Maoism*. M, Progress.

Kosygin, A., 1976. Guidelines for the development of the national economy of the USSR for 1976–1980. *Socialism: theory and practice*, 4.

Krasin, Y., 1975. *Intimidated by revolution: a critical survey of bourgeois conceptions of social revolution*. Extracts, *Socialism: theory and practice*, 11, 1976.

——1976. 'Social revolution at the present time.' *Socialism: theory and practice*, 7.

Krasso, N., 1967. 'Trotsky's Marxism.' *New Left Rev.*, 44.

——1968. 'Reply to Ernest Mandel.' *New Left Rev.*, 48.

Krymov, A., 1971. 'The debate on precapitalist relations in China.' Tr. *Soviet Sociology*, Fall 1972.

Lai En-pu, 1973. 'A cadre's self-criticism.' *China Now*, 64, 1976.

Lane, D., 1968. *The roots of Russian Communism: a social and historical study of Russian Social Democracy*. Rev. ed., L, Robertson, 1975.

——1974. 'Leninism as an ideology of development.' In E. de Kadt/G. Williams (ed.), *Sociology and Development*, L, Tavistock.

——1975. 'Ethnic and Class Stratification in Soviet Kazakhstan, 1917–1939.' *Comparative Studies in Society and History*, 17.

——1976. *The Socialist Industrial State: towards a political sociology of state socialist societies*. L, Allen & Unwin.

Levy, R., 1975. 'New light on Mao: 2. His views on the Soviet Union's *Political Economy*.' *China Qu.*, 61.

Lew, R., 1975. 'Maoism and the Chinese Revolution.' *Socialist Register* (L, Merlin Pr.).

Lewin, M., 1965. 'The immediate background of Soviet collectivisation.' *Soviet Studs.*, 17.

——1966. *Russian Peasants and Soviet Power: a study of collectivisation.* L, Allen & Unwin, 1968.

Li Cheng, 1973. 'The theory of productive forces: its counter-revolutionary essence.' *Peking Rev.*, 48.

Li Chien, 1973. 'Attach importance to the revolution in the superstructure.' *Peking Rev.*, 34.

Lichteim, G., 1970. *A Short History of Socialism.* L, Weidenfeld.

Liebman, M., 1973. *Lenin and Leninism.* L, Cape, 1975.

——1975. 'Bukharinism, revolution and social development.' *Socialist Register* (L, Merlin Pr.).

Liebzon, B., 1976. 'The Communist Movement: its attitude to historical experience.' *Socialism: theory and practice*, 12.

Lin Piao, 1965. *Long Live the Victory of People's War!* 3rd ed., P, FLP, 1967.

Liu Ching, 1964. *The Builders.* P, FLP.

Lockett, M., 1975. Review of Bettelheim 1974. *Bull. of Conference of Socialist Economists.*

Longmate, N., 1973. *As We Lived Then.* L, Hutchinson.

Lowe, M., 1966. 'The function of "China" in Marx, Lenin and Mao.' Berkely, Univ. Calif. Pr.

Lowy, M., 1976. 'From the *Logic* of Hegel to the Finland Station in Petrograd.' *Critique*, 6.

Lukács, G., 1924. 'Bernstein's Triumph.' In his 1968.

——1925. 'Technology and Social Relations' [Critique of Bukharin 1921]. *New Left Rev.*, 39, 1966, and in his 1968.

——1968. *Political Writings, 1919–1929.* L, New Left Books, 1972.

McCauley, M., 1975 (ed.). *The Russian Revolution and the Soviet State 1917–1921: Documents.* L, Macmillan.

Maccio, M., 1970. 'Parti, techniciens et classe ouvrière dans la révolution chinoise.' *Temps Modernes,* 1970. Tr. in A. Gorz (ed.), *The Division of Labour,* Hassocks, Harvester, 1976.

Macciocchi, M., 1971. *Daily Life in Revolutionary China.* NY and L, Monthly Rev. Pr., 1972.

Machetzkai, R., 1974. 'China's education since the Cultural Revolution.' *Pol. Qu.*, 45:1.

McLellan, D., 1969. *The Young Hegelians and Karl Marx.* L, Macmillan.

——1973. *Karl Marx: his Life and Thought.* L, Macmillan.

Madian, A., 1967. 'The organisation of ideology: variations on a revolutionary Chinese theme.' *Brit. J. of Sociology*, 18:1.

Male, D., 1971. *Russian Peasant Organisation before Collectivisation: a study of commune and gathering.* Cambridge, Univ. Pr.

Mandel, E., 1968a. *Marxist Economic Theory.* 2 vols, L, Merlin Pr.

——1968b. 'Trotsky's Marxism: an anti-critique.' *New Left Rev.*, 47.

——1969. 'The inconsistencies of State capitalism.' In his 1973.
——1970. 'The mystifications of State capitalism.' In his 1973.
——1971. *The Leninist Theory of Organisation*. L, IMG Pubs.
——1973 (*et al.*). *Readings in State Capitalism*. L, IMG Pubs.
——1974a. 'Ten theses on the social and economic laws governing the society transitional between capitalism and socialism.' *Critique*, 3.
——1974b. Comments in Ticktin, 1973. Ibid.
——1975. 'Liebman and Leninism.' *Socialist Register* (L, Merlin Pr.).
Matthews, M., 1972. *Class and Society in Soviet Russia*. L, Allen Lane.
Mauger, S., 1973. 'The political theory of Mao Tsetung.' *China Now*, 31–3.
Mavrakis, K., 1973. *On Trotskyism: problems of theory and history*. L, Routledge, 1976.
Mehnert, K., 1952. *Stalin versus Marx: the Stalinist historical doctrine*. L, Allen & Unwin.
Meisner, M., 1969. *From theory to practice, science and revolution: the 'three great revolutionary movements' in China, 1963–67*. Hong Kong, Centre for Asian Studies.
——1970. 'Yenan communism and the rise of the Chinese People's Republic.' In J. Crowley (ed.), *Modern East Asia*, NY, Harcourt.
Mepham, J., 1972. 'The theory of ideology in *Capital*.' *Radical Philosophy*, 2.
Milenkovitch, D., 1971. *Plan and Market in Yugoslav Economic Thought*. Yale Univ. Pr.
Miliband, R., 1973. 'Stalin and After.' *Socialist Register* (L, Merlin Pr.).
——1975. 'Bettelheim and Soviet Experience.' *New Left Rev.*, 91.
Millar, J., 1971 (ed.). *Soviet Rural Community*. Univ. of Illinois Pr.
Moore, Barrington, 1966. *The Social Origins of Democracy and Dictatorship*. L, Penguin, 1969.
Mukhina, G., 1975. *Socialist Revolution and the State*. Extracts, *Socialism: theory and practice*, 12, 1976.
Myrdal, J., 1963. *Report from a Chinese Village*. L, Penguin, 1967.
——1970. *China: the revolution continues*. L, Penguin, 1973.
Narkiewicz, O., 1970. *The making of the Soviet State Apparatus*. Manchester, Univ. Pr.
Nicolaus, M., 1970. 'The Universal Contradiction.' *New Left Rev.*, 59.
——1973. Foreword to Marx, 1858a (Penguin ed.).
Notkin, V., 1975. 'New works on the history of the Soviet working class in Anglo-American bourgeois historiography.' *Istoriya SSSR*, 1.
Nove, A., 1962. 'Was Stalin really necessary?' *Encounter*, April. Repr. as Ch. 1 of his book of the same title, L, Allen & Unwin, 1964.
——1969. *An Economic History of the USSR*. L, Penguin.
——1973a. 'Back to the Soviet drawing board.' *Times*, 16 Mar.
——1973b. 'Why habits and vested interests hinder Russian economy.' *Times*, 19 Mar.
——1974a. 'Uncle Joe in charge.' *New Society*, 16 May.
——1974b. 'A sense of proportion.' *Times Higher Educ. Supp.*, 14 June.
——1975. *Stalinism and After*. L, Allen & Unwin.
Obradovic, J., 1970. 'Participation and Work Attitudes in Yugoslavia.' *Industrial Relations*, 9:2.

Obradovic, J., 1975. 'Workers' Participation: Who Participates?' *Industrial Relations*, 14:1.

Ollman, B., 1971. *Alienation: Marx's conception of man in capitalist society*. Cambridge, Univ. Pr.

Owen, L., 1937. *The Russian Peasant Movement, 1906–1917*. NY, Russell, 1963.

Parker, W., 1973. *The Russians: how they live and work*. Newton Abbot, David & Charles.

Parkin, F., 1974 (ed.). *The Social Analysis of Class Structure*. L, Tavistock.

Perkins, D., 1974. 'The Chinese economy in historical perspective: report on a Conference.' *Items*, 28:1.

Perrie, M., 1972. 'The Russian Peasant Movement of 1905–1907: its social composition and revolutionary significance.' *Past and Present*, 57.

——1976. *The Agrarian Policy of the Russian Socialist-Revolutionary Party from its origins through the revolutions of 1905–1917*. Cambridge, Univ. Pr.

Philosophy is no mystery: peasants put their study to work. P, FLP, 1972.

Pipes, R., 1974a. 'The pock-marked god.' *Times Lit. Supp.*, 14 June.

——1974b. *Russia under the Old Regime*. L, Weidenfeld.

Plekhanov, G., 1895. *The Development of the Monist View of History*. M, Progress, 1972.

——1905. Forewords and Notes to Russian eds of Engels, 1886b. With P ed. of the latter.

Ponomarev, B., 1974. 'The world situation.' *Problems of Peace and Socialism* (M), July.

Poulantzas, N., 1970. *Fascism and Dictatorship: the 3rd International and the problem of fascism*. L, New Left Books, 1974.

Ramsay, H., 1973a. 'Conceptual confusion and contradiction: workers' control and the lone monk with the leaky umbrella.' *Bull. of North Staffs Labour History Group*, 1974.

——1973b. 'Political Economy and Conventional Theory.' Durham, Political Economy Group paper.

——1974. 'The Political Economy of the Impermanent Revolution.' Durham, Political Economy Group paper.

——1976. 'Economics or Socialism?' Mimeo.

——1977. Review of Bettelheim, 1970a. *Sociological Rev.*, 25:2.

Ratcliffe, M., 1974. 'A bad man with yellow eyes.' *Times*, 2 May.

Reed, J., 1919. *Ten Days that Shook the World*. L, Penguin, 1966.

Revolutionary CPSU (B), 1966. Draft Programme. *Hammer and Anvil*, Supp. No. 6.

Revolutionary Union, 1974. *How capitalism has been restored in the Soviet Union*. Chicago, RU.

Rey, A., 1908. *La Philosophie Moderne*. Paris.

Rice, E., 1972. *Mao's Way*. Berkely, Univ. Calif. Pr.

Rimlinger, G., 1960. 'Autocracy and the Factory Order in early Russian industrialisation.' *J. Economic History*, 20.

——1961. 'The expansion of the labour market in capitalist Russia, 1861–1917.' *J. Economic History*, 21.

Robinson, G. T., 1932. *Rural Russia under the Old Regime*. L, Macmillan, 1961.

Robinson, J., 1968. *The Cultural Revolution in China*. L, Penguin.

——1973. *Economic Management, China 1972.* L, Anglo-Chinese Educational Institute, Modern China Ser. no. 4.

Rossanda, R., 1970. 'Mao's Marxism.' *Socialist Register* (L, Merlin Pr.).

——1974. 'Revolutionary Intellectuals and the Soviet Union.' *Socialist Register* (L, Merlin Pr.).

Rubel, M., 1956. *Bibliographie des oeuvres de Karl Marx*. Paris, M. Rivière.

——1960. *Supplement* to his 1956. Paris, M. Rivière.

Rubin, I., 1928. *Essays on Marx's Theory of Value*. Detroit, Black & Red Pr., 1972.

Rue, J., 1966. *Mao Tsetung in Opposition*. Stanford Univ. Pr.

Rumyantsev, A., 1969. *Categories and Laws of the Political Economy of Communism*. M, Progress.

——1972 (*et al.*). *Soviet Economic Reform: Progress and Problems.* M, Progress.

Rus, V., 1970. 'Influence structure in Yugoslav enterprises.' *Industrial Relations*, 9:2.

Sahlins, M., 1972. *Stone Age Economics*. L, Tavistock, 1974.

Salisbury, H., 1973. *To Peking and beyond*. L, Fontana.

Samsin, A., 1976. 'The "third way" – a way leading up a blind alley: criticism of Marcuse.' *Planovoye Khozyaistvo*, 5.

Sayer, D., 1975a. 'Method and Dogma in Historical Materialism.' *Sociological Rev.*, 23:4.

——1975b. *Some Issues in Historical Materialism*. Durham, PhD thesis. [Harvester Pr., forthcoming as *Marx's Method*.]

——1977. 'Precapitalist Societies and Contemporary Marxist Theory.' *Sociology*, 11:1.

Schram, S., 1973a. Contribution to 'Mao Tsetung and Maoist Society', *Listener*, 7 June.

——1973b. 'The Cultural Revolution in Historical Perspective.' Introduction to his 1973c.

——1973c (ed.). *Authority, Participation, and Cultural Change in China*. Cambridge, Univ. Pr.

Schurmann, F., 1966. *Ideology and Organisation in Communist China*. Univ. Calif. Pr.

——1967. And O. Schell (eds). *China Readings*, I, II, and III. L, Penguin, 1968.

Schwartz, B., 1954. 'A Marxist Controversy on China.' *Far Eastern Qu.*, 13 Feb.

Scott, H., 1974. *Does Socialism Liberate Women?* Boston, Beacon Pr.

Sedgewick, P., 1963. Introduction to Serge, 1943.

Selden, M., 1969. 'The Yenan Legacy: the Mass Line.' In A. D. Barnett (ed.), *Chinese Communist Politics in Action*. Univ. Washington Pr.

——1970. 'People's War and the Transformation of Peasant Society.' In M. Friedman/M. Selden (ed.), *America's Asia*, NY, Vintage, 1971.

——1971. *The Yenan Way in Revolutionary China*. Harvard Univ. Pr.

Serge, V., 1937. *From Lenin to Stalin*. NY, Monad Pr., 1973.

——1943. *Memoirs of a Revolutionary*. Oxford Univ. Pr., 1967.

Serving the People with Dialectics: essays on the study of philosophy by workers and peasants. P, FLP, 1972.

Shanin, T., 1966. 'The Peasantry as a Political Factor.' *Sociological Rev.*, 14:1. Repr. in his 1971a and 1972.

Shanin, T., 1971a (ed.). *Peasants and Peasant Societies*. L, Penguin.
——1971b. 'Peasantry: delineation of a concept and a field of study.' *Eur. J. of Sociology*, 12:2.
——1971c. 'Socio-economic Mobility and the Rural History of Russia, 1905–1930.' *Soviet Studs.*, 23:2.
——1972. *The Awkward Class: political sociology of peasantry in a developing country, Russia 1910–1925*. Clarendon Pr.
——1973. 'Nature and Logic of the Peasant Economy: I. A Generalisation.' *J. Peasant Studs.*, 1:1.
——1974. 'Nature and Logic of the Peasant Economy: II. Diversity and Change. III. Policy and Intervention.' *J. Peasant Studs.*, 1:2.
Sinel, A., 1968. 'Educating the Russian peasantry: the elementary school reforms of Count Dmitry Tolstoi.' *Slavic Rev.*, 27:1.
——1973. *The Class Room and the Chancellery: State Education under Count Dmitry Tolstoi*. Harvard Univ. Pr.
Smedley, A., 1938. *China Fights Back*. L, Gollancz (Left Book Club).
Snow, E., 1937. *Red Star over China*. L, Gollancz (Left Book Club).
——1941. *Scorched Earth*. 2 vols. L, Gollancz (Left Book Club).
——1961. *Red Star over China*. Rev. and enl. ed. L, Gollancz, 1968.
——1966. 'The Chinese Equation.' *Sunday Times*, 23 Jan.
——1970. *Red China Today*. Rev. ed., L, Penguin.
——1971. 'The Open Door' [Interview with Chou En-lai]. *China Now*, 15.
——1973. *The Long Revolution*. L, Hutchinson.
Snow, H., 1972. *China's Communists*. Greenwood, 1972.
Solomos, J., 1976. 'The role of Trade Unions, Soviets, and Factory Committees in the transition period: aspects of Soviet experience, 1917–1921.' Unpublished BA dissertation.
Sontag, J., 1968. 'Tsarist Debts and Tsarist Foreign Policy.' *Slavic Rev.*, 27:4.
Spencer, F., 1967. *1918–1945*. L, Pan, 1970.
Starr, S., 1972. *Decentralisation and Self-government in Russia, 1830–1870*. Princeton Univ. Pr.
Stein, G., 1945. *The Challenge of Red China*. L, Pilot Pr.
Struggle between Two Roads in China's Countryside, The. P, FLP, 1968.
Stuart, R., 1971. 'Structural change and the quality of collective farm management, 1952–66.' In Millar, 1971.
——1972. *The Collective Farm in Soviet Agriculture*. Lexington, Mass., D. C. Heath.
Suslov, M., 1976. 'Our epoch is the epoch of the triumph of Marxism-Leninism.' *Socialism: theory and practice*, 8.
Sweezy, P., 1971. His contributions to C. Bettelheim/P. Sweezy, *On the Transition to Socialism*, NY and L, Monthly Rev. Pr.
——1974. 'The nature of Soviet Society.' *Monthly Rev.*, 26: 6 and 8, 1974–5.
Three Major Struggles on China's Philosophical Front. P, FLP, 1973.
Thomson, G., 1971. *From Marx to Mao Tsetung: a study in revolutionary dialectics*. L, China Policy Study Group.
——1973. *Capitalism and After: the rise and fall of commodity production*. L, China Policy Study Group.

Thornton, R., 1969. *The Comintern and the Chinese Communists*. Univ. of Washington Pr.

Ticktin, H., 1973. 'Towards a political economy of the USSR.' *Critique*, 1.

——1976. 'The contradictions of Soviet society and Professor Bettelheim.' *Critique*, 6.

Tito, J., 1948. Report to the 5th Congress of the Communist Party of Yugoslavia. In his 1970.

——1950. 'On Workers' Self-management in Economic Enterprises.' In his 1970.

——1968a. Speech of the President to the 6th Congress of the CTUY. Belgrade.

——1968b. Address to the Jubilee Session of the Anti-Fascist Council of the National Liberation of Yugoslavia – the 25th Anniversary of the New Yugoslavia. In his 1970.

——1970. *The Essential Tito*. Newton Abbot, David & Charles.

——1974. 'The struggle for the further development of socialist selfmanagement in our country and the role of the LCY.' Speech to the League of Communists of Yugoslavia. Belgrade.

Treadgold, D., 1973. *The West in Russia and China*. 2 vols. Cambridge, Univ. Pr.

'Tsarist Takeoff.' Full-page review. *Times Lit. Supp.*, 21 Apr. 1972.

Tucker, R., 1974. *Stalin as a Revolutionary, 1879–1929*. L, Chatto.

Ulam, A., 1974. *Stalin: the Man and his Era*. L, Allen Lane.

USSR, The. M, Novosti Press Agency Yearbook. Published Annually.

Valyuzhenich, A., 1976. *American Liberalism: Myth and Reality*. 2 vols. M, Novosti.

Vladimirov, P., 1973. *The Special Regions of China*. M, Nauka.

Von Laue, T., 1961. 'Russian Peasants in the Factory.' *J. Econ. Hist.*, 21:1.

Vucinich, W., 1968 (ed.). *The Peasant in 19th Century Russia*. Stanford.

Walicki, A., 1969. *The Controversy over Capitalism: studies in the social philosophy of the Russian Populists*. Clarendon Pr.

Walkin, J., 1954. 'The attitude of the Tsarist government toward the labor problem.' *Am. Slavic and E. European Rev.*, 13.

Watters, F., 1968. 'The Peasant and the Village Commune.' Ch. 5 of Vucinich, 1968.

Weintraub, W., 1949. 'Marx and Russian Revolutionaries.' *Cambridge J.*, 3.

Wheelright, E., and McFarlane, B., 1970. *The Chinese Road to Socialism*. NY and L, Monthly Rev. Pr.

White, S., 1974. 'Soviets in Britain: the Leeds Convention of 1917.' *Int. Rev. of Social History*, 19.

——1975. 'Ideological hegemony and political control: the sociology of anti-Bolshevism in Britain.' *J. Scottish Labour History Soc.*, 9.

Wilczynski, J., 1972a. *The Economics of Socialism*. L, Allen & Unwin.

——1972b. *Socialist Economic Development and Reforms*. L, Macmillan.

——1973. *Profit, Risk and Incentives under Socialist Economic Planning*. L, Macmillan.

Wiles, P., 1971 (ed.). *The Prediction of Communist Economic Performance*. Cambridge, Univ. Pr.

Wolf, E., 1969. 'Russia.' Ch. 2 of his *Peasant Wars of the 20th Century*. L, Faber.

Woods, A., and Grant, T., 1969. *Lenin and Trotsky: what they really stood for. A reply to Monty Johnstone*. L, World Books, 1972.

Yahuda, M., 1974. 'Chinese conceptions of their role in the world.' *Pol. Qu.*, 45:1.

Yakhontoff, V., 1934. *The Chinese Soviets*. Greenwood, 1973.

Yaney, G., 1971. 'Agricultural Administration in Russia.' Ch. 1 of Millar, 1971.

——1974. *The Systematisation of Russian Government, 1711–1905*. Univ. of Illinois Pr.

Yung Pin-chen, 1966. *Chinese Political Thought: Mao Tsetung and Liu Shao-chi*. Hague, Nijhoff.

Zangeldin, T., 1971. 'Development by Karl Marx and Frederick Engels of the concept of the dictatorship of the proletariat.' *Voprosi Filosofii*, 3.

Zarodov, K., 1975. 'Lenin's strategy and tactics of revolutionary struggle.' *Pravda*, 6 Aug.

Zelnik, R., 1968. 'The Peasant and the Factory.' Ch. 6 of Vucinich, 1968.

Zukin, S., 1975. *Beyond Marx and Tito*. Cambridge, Univ. Pr.

Index

Note. All proper names are indexed. Concepts are indexed only where they are directly discussed (rather than employed) in the text. In some cases (e.g. Bolshevism, Union of Soviet Socialist Republics), we do not list minor mentions since to do so would have made the index unusable.